JAN 0 7 2020

Biography  S0-AKP-698
Making a difference :my
 fight for native rights and
social justice /
Deer, Ada Elizabeth,

WITHDRAWN

Making a Difference

NEW DIRECTIONS IN NATIVE AMERICAN STUDIES
Colin G. Calloway and K. Tsianina Lomawaima, General Editors

Making a Difference

MY FIGHT FOR NATIVE RIGHTS
AND SOCIAL JUSTICE

▪ Ada Deer ▪

with Theda Perdue

Foreword by Charles Wilkinson

UNIVERSITY OF OKLAHOMA PRESS : NORMAN

This book has been selected to receive the
Julian J. Rothbaum Prize for the highest standards of scholarship.

Publication of this book is made possible through
the generosity of Edith Kinney Gaylord.

Library of Congress Cataloging-in-Publication Control Number: 2019016534
ISBN 978-0-8061-6427-4 (hardcover : alk. paper)

Making a Difference: My Fight for Native Rights and Social Justice is Volume 19 in the New
Directions in Native American Studies series.

The paper in this book meets the guidelines for permanence and durability of the Committee
on Production Guidelines for Book Longevity of the Council on Library Resources, Inc. ∞

Copyright © 2019 by the University of Oklahoma Press, Norman, Publishing Division of the
University. Manufactured in the U.S.A.

All rights reserved. No part of this publication may be reproduced, stored in a retrieval
system, or transmitted, in any form or by any means, electronic, mechanical, photocopying,
recording, or otherwise—except as permitted under Section 107 or 108 of the United States
Copyright Act—without the prior written permission of the University of Oklahoma Press. To
request permission to reproduce selections from this book, write to Permissions, University of
Oklahoma Press, 2800 Venture Drive, Norman, OK 73069, or email rights.oupress@ou.edu.

1 2 3 4 5 6 7 8 9 10

In memory of
Constance Wood Deer
and
Michael D. Green

▪ Contents ▪

▪ Illustrations ▪

■ Foreword ■

The extraordinarily productive and inspiring life of Ada Deer began in what might seem to be unlikely circumstances. She was born and grew up in poverty on the Menominee Reservation in northeastern Wisconsin, in a remote cabin without indoor plumbing or electricity. She and her brothers and sisters hauled water in from the river. As with all Indian people at the time, this young Indian girl's future looked grim. Congress's official policy, now universally discredited, was to "terminate" all Indian tribes by abrogating treaties; selling off the reservations; and eliminating federal health, education, and economic programs. Indian people would move to cities, where they would abandon their cultures and homelands and assimilate into the larger society. With the threat of termination, a thick foreboding hung over the Menominee Reservation and all of Indian Country.

These circumstances hardly seemed likely to produce a champion for Indian people, but by the time Ada was in law school, she had developed the confidence and a set of ideals that would bring lasting benefits to the Menominee Tribe, the Native people across Indian Country, and the nation. Part of her success was due to her mother. Constance "Ma" Deer grew up in a prominent family in the East. Intellectual and idealistic, she set out on her own for the Menominee Reservation, where she married Joe Deer, a traditionalist Menominee and Ada's father.

The best memoirs and biographies often contain detailed portrayals of a person's early life. The pages that follow hold a scintillating account of Ada's childhood and young adulthood and will be useful to scholars and anyone who is interested in tribal life in Indian Country during this important era. In Ada's case, her youth was laced with stresses and pressures of grasping churches, the paternalistic Bureau of Indian Affairs, racism in many forms, moves from the reservation to Milwaukee and back, and the near absence of financial resources. And, as the pages also will tell you, her early life was also laced with opportunities that it would have been easy to ignore. Ada, though, was quick to grasp them, and the multifaceted successes of her early life equipped her to be a change agent on the reservation and in the outside world.

As I say, Ma Deer had a lot to do with that. Oh, how she loved and respected this girl! She believed in Ada absolutely. Deeply committed to Indian people, Ma Deer immersed herself in Native American history, law, policy, and culture. She told Ada what she knew and gave her readings. Ada's self-confidence and a sense of possibilities flourished. I didn't know Ada in her late teens and early twenties, but I am confident that many people who met her then must have thought, "Talk about a can-do attitude!"

Ada's father was much more distant, and his many bad experiences with white people wore him down. At the same time, he was a traditional Indian man through and through, raising horses and loving to hunt and fish. He could still speak the Menominee language. His Indian ways moved Ada and deepened her appreciation of, and commitment to, Indian culture.

Ada's life and work are also rooted in the land. Yes, Ada grew up in a home that lacked many material goods but she also grew up in splendor: that cabin stood on a low hill above the Wolf River, one of America's greatest rivers. The force and sounds of the Wolf sounded in her ears when she bedded down at night and woke her up in the morning. Every day, one way or the other, she would see that rushing beauty and receive the bracing river smells. Of course, the wondrous, 367-square-mile landscape of the Menominee Reservation lay beyond the cabin, with its deep forests, the Wolf and its many tributaries, wild rice colonies, and all manner of wildlife, including wolves, bear, turkey, and elk. The profound meaning of Menominee land to Ada is exemplified by its placement on the first page of chapter 1 of this book.

By the time Ada headed off to college at the University of Wisconsin, then, the contours of her aspirations had been set. She wanted to help her tribe. She wanted to help Indian people broadly. Beyond Indian affairs, she felt a commonality with dispossessed peoples, concerns that would in time evolve into commitments to young people and women. Of course, at that time neither Ada nor anyone else could possibly have imagined how much she would accomplish in furtherance of that vision, or how much good she would create over her long lifetime.

■ ■ ■

In 1971, Ada, on behalf of the Menominee, requested legal assistance from the Native American Rights Fund (NARF) and I was assigned to the case. For us lawyers—my colleagues were Joe Preloznik at Wisconsin Judicare and Yvonne Knight of NARF—and the Menominee tribal leaders, this work was top priority, bar none. The Menominee Termination Act of 1954 was an absolute disaster: it abrogated the treaty that established the reservation; created health, education, and economic chaos; and eliminated the tribe's sovereignty. The land itself—the entire, magnificent Menominee Reservation, with all of its history, culture, wildlife, and beauty—was in great jeopardy, subject to being thrown open for sale to timber companies and second-home developments.

Ada was the leader. That wasn't because of a title or a power grab on her part. It was because she knew all the facts, fully understood what Congress needed, knew how the tribe could effectively influence Congress and the White House, and was so compelling and articulate in putting the tribe's positions forward to the public. Within the tribe, she was fully inclusive and always made sure everyone's points were presented, letting sessions go on as long as needed so that every last detail was discussed.

Ada also was savvy about dealing with Washington, D.C., officials. The Wisconsin delegation wholeheartedly supported the bill. So did many other leaders on Capitol Hill, realizing that restoration was fervently supported in newly active Indian Country. Ada was always comfortable and respectful, but never intimidated, even with such lions of Congress as Wisconsin Senators Gaylord Nelson and William Proxmire, Senator Ted Kennedy, Senator Henry Jackson, and Congressman Morris Udall. With some regularity these men, or their staffs, got too far out in front, and it was Ada's job to explain diplomatically that their approach was not in line with the tribe's. Virtually without exception, they acceded. As for the small group of prominent legislators who opposed the bill, Ada acknowledged them but found ways to bring them on board or go around them. Both Republicans and the White House were 100 percent behind the Menominee Restoration bill. In the end, the bill passed both houses with near-unanimity and was signed by President Nixon in December 1973, just eighteen months after it had been introduced. The adoption of the Menominee Restoration Act announced the end of termination and the beginning of the tribal self-determination era. Without question, the single most important person in this transition was Ada Deer.

As Ada explains well in this book, her four years as assistant secretary of the interior for Indian affairs—the highest federal office dedicated to Indian affairs–during the Clinton administration frustrated her in many ways. But her dynamic personality and dedication to Indian people nonetheless all were evident in many ways.

Perhaps most notable was her brave and unexpected vindication of Alaska Native sovereign rights. In 1971, Congress passed the Alaska Native Claims Settlement Act. We can see now that it was the last vestige of the termination era (the Menominee Restoration Act was introduced just a few months later). An enormously complex and sweeping piece of legislation, ANCSA was premised on a belief that Indian people would benefit from corporate status rather than sovereign government status. As a result, the tribal land in Alaska was transferred to new Native-controlled corporations and away from sovereign Alaska Native nations. The complexities of ANCSA, like the Menominee Termination Act, made it almost inevitable that the big corporations—the energy industry in Alaska—would end up owning what had been Native land. ANCSA came to be known as "termination in disguise," which it was. Ada identified this threat to sovereignty from the beginning, and carried it with her through the years, often explaining it to groups in public meetings.

As assistant secretary, Ada moved quickly to address the issue of Alaska Native sovereignty. Each year her office published an official list of federally recognized sovereign tribes. Over the years, even as Alaska Natives steadily increased their insistence that they still possessed sovereignty, the Alaska governors and congressional delegation stood firm that Alaska Native tribes were not sovereign and could not be included on that list because of ANCSA.

When it came time to publish the list for 1993, her first year in the office, she knew that her authority to include Alaska tribes was not entirely clear. She also knew that Alaska politics would erupt if she included Alaska tribes on the list. Still, when the new list was released, it included all 228 Alaska tribes. The Alaska delegation, comprising Senator Ted Stevens, Senator Frank Murkowski, and Congressman Don Young, were all powerful, long-standing opponents of Native rights who made their feelings loudly known. But Ada held firm, and since then Congress and federal courts have upheld her action. Alaska Natives still have a long way to go, but they have used their sovereign status extensively, and to this day they see Ada's initiative as a critical foundation piece for all of their efforts.

Speaking personally, I feel privileged to have known Ada for half a century (she is "Aunt Ada" to my boys) and to have had the opportunity to follow her public life closely. Beyond that—like so many people in her family, tribe, and far beyond—I have been blessed by Ada's warmth, loyalty, good humor, and lasting friendship. What a full life! For the readership of *Making a Difference*, whether or not they may know Ada personally, it will be comforting and inspiring to be reminded of our possibilities, regardless of how seemingly modest our beginnings may be.

Charles Wilkinson
Distinguished Professor
Moses Lasky Professor of Law Emeritus
University of Colorado

▪ Preface ▪

We first met in 1993, on the sidewalk in Tahlequah, Oklahoma, watching the Cherokee National Holiday parade. I remember the meeting vividly: Ada had just become assistant secretary of the interior for Indian affairs. Ada does not remember this meeting, but, after all, she was surrounded by well-wishers. Our next encounter was in November 2000, in Chapel Hill, North Carolina, when Ada delivered the American Indian Heritage Month lecture at the University of North Carolina (UNC). Ada; my husband, Michael D. Green; and I talked about places we had traveled and places we wanted to go. Suddenly, Ada and I said in perfect unison, "I want to go to Machu Picchu!" And so we did. Other trips followed—Mexico, Guatemala, Cuba, Italy, the Panama Canal, Egypt. The three of us drove across the South, calling on the Alabama-Coushattas, Coushattas, Chitimachas, and Houmas. And we visited each other in our homes. Ada took Mike and me to the Menominee Reservation; we sent Ada to visit the Lumbees.

When Ada retired in 2007, Mike and I began to pester her about writing her autobiography. Few individuals have had as profound an impact on U.S. Indian policy as Ada has had. In the 1970s, she led the effort to reverse the termination policy. She then went on to serve as assistant secretary of the interior for Indian affairs in a period when Congress dramatically reduced the Bureau of Indian Affairs (BIA) budget, tribes and individual Indians sued the BIA over the mismanagement of their trust funds, and casino gaming expanded rapidly on reservations. We knew hers was a story that needed to be told.

But Ada is no writer; she is a talker and a doer. So in 2011, the American Indian Center at UNC, under the leadership of Clara Sue Kidwell, provided support for a series of interviews. By the time we ended, Clara Sue, Mike, and I had conducted more than sixty hours of interviews with Ada, which Deborah Mitchum, who had worked for UNC's Southern Oral History Project, carefully transcribed. Ada's memories of her childhood and the struggle for restoration were particularly vivid; those of her time at the BIA were less so. Fortunately, Ada's longtime assistant, Lydia Bickford, had an impeccable memory and helped fill in gaps. The autobiography also required substantial additional research in newspapers, public records, and Ada's private papers. When Lydia died just before the completion of this project, we discovered that she had stored Ada's private papers from her time at the BIA at her house.

The executors of Lydia's estate delivered fifty boxes of papers to Ada's house, but there was no place to put them except in the garage. Several months later, I went to Wisconsin to see what was in them. When I opened the second box, a rat that was at least three feet long jumped out of the box and over my left shoulder, but I persevered. The papers were a treasure trove, and they explained much about Ada's memory lapses in the BIA period of her life. The workload at BIA was formidable, the attitudes of congressmen such as Washington Senator Slade Gorton toward Indians were despicable, the budget battles were grueling, and the support from the secretary of the interior and the White House was less than enthusiastic. Going through the papers together, however, jogged Ada's memory and gave a personal perspective on those four years.

Many people contributed to this autobiography in various ways. I compiled it from the transcripts of the interviews, follow-up conversations, and research to fill in and check factual information. The ideas and opinions, as well as the deeds, all belong to Ada. In conversation and interviews, she normally uses "Indian" instead of "Native" or "Indigenous" (except where Alaska is concerned), "tribe" instead of "nation," and "member" instead of "citizen." In some cases, her word choice is habit; in others, it is intentional. She has few inhibitions, never met a stranger, and is blessed with a wonderful sense of humor. I hope all of that shines through in her autobiography.

People normally write autobiographies at the end of their productive lives, but I do not think Ada is anywhere near that point. As I wrote this preface, Ada called to discuss new issues confronting her tribe. So this autobiography is not likely to be Ada's last word. For all who care about justice, let's hope not.

Theda Perdue

▪ Acknowledgments ▪

We would like to thank a number of people who contributed to this memoir. The project never would have gotten off the ground without the support of the American Indian Center at the University of North Carolina, Chapel Hill, and its director, Clara Sue Kidwell. Clara Sue also participated in the early interviews with Ada. At the American Indian Center, Randi Byrd handled technical issues ranging from operating the tape recorder to emailing the interviews to our transcriber to printing out the transcriptions. We are enormously grateful to her for her competence, tolerance, and genial disposition. Deborah Mitchum, our transcriber, did a magnificent job, especially considering that Mike and I tended to finish each other's sentences and we all often spoke simultaneously. John Wunder, professor emeritus of history at the University of Nebraska, read and commented on chapters 8 and 9. Francis Flavin of the Office of Federal Acknowledgment graciously answered questions about the workings of the BIA. We both appreciate Patrick Delabrue's insightful columns on recent Menominee events in the *Menominee Nation News*, which provided background on current struggles. In Theda's opinion, Tim Giago is a national treasure. His columns in *Indian Country Today* often criticized the BIA during Ada's tenure, but they did so sensitively, thoughtfully, and never personally. We also acknowledge David R. M. Beck's fine book, *The Struggle for Self-Determination: History of the Menominee Indians since 1854* (University of Nebraska Press, 2005), which provided Theda, primarily a historian of the Native South, with essential background. Nicholas C. Peroff's *Menominee Drums: Tribal Termination and Restoration, 1954–1974* (University of Oklahoma Press, 1982) also proved valuable.

Several other people have contributed indirectly to this project. Ada emphasizes the influence of her remarkable mother, Constance Wood Deer, to whom this book is dedicated. Reflection has brought a renewed appreciation for her siblings, Joe Deer, Ferial Skye, Connie Deer, and her late brother Robert Deer, and for their love. Among the many people who enriched and expanded Ada's life were Commissioner of Indian Affairs Philleo Nash, Common Cause founder John Gardner, University of Wisconsin Chancellor Edwin Young, and social worker Helen Isabel Clarke.

Ada is grateful to the Menominee Indian Tribe and to the people who helped save it, especially the members of Determination of Rights and Unity for Menominee Shareholders (DRUMS) and the Menominee Restoration Committee. She is forever indebted to Joseph Preloznik, the Native American Rights Fund, and Charles Wilkinson and Yvonne Knight, the NARF attorneys who worked on Menominee restoration. She recognizes that restoration was a group effort, and that she, as well as the tribe, are beholden to Verna Fowler, Sylvia Wilber, Shirley Daly, Lloyd Powless, Jim White, Deborah Shames, and many others. She acknowledges the support of Governor Patrick J. Lucey and Senator Gaylord Nelson in the struggle for restoration. LaDonna and Fred Harris assisted restoration in many ways. They provided Ada a place to live in Washington, taught her how Congress really worked, and provided her insights and introductions. She thanks them for their support and their decades of friendship.

Lydia Bickford and her husband, Jon Holtshopple, managed Ada's political campaigns. Lydia later worked for her at the BIA, and after Ada retired, Lydia managed much of her life. Lydia died before the conclusion of this book, and we both miss her. Ada appreciates the support of others in her public life, especially Senator Ted Kennedy, President Bill Clinton, and Vice President Al Gore. Among the many people with whom she worked at the BIA, she would like to acknowledge especially the commitment and dedication of Elizabeth Homer and Robyn York.

Friends are the icing on the cake of life, and Ada's icing includes Pearl Mitchell Jackson, Irene Long, Lynn McDonald, and Betty Zeps. Betty has been particularly important to this project. Ada does not use a computer, so in the final days of putting this memoir together, Betty relayed email messages, scanned newspaper articles, read problematic sections, and offered advice with remarkable cheerfulness.

Theda would like to thank the faculty of the American Indian and Indigenous Studies Program at UNC, especially Danny Bell, Dan Cobb, Kathleen DuVal, Ben Frey, Valerie Lambert, Malinda Lowery, Keith Richotte, Vin Steponaitis, and

Jenny Tone-Pah-Hote. As always, she is grateful to her former doctoral students, who are all employed, tenured, and able to buy her a glass of wine at professional meetings. One of the really good things about marrying Mike Green at middle age was that, in the bargain, she got three children who were past adolescence. Dan, Tom, and Julie Green as well as daughters-in-law Neda Shashani-Green and Vicki Mountain (and the grandchildren and great-grandchild) have enriched her life. And their father, to whom this book also is dedicated, is always in her heart. Theda thanks the women of Gossip and Guzzle, the Monday afternoon knitting group at Helen Wilson's (Theda *does not* knit), and the crews of the *Joares* and the *Maguelonne* who provided their labor and superb company on the Canal du Midi. Had these women not been a part of her life, she probably would have finished this book sooner but in a far worse mood.

Finally, we would like to thank the University of Oklahoma Press and acquisitions editor Alessandra Jacobi Tamulevich, as well as the series editors K. Tsianina Lomawaima and Colin G. Calloway. We appreciate the comments of readers Sherry L. Smith (historian) and Nicholas C. Peroff. Working with the staff at OU Press, especially Amy Hernandez and Emily Jerman Schuster, has been a pleasure. Copyeditor Kirsteen Anderson did a fine job of identifying infelicitous wording, inconsistencies, and, yes, misspellings and grammatical errors. Sherry L. Smith (indexer) compiled the index. The Wisconsin Historical Society granted permission to reproduce two of the photographs in this book.

▪ Acronyms ▪

AIM American Indian Movement

AIS American Indian Studies

ANCSA Alaska Native Claims Settlement Act

BIA Bureau of Indian Affairs

BAR Bureau of Acknowledgment and Research

CAAMP Citizens' Association for the Advancement of Menominee People

CAP Community Action Program

CIM Committee for Independent Menominees

DNC Democratic National Committee

DRUMS Determination of Rights and Unity for Menominee Shareholders

EPA Environmental Protection Agency

FHA Future Homemakers of America

FY Fiscal Year

HUD Housing and Urban Development

ICWA Indian Child Welfare Act

IHS Indian Health Service

ILS Integrated Liberal Studies

IRA Indian Reorganization Act (Wheeler-Howard Act)

MEI Menominee Enterprises, Inc. (managed our forests in the termination era)

MRC   Menominee Restoration Committee

MTE   Menominee Tribal Enterprises (managed our forests before and after termination)

NARF   Native American Rights Fund

NIGA   National Indian Gaming Association

NIGC   National Indian Gaming Commission

NOW   National Organization for Women

OEO   Office of Economic Opportunity

ONEO   Office of Navajo Economic Opportunity

PAC   Political Action Committee

PL   Public Law

PRIDE   Program for Recognizing Individual Determination through Education

UW-M   University of Wisconsin, Madison

VISTA   Volunteers in Service to America

Making a Difference

CHAPTER 1

▪ Growing Up Menominee ▪

I am a Menominee Indian. That is who I was born and how I have lived. I am tall like the trees that blanket my reservation in northern Wisconsin, and my skin is brown like their bark. Although I have not lived there in years, my roots grow deep in that rocky soil. That soil has anchored me during tumultuous times. I have roots elsewhere—geographically, ancestrally, and intellectually—and they too produced and nurtured the person I have become. But my taproot is Menominee.

The Menominee Reservation, where I was born, is just a fraction of the Menominee homeland, which once comprised 10 million acres. Today, the reservation consists of only 235,523 acres, most of it heavily forested. The Wolf River, on whose banks I grew up, bisects the reservation. Keshena is the main town, where the tribal headquarters and most tribal services are located. The lumber mill, which has employed most Menominee men for more than a hundred years, is located at Neopit. The "white" town of Shawano, where I graduated from high school, is just south of the reservation.

No description of the Menominee Reservation can do it justice. More than a century of sustainable forestry has produced a green canopy high above a landscape largely free of underbrush and now unmarred by the stubble of clear-cutting. Almost the entire reservation lies within the basin of the Wolf River. The sparkling waters, rugged boulders, and tree-shrouded banks of the section of the river that flows through the reservation has justly earned designation as a National Wild and Scenic River. Crystal-clear lakes dot the reservation, and their sparkling waters provide relief from the dark green forests.

The Menominees were a powerful and self-sufficient people when Europeans arrived in the seventeenth century. For nearly two centuries, the Menominees adapted to the European presence by supplying pelts for the fur trade. By the early nineteenth century, however, white Americans had become more interested in land than furs, and in a series of treaties culminating in the treaty of 1854, Menominees surrendered most of their territory. With their economy devastated, they struggled to find a way to provide for their families. The U.S. government demanded that they become farmers, and some Menominees tried to do as the federal government bid them, but most of the land reserved for them was not suitable for farming. Then whites discovered that the Wisconsin forests had commercial value. They hastened to exploit Menominee timber, frequently by clear-cutting with the blessing of the federal government, which saw the denuded land as agricultural fields in waiting. Menominees saw it as patrimony lost and future forsaken. Although they often disagreed about how to confront their desperate situation, Menominees loved their land and their tribe, and I was brought up understanding the necessity of preserving both.

Like many Indian people, I have European ancestry. Menominees began marrying French traders in the seventeenth century. In the 1870s, the federal government restricted reservation logging to Menominee men, but whites could get access to tribal timber by marrying Menominee women. By the 1930s, many Menominees had white fathers or grandfathers. My father's sister Rose, for example, married a white man, but like many others in interracial marriages, she and her husband lived on the reservation and raised their children there. So-called mixed-blood Indians usually either do not think of themselves that way or struggle to come to terms with their parents' disparate races and cultures. They become the people they are brought up to be, and if they are brought up in an Indian community, Indian usually is who they become, despite having a non-Native parent. I know because I am one of those people.

My Menominee father was born on the reservation; my white mother arrived in Wisconsin as an adult. My parents' marriage was made not in heaven but on an Indian reservation in the midst of the Great Depression, and they struggled to get along with each other and raise a family. Both lost their mothers at an early age, but otherwise they came from radically different backgrounds. My parents were reluctant to tell us anything about their childhoods, so I have had to piece together their stories. My mother had been a child of privilege, while privation marked my father's childhood. I always have wondered what drew them together. Perhaps it was merely physical attraction, or perhaps a love of the place where they met, courted, married, had children, and lived out their lives.

My mother, Constance Stockton Wood Deer, was the daughter of a minister in Philadelphia, and she had an identical twin, Adah. Their mother died when the twins were born in 1904, and they grew up in their maternal grandmother's household until they were thirteen, when their father remarried. Neither of them liked their stepmother. While Adah was quite conforming, my mother was the source of much consternation. She liked challenge and adventure. She also had a strong sense of moral purpose that led her to places and people her family found inappropriate. The twins went to Cazenovia Seminary, a Methodist institution near Syracuse, New York, for high school. Young women at that time had few career opportunities, especially ones that appealed to my adventurous mother. She wanted to do something meaningful with her life, so she went to nursing school. Upon graduating from the Children's Hospital of Philadelphia School of Nursing, she worked first in Appalachia, then in the early 1930s she moved to the Rosebud Indian Reservation in South Dakota. At this time responsibility for Indian health care rested with the BIA not the Indian Health Service or individual tribes, as it does today. This was my mother's introduction to Indian people and to the federal bureaucracy that delivered the services for which Indians had paid with their lands.

Rather than distancing herself from the people she served, my mother wanted to know them as friends. This may sound obvious to us today, but at that time the BIA did not encourage or even approve of such interaction between white employees and Indian people. My mother visited Lakota people in their homes, tried to learn their language, and attended some of their ceremonies. In particular, she loved horses and often went horseback riding with Noah Broken Leg, a Lakota X-ray and laboratory technician who later became an Episcopal priest. She became friends with his family, including his father, who was a Lakota medicine man. When I was a young social worker I met his son Martin, who was then a student at Macalester College, and told him how fondly my mother remembered his grandmother and other relatives. She did not get along as well with the clinic administrators as she did with the Indians, however, and after several disagreements, the BIA shipped her off to the Menominee Reservation in Wisconsin. There she met my father, who was four years younger than she was.

When she arrived in Wisconsin, my mother decided she wanted a horse, and people told her that Joe Deer had horses. As it turned out, she went to get a horse and got the horseman as well! My mother had a somewhat romantic attraction to Indians in general, so perhaps it is not surprising that she married one. I remember her happy outburst when my sister married: "Oh! Ferial married a Sioux!" My father also was a very handsome man, and I can understand her attraction to him, but they were badly mismatched.

My father was less talkative than my mother, so I know even less about his family or his life before he met her. He was born in 1908, perhaps in the West Branch community where his father, Joseph, engaged in logging. In 1918 when he was ten, his mother, Elizabeth Gauthier Deer, died in the flu pandemic. Unable to care for the children, Joseph took them to a boarding school in Keshena run by the Catholic Church. There was no high school on the reservation at that point, so my father only finished the eighth grade. Then he had to go to work, but I am not sure what he did. It is possible he worked with his father as a logger, felling trees and using his enormous horses to drag them to a railhead or to the mill in Neopit. Certainly that is how most Menominee men made a living, since the farms that the government encouraged could not support them. He also might have made some money from breeding his horses or from odd jobs on the reservation.

My parents married in December 1934 in Oshkosh, Wisconsin. Since intermarriage was acceptable to Menominees, my father's family probably had little objection to Joe's marrying a white woman. My mother's family was less welcoming. My grandfather adamantly opposed her marriage to an Indian. He expected her to marry someone from her race and class, preferably a minister's son. She had been out with a few such men, she once told me, and didn't like them, so that was that. She was a very decisive person. I find it interesting that she chose the path in life she did, and I can understand her attraction to Indian people. The breach with her family never healed, however, although she continued to correspond with them periodically. Only her brother and sister-in-law acknowledged her marriage—they sent her a set of pots and pans, which, though she needed them, served as a reminder that her privileged upbringing did not include cooking lessons.

My parents started married life with very little else. My father had bought 160 acres along the Wolf River before they married. He acquired this land from an elderly Menominee man, probably in trade for a horse, because reservation land could only be sold to another member of the tribe and, therefore, had little commercial value. My mother had saved some money from working as a nurse, and she used it to build a log cabin and a barn on the land. Once pregnant with me, my mother could no longer work in the hospital. She bought a few cows, which she hoped would generate income, and my father still had his horses, which provided some money through sales and stud fees. He also got a job in our Menominee tribal lumber mill, where he worked for thirty-eight years. It was hard work but he did it. Every morning he got up and went to work, in rain, hail, or snow. Occasionally he had a car, but usually he walked down the road, and another man picked him up.

The mill was the only real source of employment on the reservation at that point. In 1908 the U.S. Congress had enacted legislation, the La Follette Act, which provided for the construction of the mill so that Menominees could reap greater rewards from their forests. Previously, whites had processed logs from Menominee forests (and often illegally cut them as well). The legislation was an admission that there was little future in farming and represented an effort to employ Menominee men in a different occupation. The law also mandated sustainable-yield logging rather than clear-cutting. BIA agents responsible for implementing the legislation, however, did not share the perspective of Congress and continued clear-cutting. Under BIA management, the mill discriminated against Indians and reserved managerial positions for whites, but still it was the main employer of Indian men on the reservation.

I was born in August 1935. I am the oldest child in our family. My mother named me Ada after her mother, Adah, and also her twin sister. She always emphasized that my name was A-d-a, not A-d-a-h. I don't know why she spelled it differently, but I think she was trying to be respectful to me as an individual. I got my middle name, Elizabeth, from my Menominee grandmother. I have two brothers and two sisters; four other children died in infancy. I was nearly two years old when my brother Joseph Edward, named for my father, was born in 1937. When my first sister was born in 1940, my father took Joe and me to the hospital to see her. She was in my mother's arms when we came into her room. This was one of the few tender moments I recall between my parents. My father asked my mother what she wanted to name the baby, and she uncharacteristically deferred to him. "How about Nebuchadnezzar?" he teased her. "No!" she replied, clearly amused. "How about Ag-nes?" he said, drawing out the syllables as my mother vehemently shook her head. He knew these objectionable names would make my mother more amenable to the name he really wanted to give the baby. He had been reading a book about King Farouk of Egypt, who had a daughter named Ferial. My father liked the sound of the name, so that was his third suggestion. My mother agreed, and my sister became Ferial Evelyn. By the time my brother

Ada Deer as a child on the Menominee Reservation, ca. 1939.

Robert Earl (1944) and sister Constance Ellen (1948) were born, I was old enough to name them. My father had wanted Rose to be a part of Connie's name, but they forgot to include it, so all our middle names begin with E.

I always enjoyed the little babies. They were beautiful kids, a wonderful combination of my father and mother. Today they claim I was always telling them what to do, so I tease them, "Well, somebody had to tell you." We didn't fight a lot because our mother was a good mother and our father went to work to provide for us. Although cousins came to visit, we were each other's playmates. My father's enormous workhorses were a constant source of entertainment for us. He used them to plow and haul, but we regarded them as pets, just like the cats and dogs. I still remember the names of the two mares, Babe and Daisy. My brother Joe and I would gently pull their tails and stroke their legs. They would just look back to see what was happening. We weren't the least bit afraid of them.

I think my brother had a sense of sibling rivalry, and he could be quite contentious. We didn't have many toys, so we played with adult tools and imitated our parents. When I was four or five, I was outside sweeping the yard around the cabin, and he picked up an ax and chopped up the ground where I was sweeping. I said, "Get out of here! I'm keeping this clean." But he wasn't going to listen to me. Pretty soon he chopped my foot. I was just standing there with my broom. He picked up this ax, and he chopped my foot. All of a sudden the blood started spurting, and I screamed. My mother came out, and she saw all this blood. She called to my dad, and we rushed to the hospital. I was all right, but afterwards I kept a close eye on my brother Joe when there was an ax lying around.

I was thirteen when Connie was born. That is also when my mother decided it was time for me to learn how to drive. I always tell everybody that I was born an adult, but driving a car seemed like too much responsibility for a thirteen-year-old. I suspect that my mother doubted my father's dependability, since he had begun drinking pretty heavily, and she thought we needed another driver in the house. One day we were driving down the road when she stopped the car and told me, "Get over here and start driving." I said, "I'm only thirteen. I don't want to do that." She insisted, "It's time for you to learn." We argued, but finally I caved in. The car had a stick shift. She explained the shift pattern, I put the car in first gear then released the clutch, and we lurched along. I practiced a little bit the next day, then the day after that my mother said, "You have to take me to the hospital." Whoa! We were at the cabin, she was having labor pains, my father was not there, and I was scared for her. But we had to get to the hospital, which was several miles down the road from where we lived. I don't know how I did it, but I drove her to the hospital, and I brought the car back home. I think I earned the right to name Connie.

■ ■ ■

Our cabin was on a hill overlooking the river. I would wake up in the morning to the sound of the river running and the birds singing. I acquired a deep love of the land and the water and the animals, a love which remains with me. But our life was hard. With so many small children, my mother could not work outside the home. In addition to his job at the mill, my father hunted and fished, and in the summer he hitched his big horses to a plow and prepared a garden. All of his work helped feed us. We never went hungry. For other necessities, we drove about ten miles down the road to Shawano. Sometimes a box of clothes arrived from my mother's brother or other relatives in the East. We did not have running water: there was a pump outside for drinking water, but we also hauled water from the river for washing clothes, and we had an outhouse. As we got older, my sister Ferial and I would walk to the hospital a couple of times a week to take a bath; at other times we took sponge baths. We didn't have any electricity until the early 1950s and then only briefly. We chopped wood to heat and cook with, and I did my schoolwork by lamplight. I didn't mind any of those chores, but altogether they took the whole day and there was hardly any time left for what I wanted to do, which was read. As poor as we were, we lived no worse than most Menominees and better than many.

My father had been raised Catholic and placed in a Catholic boarding school, and my mother was raised Quaker and attended a Methodist school, but neither had much interest in organized religion. If my mother ever professed a religious affiliation, it was Quaker. She did sometimes validate her largely secular views by paraphrasing the Bible—"God will do the impossible; you do the possible" was a favorite—but she seemed to be interested in Christianity primarily as a philosophy of life. In her later struggles for Menominee rights, she sometimes invoked God and the Bible to challenge those who violated the tribe's sovereignty, seized Menominee resources, and impoverished Indian people. She never expected God to make things right; she simply demanded that human beings do what she believed the Bible commanded: treat each other justly.

Most Menominees were at least nominally Catholic, but some practiced an Indigenous religion called Midewiwin, which focused on spiritual power received through participation in a cycle of seasonal ceremonies. While Catholicism tended to emphasize individual salvation, Midewiwin stressed the importance of believers joining together and calling on their spiritual power through song or other ceremonial practices. In 1914 a small Native American Church (a religion originating in Oklahoma and incorporating peyote in its ritual) was established on the reservation.

My parents decided early on that they would not raise us Catholic. Midewiwin was not an option because my mother, and perhaps my father, knew little about its practices or beliefs, and neither was the Native American Church. Nevertheless, I vaguely remember my father taking me to some sort of ceremonial events at the reservation community of Zoar, where the language was Menominee, but no one explained to me what was going on. I do not think it was a Midewiwin ceremony, but my memories suggest to me that my father had survived the brainwashing of boarding school with some appreciation for his culture intact.

In the period when my father attended boarding school, the United States was pursuing a policy of extinguishing American Indian cultures and tribes' common titles to their land. Menominees resisted repeated attempts to allot their tribal lands, especially their forests, to individuals, so their lands remained intact. But the culture took a beating, largely because of boarding schools. Two boarding schools operated in Keshena, one government and one Catholic, along with a day school in Neopit. Children who lived near Keshena could attend the schools as day students, but those whose families lived farther away, or who had no one to care for them, boarded at the schools. Most teachers at all the reservation schools had little use for Menominee traditions. Language was one of the most obvious expressions of culture and, in an instructional setting, one of the most easily attacked. The schools prohibited children, including my father, from speaking their native language. One result, I think, was that children came to regard their language as something to be embarrassed about. Even as adults, they rarely spoke it within the hearing of English speakers, nor did they teach it to their children. As a result, today fewer than twenty Menominees speak their own language, and the success of tribal efforts to recover the language remains uncertain.

I became aware of the fact that my father spoke Menominee when I was a small child. People knew that he was fluent in the language, and old-timers who used to call on us spoke Menominee with my father. One day Mr. Napone Perrote was visiting, and I noticed that I could not understand what they were saying. I became very upset and ran to my mother for an explanation. "They are speaking your language, Ada," she told me. I was shocked: "*My* language?" "Your tribal language," she said. "Can I learn it?" I asked. She replied, "You are going to have to talk to your father about that because I don't know it and he does." I think that was my first key to understanding what it meant to be Menominee—Menominees speak a different language. So periodically I would ask him, "Dad, can I learn the language? Will you teach me?" "Oh, just get out of here," he would say. "No, I'm not doing that." When I got older, he would take me with him when he went to visit some of the elders, and they would speak Menominee. He might have thought I would just pick up the language, but I didn't. Later on I asked him why he did not teach me, and he said he didn't want his children to go through what he had been through—the burdens he carried and the struggles he experienced.

I wish my father and his siblings had been willing not only to teach me the language but also to share more about being Menominee. My father's half-brother Bob, for example, was an amiable man who liked us children, and I enjoyed having him around. But he was a bit aimless. He lived in a horse barn and spent his time hunting, fishing, and doing odd jobs. I asked my Aunt Teresa, his sister, why he never married and had a family of his own. She curtly replied that he was too selfish. I later learned that he, too, had been sent to boarding school. I do not know if that experience explains his life choices, but when I see the beautiful pair of floral beaded moccasins with puckered toes that he wore and which my brother Robert donated to the Menominee museum, I feel a great sense of loss for all the things he knew but did not tell us.

My mother always seemed to enjoy her children, but my father did not. He was not proud of being a Native person, and he seemed to have a deep sense of inferiority or inadequacy. I sometimes think he would have been happier living two hundred years earlier, when subsistence depended on men hunting and fishing rather than working in a mill. I suspect his own history as well as the difficulty of providing for us was to blame for the deep sadness that seemed to haunt him. There were, however, more pervasive, less personal reasons for it. Native people had suffered tremendous loss of land and resources, a catastrophe that few non-Indians even acknowledged. Adding insult to injury, those exercising authority over Indian lives demeaned Native languages and cultural practices. Furthermore, when Indians tried to make decisions for themselves, the very people charged with helping them—U.S. agents and missionaries—threw up roadblocks.

My father, like so many people around him, became addicted to alcohol. Drinking was part of the social, cultural, and historical pattern of their lives. I can understand my father's alcoholism from a social scientific point of view, but the impact on my family makes it difficult to face. My mother never knew whether or not he would drink up his paycheck. When my father drank, he often became violent. In 1940, just before my sister Ferial was born, he beat up my mother. I couldn't believe it. My mother hunched over to protect her unborn infant, and I started screaming at him to stop. My father's violence made a profound impact on me. I decided early in life that I would never allow any man to have any control over me—and I haven't. I have dated men and I have male friends, but I am not willing to surrender one bit of my autonomy to anyone. I like to say that, by staying single, I saved myself from my first divorce.

My father was not alone in his drinking. All his siblings drank. His sister Rose and her husband drank excessively long before it became a problem for my father.

They would arrive at our house falling-down drunk, fighting with each other, and behaving stupidly. I asked my mother, "Why are they acting that way?" and she replied, "Well, they're drinking." I was confused since I knew about drinking water and milk. When I drank, I did not behave that way. And so I asked, "What are they drinking?" "They're drinking alcohol." "Oh, that's what happens when you drink alcohol," I thought to myself. "Alcohol is bad. Don't drink."

If they were on a bender, Aunt Rose and her husband neglected their six children. When these cousins came to visit, they would jump out of the car and run into our house, which they proceeded to ransack, looking for food. "Mom, why are they doing that?" I asked, and she replied, "They're hungry." And she fed them. My mother didn't put them down, but she did ask friends and relatives to stay away from us when they were drinking. I don't think any of them ever honored her request. Because of my father's drinking, we never knew how much money there would be, but my mother made sure that we had food.

Unfortunately, my brother Joe followed in my father's footsteps. He started drinking as a teenager. When he finished school, he went into the military. After he came home, he worked at the mill as a lumber grader and made decent money. My father enjoyed his company, and they drank together. Joe married, but after several years his wife divorced him because of his drinking. He remarried, and his second wife told him that she would leave him if he continued his drinking. At the age of forty, he stopped. I asked him, "How did this happen? What did you do?" He said, "I just quit." I think it is testament to his character and his strength that he could stop drinking cold turkey. To my knowledge, he hasn't had a drink since then, and I am very proud of him for that.

I decided early on that alcohol was trouble. I was enormously conflicted when I saw my aunt and uncle drinking because I really liked them. My mother didn't criticize them, but she never joined in. My father was always happy to see them, and he would visit them from time to time. Alcohol was their social lubricator. I was really afraid to engage in any kind of drinking when I was growing up, and even now, I only have an occasional glass of wine with friends. I have learned, of course, that not all Indians drink, and that not all people who drink excessively are Indians. The causes of alcoholism are complex and not fully understood, but I regard the plague of alcoholism, which historically has crippled many Indian communities, to be a legacy of European conquest. Europeans first introduced whiskey to Indians and, through their own behavior, encouraged binge drinking. Liquor flowed at treaty negotiations that resulted in the loss of Indian land and resources.

My mother must have had a lonely life, at least when we were small. She was something of a loner, but because she was a nurse, women in the community sought her out for childcare advice and treatment of minor medical problems. I do not think she developed close friendships with any of these women until the 1950s, when threats to the tribe brought them together. I think she could have been closer to Rose had it not been for my aunt's alcoholism. She did not much like my Aunt Teresa—and the feeling was mutual—but Aunt Teresa liked me. Teresa had only one son; she had always wanted a daughter, but she could bear no more children. When I was four or five years old, my mother decided that I was old enough to spend a night away from her, so she sent me to stay with Aunt Teresa. Then Aunt Teresa concluded that my mother was not raising me properly—she had her own ideas about raising kids—and decided I should come to live with her. My mother, after all, had other children. She was eager to take me away, but my mother, of course, refused to let me go. My mother also rebuffed her sister-in-law's childcare tips, partly because she was equally opinionated. She knew what she was doing, and she was not about to be told by anyone else how to raise us. "I'll raise my kids, you raise your kid, and we'll see what happens," my mother said. She was civil to Aunt Teresa, but they were never very friendly.

I do not think I was aware that my mother was white until I was about five years old. I certainly had seen other white people—clerks in Shawano, BIA personnel, Aunt Rose's husband—but I did not draw an analogy with my mother, who was primarily, of course, my mother. Even as a young child, however, I did begin to distinguish between who was white and who was Indian. My father had these white so-called friends. They were always asking my father to do something for them, and he would, but they never seemed to do anything for us in return. One white farmer, Otto Schulz, used to bring his mares to breed with my father's stallion, but he would not pay a fair price for these services. My father's reluctance to demand fair payment usually precipitated an argument with my mother because we desperately needed the money. I knew these men were white and that I did not like them, but I do not remember whether or not I connected their dishonesty with their race.

I certainly associated the BIA with whites, as did all Menominees. In Neopit, there was a row of white frame houses, which Menominees referred to as the "White City." I first thought it was because of the color of the houses, but then someone told me that it was because that was where the government people lived. Almost all of them were white, so that is how the neighborhood got its name. As a child, I was not sure what those people did, but I sure knew what race they were. Although I remember these early impressions of whites, the negative racial messages of childhood did not have a lasting impact on me because I also knew whites, especially my teachers, who were generous and kind.

My most painful experience around race came from my grandfather Wood. When I was about five years old, a shiny blue car drove up to our house. My mother was inside our house, but my brother Joe and I were outside playing in the dirt. It was summer, and we were brown as berries as well as caked in mud. A man and woman got out of the car. The man had white hair and wore a suit. The woman, wearing a stylish silk dress, looked exactly like my mother. They were my grandfather and my Aunt Adah. I was befuddled. If I had ever been told my mother had a twin, I had not understood what that meant. I knew that the woman stepping from the car was not my mother because my mother was in the cabin, but here she stood, right in front of me. I ran up to her, and she cringed, fearful no doubt that I would touch her with my grimy little hands. Then my mother came out. I don't know what they all talked about, but the conversation was heated. Finally my grandfather blurted out: "All right, Constance, stay in the backwoods with your half-breeds." They got into the car and left.

Upset by the mystery of my mother's double and the tenor of the encounter, I ran to my mother. "Mom, what's a half-breed?" I asked. She had tears in her eyes, and she could not speak. Later she told me that they had wanted her to give up this "nonsense," put us in an orphanage, and come back East to lead a proper life. She refused, of course. She loved us dearly, she still loved my father, and, despite the hardships, she liked living on the Menominee Reservation. She and her father wrote to each other, but she tore up his letters after reading them. Ever curious, I asked what was in the letters. "I don't want you to read them," she replied. "They're bad letters, they're wrong letters, they're angry letters."

My mother never reconciled with her family, but I saw my grandfather again when I was fourteen. Through my school, I acquired a pen pal who lived in Altamont, New York, which is near Albany. She invited me to visit her, and my mother let me go alone from Wisconsin to New York by bus. I spent a wonderful summer with them. While in the East, I met my uncle Morris and aunt Betty, who took me sightseeing in New York City, a thrilling experience. Then they took me to see my grandfather. I had only two or three dresses and one pair of good shoes, but I made a favorable impression. My grandfather was astonished that I spoke English correctly, that I liked to read, and that I had very good manners. I was polite and respectful, and I could carry on an intelligent conversation with adults. Even without Aunt Teresa's help, my mother had managed to raise a perfectly presentable young woman. My grandfather began making plans to visit my mother the next summer. Unfortunately, both he and his wife died before they could make the trip. I would like to believe that my trip East precipitated a kind of reconciliation between my mother and her father. As for me, my second meeting with my grandfather did not erase the memory of my first.

In 1941 my mother divorced my father on the grounds of cruelty, and we moved to the south side of Milwaukee. Despite the divorce, my father followed us. Employment opportunities were better in Milwaukee, and my father worked for a while in a foundry. I do not think my father lived with us initially, but he continued to contribute to our support. By the time we moved to Milwaukee, my sister Ferial had arrived, and Robert was born in 1944, following a reconciliation between my parents. My father, who was classified 3-A because of his dependents, finally got drafted in January 1945. I am not sure how a man with four small children ended up drafted, but draft boards were white and my father, of course, was not. When my father left for basic training, we stayed in Milwaukee because my mother thought it would be easier to take care of us there than on the reservation. I also think she was uncertain about a future with my father and probably saw this as the beginning of a real future without him.

After my mother died in 1984, my brother Joe mentioned something to my sister Connie about our mother having had another baby besides Robert in Milwaukee, and having given it up for adoption. When Connie asked me about it, I was absolutely flabbergasted. I was older than Joe, certainly old enough to remember our mother being pregnant, but I have no recollection of this pregnancy at all. My other siblings and I couldn't believe it was true. My mother loved all of us so much that it was hard to imagine her surrendering a newborn, but Joe insisted that he remembered correctly. My parents were divorced, of course, and my father had left Milwaukee in January 1945, so it began to make sense. Our mother might have given birth to a child fathered by someone other than our father and could think of no feasible alternative to adoption. Connie, who by 1984 was a lawyer, got busy. Ultimately, she tracked down our half-sister, Carol Jones, in California. Carol, who was born in 1945, already had uncovered the identity of her birth mother and had come to the reservation several years earlier looking for her, but everyone she talked to said that they didn't know any people named Deer. When we finally met Carol, I could not believe how much she looked like our mother. I hope that Carol's father gave my mother the affection and tenderness that seemed lacking in her relationship with my father.

I started school in Milwaukee. The years I spent in the public schools there had a profound effect on me. The teachers enjoyed their jobs and were proud of their profession. They were committed to their students, guiding them, showing them warmth, and providing encouragement. They instilled in me a love of reading, and they encouraged me to be open to new ideas and experiences. I kept in contact with a couple of them over the years, and their continuing interest in me and my career was empowering. They helped me form study habits that I retained when my family returned to the reservation.

I could hardly wait to go to school each day because it was so much fun. I liked being with other children and I loved my teachers, especially my fourth-grade teacher, Mildred Raasch. I vividly remember the day I asked her how to spell the word "prejudice." She replied, "Ada, come up to the blackboard and sound it out." In front of the whole class I began to write "p-r-e"— but I did not know whether the next letter was "j" or "g." Mrs. Raasch helped me, and I finished the word. "What does it mean?" I asked. I was so intent on spelling the word correctly that I do not remember exactly what she replied, but I think it was something like "prejudice is when people have false information about others and base their dislike for them on that information without really knowing them." She was one of the teachers I kept in touch with after we left Milwaukee. Years later, I nominated Mrs. Raasch for a teaching award given by the University of Wisconsin–Milwaukee to public school teachers, which she won.

Milwaukee was our first experience living in a largely non-Indian community and, as Indians, we children faced curiosity and schoolyard hostility, hence my interest in the word "prejudice." Joe and I were conscious that, unlike our classmates, we were Indians. The only other Indian in our school was a little Oneida girl. Our teachers seemed both intrigued by us and supportive of our presence, although sometimes in ways that made me uncomfortable. Like many people, they expected me to know everything about Indians, but my mother was white, my father was reticent, my aunts and uncles were busy with their own families, and my grandparents were dead. I didn't have anyone sitting me on their knee, pouring Indian traditions into my ear. One teacher asked me how "my people" celebrated Thanksgiving. I remember thinking, "Why is she asking me this? Why isn't she asking everybody? What am I supposed to know about this?" So I said, "We just eat turkey." Her disappointment was obvious, but I could not imagine what she wanted me to say. We *did* eat turkey!

In Milwaukee, I first encountered popular representations of Indians. Through radio programs, comic books, and Saturday-afternoon movies, I learned about cowboys and Indians, but those Indians bore no resemblance to any Indians I knew. I certainly did not equate them to myself. But perhaps the movies and comic books gave our white classmates some ideas about how to deal with Joe and me—they beat us up, which made us really angry. Finally we ganged up on a couple of them and gave them a dose of their own medicine. It wasn't the Little Bighorn, but it was a great victory for us.

The hostility was not limited to children. Most of our neighbors were immigrants, many of them Polish. I remember a family that lived next door to us. They were recent immigrants, and they spoke their own language at home and with friends. I don't know why they were so mean to us. We didn't do anything to them, like throw stones or call them names. One day Joe and I were playing in front of the house, and the lady yelled in heavily accented English, "Go back to where you came from!" I was astonished. We had always lived in Wisconsin.

When the war ended, my father was on a ship headed to Japan. Soon he returned to Milwaukee, and he and my mother decided to go back to the reservation together. Both of them had missed it, and they wanted us to grow up with Menominees. My father, who had dark skin, had experienced racism in the army, which still segregated into black or white. He had served in a white unit as did most Indians, but soldiers who had never met an Indian usually thought he was African American.

Although the house in southside Milwaukee had conveniences that we lacked in the small log cabin on the Wolf River, it was a poor substitute for home. We all longed for the beauty of our reservation and missed our friends and family. Furthermore, my baby brother, Robert, suffered from lactose intolerance and almost died in Milwaukee. Goat's milk saved him. For several years he subsisted largely on goat's milk, which was hard to find in the city. Back home my mother acquired some goats and became a real proponent of goat's milk, which she also believed cured her arthritis. My father went back to work at the mill. After we returned home, my sister Connie was born.

My memory of life after we returned to the reservation is much clearer, of course, than it is for the period before World War II. My aunts and their families, friends, and neighbors visited us from time to time. After the disagreeable neighbors and bullies in Milwaukee, I found Menominee people particularly genial and, despite their poverty, happy. Even though we had been away, they welcomed us back. My father, in particular, was glad to be home where he could speak Menominee, hunt, and fish with his old friends.

After we returned home, I became more aware of how my father made me Menominee, not through self-reflection but because of the way people treated me. One person I particularly remember was Old Mike, whose real name was

Mitchell Pamonicutt. He lived down the road from our cabin in a tar-paper shack. He was always very happy to see us as we walked past him to catch the school bus, and he often gave us apples or little things he thought we would like. He would call out, "Hello, Baby Buck." It was a play on my name, Deer, of course, and he would call Joe "Joe Buck." These became our nicknames, different from our father's name but reminding us—and everyone else—who we belonged to.

My father connected me to Menominees ancestrally and legally, but my mother connected me intellectually by recounting Menominee history. She told me about how the United States had treated Indian people and explained to me how dispossession of my own people had led to the poverty that we experienced and saw all around us. She encouraged me to channel the anger I felt about our mistreatment into trying to change things. In 1954 when Connie entered school, my mother went back to work at the tribal hospital in Keshena. Catholic nuns administered the hospital under an agreement with the BIA, but the tribe paid for it with profits from the lumber mill. My mother's broader engagement with Menominee people led her to become increasingly interested in tribal affairs. She regularly attended General Council meetings and often took us with her. She also encouraged me to attend meetings of the Menominee Indian Advisory Council, which administered tribal affairs. At that time, members were exclusively men. I was interested in what was going on, and I copied my mother by taking notes on what was said. I also wrote down words that I did not understand and found out what they meant later. Here was a young girl with glasses and braids taking notes at the Advisory Council meetings!

Menominees governed themselves under a constitution approved in 1924. It provided for a General Council in which all adult Menominees had a vote. My mother, of course, could not vote, but she was free to observe. The General Council empowered an Advisory Council, which acted as a kind of executive body and spent much of its time dealing with the BIA. The BIA administered a range of educational, medical, and social services on the reservation through the agency in Keshena. These services represented the U.S. government's trust responsibility to the tribe, and the tribe expected the nation to fulfill its obligation.

A BIA supervisor was in charge of the mill in Neopit. The La Follette Act of 1908 had mandated sustainable logging of Menominee forests and employment and advancement opportunities for Menominees in the mill. Menominees were far less interested in profits than they were in conserving their forests and providing a job for any tribal member who wanted one. Even with these objectives, the lumber industry generated sufficient income to support all the tribal services provided by the BIA. The Menominees did not cost the government a dime. The agents, however, tended to have a more capitalistic mindset. They reserved managerial positions and most skilled jobs at the mill for whites, they clear-cut large swaths of forest, and they constructed rail lines and roads that put many Menominee loggers and teamsters out of work. Menominees, however, wanted control of the resources on which their economy rested—the forests and the mill.

In 1935, the year I was born, the Menominees brought suit against the federal government for mismanagement of the forest. In 1951, they finally won a judgment of $8.5 million. This issue and others were widely debated at General Council meetings. I respected the seriousness of the matters at hand, but I also enjoyed the discussions. Although I could not understand it, I liked hearing the Menominee language, which some people still used in debate and a translator interpreted. It was through these general council meetings that I began to acquire an aware-ness of "Menominee" as something more than a racial, social, or cultural term. Menominee was an Indian tribe struggling to govern itself and wrest control of its resources from outsiders. The tribe had legal rights and political power. It would be a long time before I joined the struggle in earnest, but my understanding of myself as a citizen of a sovereign Indian nation, the Menominee Indian Tribe of Wisconsin, began to emerge in those general council meetings.

My Menominee identity is rooted in place, family, and history, not culture. The Indian New Deal, enacted in the year before my birth, purported to end the assimilationist policies that had shaped Indian affairs since the early nine-teenth century. But for the elders in my Menominee family—my father and his siblings—this shift came too late. They already had become victims of those policies. Although they spoke Menominee and perhaps knew about Menominee traditions, they had internalized the assimilationist message to the extent that did not want to burden their children with a culture that they believed had become obsolete. I am proud that some Menominees managed to preserve our language, beliefs, and practices, and that a younger generation is interested in revitalizing our culture. Despite everything, I have never had any doubt that I am Menominee. Nor have I struggled with my biracial ancestry. While some people view their mixed ancestry as a burden, for me it is not a big deal. I accept all of myself. Some Indians who write or speak about this issue see themselves as living in two worlds. I do not. Although my mother was white and I have little connection to ancient Menominee culture, I have no doubt about who I am. I am a Menominee.

CHAPTER 2

■ Preparing for the Future ■

My impoverished childhood convinced me that I did not want to be poor, and early on I decided that education was the way out. But escaping personal poverty was not my only goal. I wanted to be useful, to help people overcome obstacles and challenge the circumstances that held them back. I am sure that this commitment came largely from my mother, who had left her privileged life in Philadelphia to work in Appalachia and on Indian reservations. Furthermore, the conditions that I saw on the Menominee Reservation helped me articulate a goal of helping Indian people. I could not ignore the desperation of my own people. Before I could change things, however, I needed to prepare myself.

When we returned to the reservation, my parents decided to enroll us in the Shawano public schools, where I skipped the fifth grade due to the foundation I had received in Milwaukee. Shawano had a population of about five thousand people, almost all of them white. I suspect the decision to send us to an overwhelmingly white school was difficult for my parents, but they did not want us to attend the reservation schools, which the Catholic Church operated. My father had had a terrible experience in the Catholic boarding school, and they did not want us to repeat that. We were the only Indian students in the Shawano school until high school, when more Indians enrolled because there was no high school on the reservation. Each year at the Shawano school, however, there were fewer and fewer Indians in my grade because so many dropped out. There was a big difference between the number of Indian students who started out as freshmen and who graduated as seniors.

The Menominee students who moved from the reservation schools to the Shawano high school were at a serious disadvantage. Catholic mission schools of that era did not encourage critical thinking, curiosity, individual action, or academic excellence. My cousins, who went to the reservation school, were all very casual about learning. Education was not all that important to them whereas my siblings and I would shovel snow for half a day to get down our road just so that we could go to school the other half. The neighbor kids who lived over the hill laughed at us for doing that.

When we first enrolled in elementary school, my mother had to drive us the ten miles to Shawano. The authorities on the reservation did not like the fact that my parents refused to send us to the reservation schools, and they would not permit us to ride the school bus that carried high school students. Eventually they relented, and we rode the bus. The bus brought its own set of problems. Other kids teased me because I had dark skin, long braids, and glasses. I loved to read, so I always had an armful of books. One summer, I got permission from a teacher to read books that the school library designated appropriate for my next grade, and I read them all. Sometimes on the bus kids jostled me to make me drop my books, and called me "bookworm." I just picked up my books and told them, "I like being a bookworm. I like these books, and you should like books, too." They were trying to intimidate me, of course, but I refused to respond in kind and after a while they stopped teasing me.

I think even as a child I understood that many Indians had ambivalent feelings about education and that these children were expressing deep-seated hostility toward what books represented to them and their families—an oppressive dominant culture, disregard for their own history and culture, the boarding school experience, and lack of opportunity on reservations for educated Indians. Some Indian parents feared that education would separate them from their children and, therefore, did not encourage them to excel in school. Other parents saw education as a rejection of Menominee lifeways and even as a repudiation of their families.

My father no doubt shared many of these feelings. He wanted us to go to school, but he could not understand how much I enjoyed it and how seriously I took my education. For him, school had been an ordeal; for me, it was sheer pleasure. He constantly put me down. Our living situation heightened the friction between the two of us over my bookish ways. The one-room log cabin had one table and one oil lamp. When I studied at night, my father yelled at me to turn out the light, but I still had homework to do. My mother came to my defense,

Ada in high school.

and an argument always ensued. We usually won because there were two of us and one of him, but my bookishness clearly contributed to the tension in the household. My mother looked for solutions.

The first semester of high school, two Mormon missionaries called on us. Mormons believe that Indians are descended from the lost tribes of Israel and so missionaries have a special obligation to bring them back to the true faith. I found the missionaries interesting, probably because, unlike people in other denominations, they talked specifically about how Indians fit into their faith and their version of history. Indians were not villains or victims; they were instead God's chosen people who had simply strayed from the right path. They were genuinely interested in the reservation, unusual for white people, and my mother was happy to answer their questions. I had no intention of converting, but I did like to talk to them.

The Deer family. *Back row*: Ada, brother Joe, Ferial;
Front row: Connie, Constance "Ma" Deer, Robert.

The missionaries ultimately raised the issue of my leaving the reservation and living with a Mormon family in Utah while attending high school. My mother thought it was a good idea, and I agreed. The Mormons bought me a bus ticket, and I went to live in the little town of Gunnison, Utah, with the Luris P. Allen family. They had six or eight children and owned a dairy. I had to work in the dairy after school, which was okay with me, but my chores left me little time to study. They told me about their religion, and I went to various Mormon events with them, but their efforts at conversion were subtle. If I had stayed with them through my high school years, I might have become more susceptible to their

Ada's father, Joe Deer.

message, but my time with them was brief. When I went home for a visit at the end of the semester, I told my mother that I did not have enough time to study. She said, "That's why you're in school. You don't need to go back."

In my senior year of high school, my mother announced that I was going to live in Shawano with family friends: Glarus and Morrie Shectman. They owned a clothing store in Shawano, and Mr. Shectman would bring clothes up to the reservation and sell them out of his car. Mrs. Shectman's father had been the BIA farmer on the Menominee Reservation, a position that made little sense for a tribe that did very little farming. Living in Shawano meant that I could participate in lots of after-school activities. Because other Indian students had to ride the bus back to the reservation after school, few participated in these activities. Once I had the time and opportunity, I became the editor of the high school yearbook, a member of the debate team, and a competitor in public speaking, earning an A for original oration in the state contest. But I did not belong to a high school clique nor did I socialize much with other students. I just never felt that it was important, and I didn't have the money for entertainment and recreation or fancy clothes. I never got to the prom, I like to say, but I did get to the White House.

I enjoyed all the subjects in school that required reading. Math and science were harder. That is not where my talents lie, although I did not realize it at the time. I had a really good memory so if I needed to know something, I just memorized it. Somehow or other I got through algebra, geometry, and chemistry, but I never really understood those subjects. I asked questions like, "What does this formula mean?" and "Why are we doing this?" The teacher looked at me and said, "Never mind, just do it." I seemed to be alone in asking these kinds of questions. Because I missed the fundamentals and had little natural aptitude for these courses, I was ill prepared when I reached college.

Another course that posed a major problem for me in high school was home economics, which my high school required all girls to take. My mother had little interest in domestic skills and even less knowledge about how to perform them. She did not sew, and her cooking was so bad that my father often fed what she made to the dogs. "This is going to be a problem," I thought when I showed up for class. Many of the students were from the surrounding farms, and they participated in 4-H and Future Homemakers of America (FHA). They already knew all this stuff. So did the town kids, most of whom were only a generation removed from the farm.

First off, the teacher, Irene Crouse, said, "Girls, we're going to start our sewing unit by making a dirndl skirt." Dirndl? I had no idea what that was. Then she told us how much material and thread to bring to the next class. So I got the yardage and I got the thread. At the next class meeting, she assigned each of us a sewing machine and said, "Now, you have to thread your bobbins." I looked at my machine. There was nothing that said "bobbin" on that machine. Finally I raised my hand: "Excuse me, Miss Crouse, what's a bobbin?" She stared at me in disbelief. She doesn't know what a bobbin is? So I explained that my mother did not sew and that I did not know much about sewing. In fact, I knew nothing about sewing. She must have groaned silently, but she showed me how to do it. This, of course, was only the first of many steps, each equally new to me, and so this scene was repeated at every class. It took me the whole semester to make that darned dirndl skirt, a task my fellow students completed in days.

Near the end of the school year, Mrs. Crouse announced, "Girls, you all have been invited to the FHA convention, and we have to select people to represent our school." I recoiled in horror, an instinctive but no doubt unnecessary response to the prospect of displaying my ineptitude on a broader stage. Then she said, "We also need a master of ceremonies." All the girls immediately nominated me. I knew nothing about home economics, but I certainly could talk. So I went off to the FHA convention and presided. At first I thought the class just did not want me to embarrass them with my poorly made project, but then I discovered that, in fact, they all were terrified of public speaking. At the end, they congratulated me and told me, "I couldn't do that." I said, "Well, I can't do what you can do, so we are even."

I regret that I never had an opportunity to take courses in women's studies, African American studies, Chicano studies, or American Indian studies, either in high school or college. These courses resulted from the activism of the 1960s and 1970s, and they have enriched both students' understanding of the society in which they live and their appreciation for people who are not like them. They also enable students to discuss troubling episodes in our nation's past that they may not be able to process on their own. Since I was an avid reader, I learned about the history of Native people through books not classes. I absorbed alone the tragedies of the Indian wars and the confinement of Indians to reservations and the magnitude of Indian land loss. My anger led to depression. Finally, my mother told me that, rather than becoming depressed, I needed to put my anger to use. She said, "You were put on this earth for a purpose. You are here to help people. You are here to help *your* people." I took what she said to heart.

How I was going to help was the issue. I helped at home by taking care of the babies, hauling water, carrying wood. But how could I help other people, especially Indians? I knew that Indians were very poor, a fact that going to school in Shawano with middle-class white kids drove home. What could I do to help since we were very poor, too? Once again, my mother provided the answer: "You have a brain, use it." If I was going to help Indians, I had to continue to study hard, finish high school, and go to college, rare accomplishments for Menominees of my generation. I had to learn as much as I could and figure out how to put that knowledge to use for my people.

Concrete ideas about how I could help began to develop while I was in high school. Two avenues opened to me. I was conscious of one but not the other. I thought that I would enter the medical field. In particular, I wanted to be a doctor. My mother's profession as a nurse probably inspired me because she helped individuals in very obvious ways. She worked at the reservation hospital for a while after we returned from Milwaukee, but even when she was not employed as a nurse, people came to her with medical problems and sought advice.

The more obscure avenue that opened was political activism, which I did not recognize as a possibility until years later. Between my junior and senior years in high school, I had the opportunity to participate in Badger Girls State, a program founded in 1941 by the American Legion Auxiliary to prepare young women for leadership roles. Held in Madison, the state capital, the program introduced participants to how government worked and asked them to develop political platforms and outline the means to accomplish them. Several state legislators met with us, and the experience really got me interested in government. For the first time, I began to understand how political institutions and policies affected people's lives.

The extracurricular activity that had the greatest impact on me was the Youth Advisory Board of the Governor's Commission on Human Rights. The Governor's Commission brought together people from different races and religions and published materials about various groups in Wisconsin. When commission members set up the Youth Advisory Board, my teachers nominated me for a position. As a member, I read the commission publications, including *Housing in Wisconsin* and *Migrants in Wisconsin*. I learned about a Wisconsin that I never knew existed. I do not think I had ever met an African American, Jewish, or Asian person until I joined the board. I found their different histories and cultures fascinating, but I also appreciated how similar we all were in terms of our values and aspirations. This experience broadened my horizons considerably.

A state social worker who was recruiting a diverse group of Wisconsin high school students to participate in statewide youth programs encouraged me to attend Camp Miniwanca, an interfaith leadership training camp in Michigan supported by the American Youth Foundation. Four visionary men had established the foundation for the purpose of developing young leaders. My mother agreed, so I went for two weeks and had a wonderful time. The camp program was based loosely on American Indian philosophy. The campers belonged to tribes, which engaged in various competitions. I now recognize how artificial the Indian theme was, how it embodied a number of stereotypes, and how absurd it was that white people were teaching me how to be an Indian. But this was the first time I had encountered a positive image of Indians or genuine respect for what camp organizers thought was an Indian way of life. My Menominee father and his family had little pride in their Native heritage; if anything, it made them feel ashamed and embarrassed. But these white people believed that Indians had valuable lessons to impart to young people. The portrayals might have been inauthentic and stereotypical, but they were positive and they helped me think about myself as an Indian in a positive way. I think many Native people embrace such stereotypes for similar reasons—they counteract not only fictional images of savage Indians but also preconceptions of Indians as impoverished, dysfunctional people with little to offer.

The camp program focused on our mental, physical, social, and spiritual development, what the founders called the Four-Fold Way of Life. We learned the importance of balancing these dimensions of our lives and using them in service to our communities. In addition to doing typical camp activities like swimming and crafts, we took classes and met individually with advisors. Every night at sunset we attended vespers on the sand dunes overlooking Lake Michigan, a spectacular view. I continued to attend the camp after I went to college, and each summer, I filled out a camp questionnaire that was supposed to show how well balanced my life was. After filling out the questionnaire, campers discussed their progress with an advisor, many of whom were prominent people. One year my advisor was Margaret Hickey, a lawyer and journalist who was public affairs editor for *Ladies Home Journal.* According to the questionnaire, my life was never very balanced—it was high on mental and social, low on physical and spiritual.

My family had very little money, but my mother encouraged me to take advantage of every opportunity I had to learn about the broader world—visiting my pen pal and her family in New York, participating in Girls State, going to Camp Miniwanca. Sometimes her enrichment efforts were more eccentric. In the late 1940s, she got some money from her family's business enterprises. She used some of it to send my brother Joe and me to a riding school at the White Horse Ranch in Nebraska. The ranch was renowned for its herd of trained white horses and its traveling shows in which children performed on horseback. We stayed for six weeks and learned horsemanship and jumping. I also managed to ride Roman style, standing with one foot on each of two bareback horses. I am not sure what my mother's objectives were in sending us there. We had not asked to go and, in fact, I was quite reluctant. Given my mother's lifelong love of horses and romantic view of Indians, maybe she thought we had a future as "show Indians." More seriously, she just wanted to provide us with an experience beyond the normally straitened circumstances of our childhood.

Perhaps the wackiest idea my mother had for opening my eyes to life beyond the reservation was entering me in a contest to identify the six most beautiful Indian girls in the nation. The prize was a trip to Hollywood where the girls would appear in a movie, *The Battle of Rogue River* (released 1954), with George Montgomery, Martha Hyer, and Richard Denning. I was not interested. I was about to graduate from high school, and I was going to college that fall. This silly contest was not on my agenda for that summer. But she kept bugging me: "You have to go down and get your picture taken. You have to do this."

Finally I gave in. "What do I have to do to enter?" I asked. "You have to get your photograph taken." "But Ma, I don't have anything Indian to wear." She was willing to concede that, indeed, I had nothing Indian, but she did not regard that as a major obstacle. Somewhere, she found me a fringed brown flannel dress, a headband, and a feather. I suspect this getup was a costume for a tribal pageant or a recent production on the reservation of *Hiawatha*. Laughing to myself as I put it on, I thought, "Well, finally I get to be an Indian." So I had my photograph taken to get my mother to stop pestering me. Once the photo was done, I pushed the whole business to the back of my mind.

Then the letter arrived: "Congratulations. Columbia Pictures has selected you as one of the six most beautiful Indian girls in America. You will receive an expense-paid trip to Hollywood and a part in a movie." I was surprised, but I also was worried. "I'm going to college in September," I thought. "I can't be messing around with Hollywood this summer." But my mother and Glarus, the lady I lived with, were terribly excited. Glarus notified the Shawano newspaper, which announced that I had been chosen, and there was no turning back. Since Glarus had a dress shop, she was able to provide me with the clothes I needed for my Hollywood debut.

I boarded an airplane in Green Bay, Wisconsin, my first ever flight. On arriving in Hollywood, California, I followed the instructions the studio sent me and took a cab to the Hollywood Roosevelt Hotel. I checked in at the desk and went up to the suite of rooms reserved for the six most beautiful Indian girls. The others already had arrived. Three of them looked white to me—they were from Oklahoma tribes and had hairdresser hair. The other two, a Navajo and a Sioux, had darker skin and long hair. I got along better with them. None of us was fluttering around, but we all were pleasantly excited. We had a chaperone and a driver, who gave us a tour of Hollywood and took us to the Mocambo nightclub. Our chaperone kept us on schedule for photo shoots, makeup sessions, and wardrobe fittings. For the fittings, we went to a building where there were rows and rows of all kinds of costumes. They took us to the "Indian dresses." Mine was just gorgeous. It was white leather with a fully beaded top.

The Battle of Rogue River was a B Western about a real conflict that took place in the 1850s, but like most historical films, it played fast and loose with the facts. In the movie, the Indians and U.S. soldiers had reached a truce after a long period of hostilities, which local white businessmen tried to reignite. They feared that Oregon statehood, which the truce made possible, would bring an end to their illegal mining, timber cutting, and ranching. George Montgomery's character exposed their nefarious plan, reconciled the Indians, and got the girl. The six most beautiful Indian girls appeared in scenes of the Indian camp. We probably were the only real Indians on the set; the rest were white men painted to look like Indians. There was one speaking line for the beautiful Indian girls. All of us were asked to read a few lines from the script, and I got the part. The director explained: "Now here's the scene. A man is going to come riding into the village on a horse, and your line is: 'Did you meet the soldiers? Then you are safe.'" The "Indian" on horseback responded disdainfully, "I don't speak with mere women. I speak with the chief." We did one, maybe two, takes and that was that.

I found it increasingly difficult to take any of this seriously. People were constantly fawning over us. My smirk became more pronounced, and I had trouble stifling my giggles. When we had our photographs taken with George Montgomery, I decided, "I'm going to have some fun here." So I said, "Oh, Mr. Montgomery. I've seen you in the movies. Little did I dream that I would ever be in a picture with you." He smiled broadly, took my hand, and began squeezing it, which I thought was hilarious. The other beautiful Indian girls were appalled, and I heard the staff muttering, "I wonder what Dinah would think about this? We're going to tell Dinah." They were referring to Montgomery's wife, Dinah Shore. I suspect Dinah would have found the whole thing as funny as I did. By the time the photos were taken, I was ready to go home. The Hollywood life, I had decided, was not for me.

I returned home a local celebrity. The Shectmans arranged for the Chamber of Commerce to hold a parade in my honor. I did not want a parade, but the next thing I knew, I was riding in this convertible waving my hand. I am sure this was the only parade the Shawano Chamber of Commerce ever held for an Indian. I felt really awkward about all the attention. I was accustomed to being praised for my intelligence and hard work, but I had no experience with attracting attention for my looks. My mother and father did not stress our appearance, nor did our relatives. Yet in Hollywood the publicist and the chaperone kept saying, "Aren't they beautiful!" I did not like all the fawning. I thought it was silly and that they were being hypocritical. But I must admit that I enjoyed the whole Hollywood escapade—almost as much as I have relished telling the story of my movie career over the years.

My formal education gave me a future, but so did the other kinds of activities in which I engaged, even the trip to Hollywood. My experience points to how important it is for children, especially poor children, to have opportunities to develop their potential. From Badger Girls State and Camp Miniwanca to trick riding and the Hollywood movie, I gained self-confidence and self-discipline. I learned how to get along with and appreciate people from diverse backgrounds, how to set goals and realize them, and how to plan for a life very different from the ones my parents led. I was extraordinarily fortunate that my mother understood the value of such experiences and that she, along with my teachers, made opportunities available to me. Few poor children have this kind of support, which is a great tragedy.

More important to me than Hollywood stardom and the Shawano parade was enrolling in my freshman year at college. My mother expected her children to go to college, and with the exception of my brother Joe, who joined the army, we did. My sister Ferial studied dance at Julliard and later got a doctorate in education and counseling. Connie has both law and nursing degrees. Robert completed two master's degrees and left graduate school after having completed all requirements for a PhD except his dissertation. By contrast, most people on the Menominee Reservation who pursued higher education went to the Haskell Institute, which was then an Indian vocational school in Kansas, or some other kind of vocational school.

Since my family had no money to spare, my options seemed limited. Haskell, which Indians could attend for free, did not appeal to me, so I thought about joining the Women's Army Corps, which would provide me with training. When I was in my senior year, I asked my guidance counselor what was the best school that I could afford. He said, "The University of Wisconsin." He helped me apply, but I worried about how I would pay the cost. Then I got a letter from the Menominee Indian Advisory Council, the tribe's governing body, announcing that I had been selected to receive the tribal scholarship, which was a thousand dollars a year for four years. That covered my tuition, books, and housing. To earn pin money, I got a job as a librarian's helper and later as a waitress in the dorm cafeteria.

My tribe's investment in me brought a new awareness of what it meant to be a Menominee. Not only were my parents responsible for me, but so was my tribe. I began to understand that we have obligations to be helpful beyond our families, and that institutions and governments can be forces for good in the lives of individuals. I was keenly aware that I had an obligation to repay that investment in some way. I think Native people who are really grounded in their tribal communities feel a sense of responsibility for the tribe and recognize the importance of reciprocity. It took me a long time to figure out how to fulfill that obligation, but looking back at my life, I am satisfied that I did so. A four-thousand-dollar scholarship made it possible for me to acquire the skills—and reinforced my sense of moral duty—to lead the tribe in an epic struggle for the historic reversal of American Indian policy and the restoration of Menominees' legal status as a federally recognized Indian tribe.

That scholarship also introduced me to the resentment that some non-Indians harbor over what they perceive as unfair Indian advantages. When some of the girls in my dorm found out about my scholarship, they did not see why I should have this money just because I was Menominee. Their parents had to pay. Of course, their parents *could* pay. They had grown up in houses with electricity and plumbing, not a one-room cabin on an impoverished Indian reservation. Since then I have arrived at a deeper understanding of their attitude. Many non-Indians resent the government funds that flow to Indian tribes and think the revenue stream should stop. They either don't realize or ignore the history of these monies. Indian tribes signed treaties with the federal government in which they surrendered their land in exchange for monetary and other considerations. The provisions of those treaties remain in force in the twenty-first century unless Congress acts to revoke a specific stipulation. Treaties reserved land for tribes, which became reservations. The federal government holds reservation land in trust and, therefore, assumes responsibility for health, education, and other social services that state and local governments normally provide. In the case of the Menominees, the tribe actually paid for most of those services from the earnings of the lumber mill. If one thinks about the Menominee tribe as one big family that shared income from a family business, then in a sense my "family" did pay my expenses.

For people who grew up in college-educated families and in communities where most people value education, it is hard to imagine how daunting college can be for those who didn't. Even the most basic things are huge hurdles. I had no idea how to select classes or programs of study. I did not know what a catalog of courses was, nor did I realize that before I enrolled I should have received an orientation packet, which apparently got lost in the mail. Still interested in becoming a doctor, I registered for premed courses. Was that ever a mistake!

Chemistry 101 met in a lecture hall with more than a hundred students. Then we had to go to lab, where I read the instructions for the chemistry experiment. I had no idea what we were supposed to be doing. Not even the periodic table made sense to me. I was equally unfit for algebra. After several weeks, I concluded that premed was not for me. By this time, I had heard of a special liberal arts program, Integrated Liberal Studies (ILS). I went to the housemother in the dorm, and I told her that I was not going to do well in my course of study. It was simply the wrong field for me, and I wanted to change my classes although we were several weeks into the semester. She said, "You have to get permission from the dean." I had no idea what deans were, who they were, or where to find them, but finally, I made it to the appropriate office. "I want to take liberal arts," I announced. "As it is, I will do well in English and German, but I probably will fail chemistry and algebra." The dean agreed, and I got accepted into the ILS program, much to the amazement of the housemother and the girls in the dorm.

After I recovered from that near debacle, I settled into college life. I could hardly believe my good fortune. Here I was at the University of Wisconsin, taking classes from incredibly impressive professors. I took courses I was genuinely interested in. I enrolled in U.S. history with Merle Curti, the distinguished American social and intellectual historian, whose class I enjoyed enormously. Many years later I met him at a political event, and he laughed when I told him, "I was one of the masses sitting in your classes." I thought about majoring in history, but I could not figure out what one would do with a history degree, so I did not major in it. But I did enjoy the classes.

I welcomed the chance to get to know faculty members. I found my historical geography class so interesting that I met with Professor Andrew Clark during his office hours, which provided an opportunity to discuss further the material he had presented. His lectures on the impact of the Appalachian Mountains on human migrations were particularly interesting. It made sense to me that the environment shapes history and society. The next thing I knew he invited me to his house for dinner with his family. We were permitted to invite faculty members to dinner at the dorm periodically, and I always took advantage of the opportunity. One of my guests was Selig Perlman, the famous economist and labor historian. I initially met Dr. Perlman because he was a member of the Governor's Commission on Human Rights. Word got around the dorm—sit at Ada Deer's table because then you get to meet all these interesting people. Other students could host guests, of course, but few seemed to do so. Someone asked me, "You got Dr. Perlman to come down? How did you do that?" I replied, "I just invited him."

I had discovered in high school that there was much to learn outside the classroom, and my conversations at Camp Miniwanca with Margaret Hickey, who was a world traveler, whetted my interest in international affairs. After attending numerous events and programs at the fabulous Memorial Union, I joined the International Club, which enabled me to get acquainted with students from around the globe. I ended up serving as president. I organized a weekend

YWCA Benefit Tea for International Students, 1956.
Wisconsin Historical Society, image WHi-92318.

trip to Shawano and the Menominee Reservation for the club members, who came from Austria, India, Finland, Germany, West Africa, Ethiopia, Colombia, Puerto Rico, Burma, Sri Lanka, and Wales. We visited the Badger Breeders Cooperative, which is one of the world's largest artificial breeding facilities, and the reservation home of the late Angus F. Lookaround, a Menominee who played football at Carlisle Indian School and the tuba with John Philip Sousa's band. After lunch, we had a tour of the Menominee mill. In the evening, students dressed in their national dress for a dinner at which Menominee dancers and drummers performed. I also joined the India Association so that I could meet South Asian Indians and learn about their cultures. When I went to the first meeting, I said, "You're an Indian, I'm an Indian; East meets West." I remained in touch with I. P. Shah, with whom I became acquainted through these groups, for well more than fifty years. Both of these clubs met at the Union, the hub of campus life, which became a big part of my student experience.

A staff member of the Governor's Commission on Human Rights suggested that I attend the American Friends Service Committee International Student Seminar held at Milton Academy in Massachusetts. In 1955, I applied and was accepted to the four-week program. Each week we studied a different region of the world with professors from a variety of colleges. Participants came from around the world. I learned to appreciate a diversity of religious beliefs and cultures. I had been attending a Presbyterian church with my roommate, but the idea that anyone who did not accept Christianity was damned troubled me. After meeting genuinely good and caring people who were Muslim, Hindu, Buddhist, and practitioners of other religions, I concluded that I could not accept the exclusivity of Christianity.

The next summer I went to the Encampment for Citizenship, a six-week program at the Fieldston School in New York City. Founded by the New York Society for Ethical Culture, this program brought together young people of diverse backgrounds and nationalities. The purpose was to engender respect for democratic principles and encourage political activism. We learned by establishing a camp government that required us to put democracy in action, participating in workshops on issues of citizenship and democracy, and interacting with prominent public figures.

Two years earlier the Supreme Court had handed down the decision in *Brown v. Board of Education* (1954) that outlawed public school segregation. I knew little about segregation since I had grown up in rural Wisconsin, so I signed up for a workshop on the subject. One of the speakers was Dr. Kenneth Clark, a psychologist who, along with his wife, Dr. Mamie Clark, devised the doll experiment in the 1940s. They had presented black children in segregated schools with a white doll and a black doll and asked them which was smarter, which they would rather play with, and other questions that required them to choose. Most of the children chose the white dolls. Dr. Clark had testified about his research in one of cases that was rolled into *Brown*, and his findings helped shape the majority opinion. I was enormously impressed. These distinguished African American psychologists had undertaken research that dramatically helped improve the situation of black Americans. "Someday," I thought, "I can do something of equal significance that will impact Indians."

Participants in the Encampment spent a whole day at the Franklin Delano Roosevelt estate in Hyde Park, New York, as the guests of Eleanor Roosevelt. The former first lady was an advisor to the board of directors of the New York Society for Ethical Culture and an ardent supporter of the Encampment. She gave a presentation about the United Nations and international cooperation, and then asked for questions. There were a hundred of us there, and no one said a word, so I piped up with a question about South Africa. My workshop on segregation had made me aware of racial injustice beyond the boundaries of the United States. The South African government was oppressing, imprisoning, and killing its nonwhite citizens who sought racial justice. "What can be done?" I asked. "Should the UN throw them out?" She looked at me very kindly and said that expulsion from the UN was not the answer, nor was violence. Change takes time, and education is the way to accomplish change. Here I am in 2018, eighty-three years old, and I still remember vividly what Eleanor Roosevelt told me in 1956. In her reply I have found motivation and strength that have guided me over the years.

Programs like the Encampment motivate young people to do more than they ever imagined was possible and provide them the skills they need. Such programs define achievement not in terms of personal accomplishments but in terms of volunteerism, community service, and political activism. They help participants measure their self-worth by what they have done to bring about positive change in the world rather than what they have accumulated for themselves. The Encampment also brought home to me an awareness that there is strength in numbers and that, by joining together, we can accomplish far more than we could as individuals. Helping an individual out of poverty is good for that person, but addressing the causes of poverty is far more helpful. The Encampment introduced me to a community of people from around the world who were committed to its ideals. Over the years, those connections helped advance the causes for which I have worked.

Late in my junior year, I realized that I needed to get down to brass tacks and declare a major. I went to my advisor, Professor John Barton in the Department of Rural Sociology. I explained my situation and told him, "I don't know what to major in. I have just been taking classes that interest me. I only know that I want to help people." He said, "You are very good with people. You should be a social worker. Think about that as a profession." So I thought about the social workers I had met, and I decided that this was a good plan. Today social work is primarily a graduate program, but in the 1950s Wisconsin offered an undergraduate degree. So I declared social work as my major.

In my senior year, I began thinking seriously about my future. To be the best social worker I could be, I thought, I needed a graduate degree. So I asked the social workers I knew, What was the best social work school? They all concurred—the New York School of Social Work. Founded in 1898, the school, which had affiliated with Columbia University in 1940, was the oldest and most distinguished in the country. Plus, it was in New York City. I applied and was accepted. I received fellowships from the John Hay Whitney and Delta Gamma Foundations and took out a loan from the Knights Templar Educational Foundation. But I had one more hurdle before I could head to the Big Apple.

I discovered that I had to take statistics. That meant summer school and a terribly long, hot, tedious summer in Madison. Class began at 7:45, and then we had to go to lab. The dean of the business school taught the class, and an assistant directed the lab. The lab assistant was really smart but he could not teach. I don't think any of us learned a thing; we just stood around looking at each other. A group of us asked if we could change labs but we could not. I flunked the first quiz and panicked. I already had been accepted to graduate school! Another woman and I started studying together, but we understood so little that we were of no help to each other. Finally, we went to the dean who was teaching the course and told him that we were learning nothing. He assigned us a tutor, but we still had to go to the lab. When it came time for the final exam, we went through every syllable of every lecture and reread all the assignments. I memorized everything that I could. It turned out that there were things on the exam that I actually recognized, but I had no idea whether I had passed or not. Then I got my final grade—I had made a 94, which gave me a B in the course. I had never worked so hard for a grade, and I have not looked at a standard deviation since. After I joined the faculty at the University of Wisconsin, I saw the tutor, Professor Jon Udell, from time to time. I always smiled and waved and told him, "Thanks for saving my life."

I was exhausted by the time I reached New York City and enrolled in graduate school at Columbia. I told my advisor that I planned to work with Indian people and that I would like to study community organizing. She looked at me and said, "We don't have that here." So I said, "Okay then, what do you have?" It turns out that they had group work and casework. I took the group work sequence my first year. Social work required field placement in agencies. The first placement they offered me was in a mental health facility. I said that I was not working with mentally ill people. Next thing I knew, they wanted to send me to the juvenile court. I told them that I was not going to deal with juvenile delinquents. By this time they were getting tired of me, but both of these placements involved one-on-one casework, which I was not studying and in which I was not interested. Someone later told me I was a macro social worker trapped in a micro world. From my experience in graduate school, that sounds about right.

I lived at the Henry Street Settlement, a social service agency founded in 1893 by progressive reformer Lillian Wald. Nearby was a housing project in which I finally found a suitable placement. There were two buildings sixteen stories high with eight units on every floor. There were Jewish people, Italian people, Puerto Rican people, and African American people living in little cubbyhole apartments and often not even knowing people on their own floor. This shocked me since I came from an Indian reservation where everyone knew everyone else. The residents were curious about who I was and why I was knocking on their doors. I explained that I was with the Henry Street Settlement just down the street, and I told them about its programs and other services available in the neighborhood. I worked with a team of four social work students—the other three already had their master's degrees—and our primary responsibility was to organize the residents and refer them to available neighborhood services. I went floor by floor visiting residents. Building-wide meetings followed. Organizing residents in public housing was such an unusual project that the *New York Times* carried a story about it. This was what I wanted to do, organize people so that they could identify their needs, set their own agendas, and work together for a better quality of life in their building and neighborhood.

As part of my placement, I worked with a Puerto Rican teenage girls' group. It was clear to me that hormones were raging and that these girls invested enormous amounts of time thinking about, talking about, and going out with boys. I decided that I needed to address the issue of sexuality. I knew little about Puerto Rican culture, and I did not want to offend the girls or their families, so I went to talk to my supervisor about how to bring up the subject of sex. I said, "What do I do about this?" He said, "Oh, that doesn't matter." I'm sitting there thinking, "What? What do you mean it doesn't matter? These are teenagers!" Then he looked long and hard at me and said suggestively, "You are so beautiful." Taken aback, all I could think to say was, "Thank you very much. Can we get back to the matter at hand?" He made a few other remarks that made me uncomfortable and that I did not know how to handle. I left as quickly as I could. Then I received his evaluation of me. It was very negative: he made me look like I was unfit to be a social worker. I challenged him and defended myself, but he refused to reconsider. I appealed the evaluation but got nowhere. My academic work was excellent, but his evaluation made me angry. I took a two-year leave of absence.

This was the 1950s, and terms like "sexual harassment" were not in use. Few people wanted to talk about such impropriety, and supervisors usually did not want to confront offenders even when victims complained. I encountered my second masher after I graduated from Columbia and interviewed for a job at a neighborhood house in Minneapolis. The executive director was sitting on a bench with me during the interview, and he started grabbing my hand. I just pulled away and he stopped. I really wanted this job, so despite his inappropriate behavior, I decided to accept the position. I knew I could handle his advances. What I had not taken into account was how pervasive his lechery was and how far it extended beyond hand-holding. I learned much later that he was really abusing the black housekeeper, touching her and doing inappropriate things. She, of course, was powerless to do anything about him since he was her boss and she desperately needed the job. One of the many positive things to come out of the modern feminist movement is sensitivity to and recourse against sexual harassment.

While I was on leave, I became a group worker in Brooklyn for a cooperative partnership program sponsored by the City of New York and the Protestant Council of New York City. Since churches largely sit empty during the week, this program put them to use as sites for a delinquency prevention program. I worked at the Siloam Presbyterian Church, which had been an activist church since the 1860s. Escaped slaves found refuge there; John Brown received a donation from the congregation; and the minister when I worked there, Reverend Milton A. Galamison, was a leader in the civil rights movement. We had after-school programs for little kids and for teenagers. I was in charge of programs for girls and my colleague, a black minister, was responsible for the boys. I had several girls' groups that met during the week, and we engaged in a variety of activities that they enjoyed. Many of my clients were from the West Indies. My supervisor was happily married, kept his hands to himself, and behaved the way a supervisor is supposed to. I had a great time. Years later, some of these girls contacted me and I had tea with them in the Plaza Hotel. By this time, they were all middle-aged, but they still called me "Miss Ada."

I benefited enormously from this experience and from friendships with several African American students. Until I moved to New York, I only knew about African Americans in the abstract, as a problem. I had virtually no personal experience with black people beyond the Youth Advisory Board. Before concerted efforts to increase black enrollment, prestigious universities often had few black students although, unlike in the South, they legally could attend. In Madison only one black woman lived in my dorm, but I did not really know her. At Columbia, many of my colleagues were African American. I especially remember Kenneth Marshall, who was a member of my field group. Through him I met many other black intellectuals, including his wife, the writer Paule Marshall. One of my other colleagues, Luther Ragin, took me to Harlem and introduced me to community activists. They played a formative role in my development and enriched my understanding of people of color in this country.

After two years, I returned to the School of Social Work, which had a new dean from Madison, Fred Delliquadri, who knew me. Even so, I had to go through the same rigmarole to get a placement appropriate to my interests and goals. I encountered problems with the curriculum's rigid division into two tracks, casework and group work. Once you selected a track, you were supposed to stay in that track. I decided that I needed to learn about both tracks, so I went to see the head of the Casework Division. I explained to her who I was and what I wanted to do, and she gave me permission to take courses in casework. I also received a casework placement with the New York Foundling Home. My responsibility was to visit infants who had been placed in foster homes and to evaluate their circumstances and foster parents. This placement and the courses proved very valuable to me since a social worker always has to work with individuals, even in a group context. This bit of flexibility in the curriculum, however, was rare. The school had its system and stuck to it.

The faculty generally took no notice of the fact that I was an Indian and that Indians have specific needs related to their special status as citizens of sovereign nations. I wanted to help Native people address those needs, but no one seemed the least bit interested in helping me learn how to do that. To graduate, I could write a thesis or participate in a group project. I went to talk with the faculty member in charge of research to discuss these options. I told him there were Indians in Brooklyn and that I would like to do research on a topic related to their experiences and needs in the city. His comment was, "First of all you have to decide if it's a social problem," and essentially dismissed the whole idea. I opted for a group project that had nothing to do with Indians. Years later I met a Lakota woman who also graduated from the Columbia University School of Social Work and likewise found it a very difficult environment.

I remain astonished that the best social work school in the country had little interest in American Indians, people who could have benefited so very much from their expertise. Imagine how surprised I was when, in 1998, I received a letter from the Columbia University Alumni Association notifying me that I was being inducted into the hall of fame. When I returned to Columbia for the awards ceremony, I sat across from one of my former professors, Alfred Kahn, who taught the history of social work. Seeing him reminded me of the really wonderful classes I had taken, including his. I told him that I thought his course was fabulous. He looked at me and said, "Miss Deer, now I see why you're such a successful politician."

The best course I took was from Richard Cloward, a sociologist who lectured on race and class. He helped me conceptualize what previously had been merely personal experience. As an activist for welfare rights, he also provided an excellent role model for how social workers can move beyond helping clients navigate government bureaucracy to organizing them to challenge the system and precipitate positive change. Professor Cloward was involved with the organization and implementation of Mobilization for Youth, a project that served as a precursor for the War on Poverty in the 1960s. Because faculty members like him embraced a relationship between academics and activism, I got an excellent education from the courses I took, but the placements were much less instructive. Most of all, I had learned a lot about advocacy, mainly through advocating for myself. I also benefited from living in New York City and experiencing its enormous diversity, but I was ready to go back to the Midwest and get down to work.

Before I went home, however, I had one more great adventure—I went to Europe. I had never traveled abroad, but my interest in international affairs went back to my undergraduate years, my membership in the international club, and my participation in the American Friends Service Committee International Student Seminar and the Encampment for Citizenship. Living in New York had intensified that interest. I had been able to visit the United Nations, including the delegates' lounge, and I had worked with immigrants to the United States. Now I wanted to see what it was like to be a foreigner. I had also retained my interest in history, and I looked forward to seeing the historic sites that, even as a child, I had read about.

When I graduated from Columbia, I borrowed money and gave myself my own European tour. I went with Edris Herman, a student friend from Wisconsin who had been working in New York. We took a charter flight and spent a summer in Europe for a thousand dollars. Edris had been in the International Club as well, and we visited several people we had met through the club. We had high tea in London with a woman I had met in New York, who lived in a big house adorned with her father's hunting trophies from Africa. In Amsterdam we visited an Indonesian friend, and then we went on to Paris, Rome, and Athens to see other people we knew. We also did plenty of sightseeing—the British Museum, Rijksmuseum, Eiffel Tower, Coliseum, and Acropolis. Edris was a classics major, and I really benefited from her education on that trip. From Greece Edris went to

Beirut, and I took a peasant boat around the Greek Islands. I could not afford a cruise, so I took the boats that local people took to Crete, Rhodes, and Mykonos. When I left Greece, I went to Germany, where I stayed with a friend in Nuremberg.

Although I sometimes embarrassed Edris, I took advantage of every opportunity to talk to people, often young men who flirted with us. In Crete a guy came along on his motorcycle and asked if I wanted a ride. I said, "Well, why not?" So I went on a glorious motorcycle ride. I got wonderful exposure to regular people. One guy I talked with at a little pensione spoke five languages. He told me about the German occupation, a memory still fresh in the minds of many Greeks. I had a great time, but by the time I got to Germany, I was getting a little homesick. It had been three months. I was very happy to have traveled so widely but I was glad to end my trip. I had spent almost my entire life preparing myself to be useful. Now it was time to put that training to work.

Like all people, I constructed several layers of identity in my formative years. The core was always Menominee, but I also had become a serious student, a social worker, and an engaged citizen of the world. I had acquired the joy of reading and learning, and I had become self-disciplined and resourceful. I had seized opportunities when they became available, met the challenges that life presented, and picked myself up and moved on when things did not go the way I expected. In preparing for the future through education and training, I also had developed character traits that would prove useful as I embarked on my professional career.

CHAPTER 3

▪ Trouble at Home ▪

While I was in college and graduate school, a crisis was developing on the Menominee Reservation. In the 1950s the United States moved away from the Indian New Deal of the 1930s, which had been intended to strengthen tribal governments, halt Indian land loss, and revitalize Native cultures. Congress initiated a new policy called "termination," which sought to end the trust relationship between the tribes and the federal government. Menominees became a prime target for termination. We had rich timber resources that we were utilizing, and a successful claim against the federal government only enhanced our appearance of prosperity. Policymakers insisted we were prosperous enough to be cut free from federal supervision, but they had little understanding of our economy, the importance of our tribal identity, or the impact termination would have on us. Most Menominees did not fully comprehend termination, but the prospect of such a radical change—abrogating treaty rights, severing ties to the federal government, becoming subject to state and county laws, privatizing our lands and lumber mill—terrified people. My mother attended General Council meetings and kept me apprised as events unfolded. It was very clear that there was trouble at home.

In retrospect, the disaster was not surprising. Although the Menominee tribe was self-supporting and paid the expenses that the BIA incurred on the reservation, BIA officials had always exercised a heavy hand, especially where tribal resources were concerned. For decades in the late nineteenth and early twentieth centuries, whites had gotten preferential treatment with regard to cutting, hauling, milling, and marketing our timber. In 1905 a windstorm blew down trees on large sections of reservation land. In response, the La Follette

Act of 1908 mandated that the federal government construct a lumber mill for the Menominees, train Menominees for managerial positions, and institute sustained-yield forestry on the reservation. Although the mill was built, agency superintendents continued discriminatory hiring practices and authorized whites to clear-cut broad swaths of our forest rather than harvesting only mature trees and planting seedlings, as sustained-yield forestry prescribed. Clear-cutting the forests damaged other resources, especially the fish and game on which many Menominees depended for food.

After World War I, agents actively promoted the allotment of tribal land to individuals, a move that almost certainly would have dispossessed and further impoverished the Menominees, just as it had many other tribes. Most of our tribal members did not object to individual ownership of their homesteads, but they wanted to continue to hold our forest in common as a tribe. In the 1920s, the tribe defeated efforts to allot our land, remove federal oversight, and dissolve tribal government. The tide of federal Indian policy and Menominee governance was about to change, but the pressure on Menominees to embrace individual ownership of what had been common property, adopt capitalist values, and assimilate into the American mainstream did not abate.

The Menominees wrote a constitution in 1924 that placed power firmly in the hands of the General Council in which every adult Menominee had a vote. Four years later, we established the Advisory Council to manage tribal affairs, but its actions remained subject to veto by the General Council. My family was not directly involved in tribal politics: seats on the Advisory Council tended to go to members of a few families who had more education, experience, and money than my Menominee relatives had. Our new tribal government not only continued to reject allotment, but it also sought control of tribal resources and indemnification for federal mismanagement of our forest. In order to seek compensation, the tribe needed a lawyer, but the tribe's request to hire one was subject to congressional approval. Finally in 1931 Congress granted us permission to engage legal representation, and in 1935, the year I was born, agreed to permit the Menominees to seek restitution in the U.S. Court of Claims. The claim was based on incidents of mismanagement, such as a BIA agent's refusal to sell timber blown down in the 1905 windstorm because he thought it would depress the price of white-owned timber. Menominees wanted compensation for those unprincipled acts. It would take sixteen years to get it.

In 1934 Congress passed the Indian Reorganization Act (IRA), also known as the Wheeler-Howard Act. This act—designed by Commissioner of Indian Affairs

John Collier and supported by President Franklin D. Roosevelt—was the basis of the Indian New Deal. It ended allotments, encouraged new tribal constitutions that established representative government, and provided for the incorporation of tribes for the management of tribal assets. The Menominees quickly accepted the IRA by a vote of 596 to 15. Then, however, the tribe rejected an IRA constitution that would have enabled them to incorporate. Because our General Council permitted broader direct participation than the representative council which would have been established under the IRA constitution, Menominees were concerned it might become a tool of the BIA. We also feared that its provisions could make our forest subject to taxation and sale. Menominees have always loved our forest, so we were committed to preserving it intact, stopping federal mismanagement, and ensuring that the timber industry benefited all tribal members. We won a victory in 1934 when Congress gave the Advisory Council a veto over the budget for the lumber mill, a power Menominees repeatedly used to force concessions from the BIA.

In 1951 the U.S. Court of Claims finally reached a decision that awarded the Menominees $8.5 million, which brought the total amount the tribe had on deposit with the U.S. Treasury to approximately $10 million. Profits from the lumber mill and success before the Court of Claims encouraged a view that had been gaining ground in Washington since the end of World War II: the Menominees should be cut loose and required to fend for themselves as individuals. The reality was that Menominees were better off than many American Indian tribes because they had resources that, with proper management, could be exploited indefinitely without dependence on outside capital. But their standing vis-à-vis other impoverished Indians reveals little about the economic situation of individuals. Most Menominee families were poor by national and even Wisconsin standards, and tribal resources merely kept the wolf from the door by providing employment, services, and a safety net.

From the perspective of the BIA and Congress, however, we appeared to be a prosperous tribe that no longer required federal services. This view, however, ignored the fact that we reimbursed not only the U.S. government but also the state and county for those services out of income from the mill. When the state agreed in 1949 that Menominees were eligible for subsidies earmarked for the elderly and indigent in Shawano County, for example, the tribe "gifted" the amount disbursed to the county. Many Menominees would have been quite happy to dispense with federal paternalism and manage our own affairs, but our relationship with the federal government entailed more than services. The United States held Menominee land in trust, which protected tribal assets from sale or seizure. Trust land could not be taxed or mortgaged, and, therefore, federal oversight prevented white timber interests or other entities from acquiring the Menominee forest and lumber mill.

The Menominees were strongly committed to the employment of tribal members and to sustainable-yield forestry rather than clear-cutting. Any Menominee man who wanted a job could find one at the mill. In the 1930s the General Council secured a work schedule at the mill that reflected not only economic hard times but also traditional Menominee subsistence practices. Instead of operating year-round on a shortened workweek to mill the timber allocated for cutting, the General Council approved a plan for ten-hour days until all the logs had been sawn. The mill then closed for the rest of the year so that workers could hunt, fish, and engage in other economic pursuits. As we gained some control over decisions affecting our forest, largely through the Advisory Council's veto power over the mill budget, Menominees reduced the percentage of the forest harvested annually in order to ensure trees—and the jobs they brought—were always available. A smaller number of trees taken annually meant that we could cut and mill timber every year. We were determined to favor employment over profits in the management of the forest and the operation of the mill. The BIA did not always endorse such business practices, but Menominees insisted on them.

When the tribe won its court claim, the Menominees voted to use some of our money to help alleviate individual poverty on the reservation. "Why should all that money go into the tribal account?" people asked. Since we all owned the forest, we thought, we should each receive a share of the claim award. Remember that this was *our* money, not a federal handout, but still we had to get Congress to release it. We decided to seek authorization for a payment of $1,500 to each of our 3,270 tribal members. This would have amounted to approximately one-half of the tribal reserve held by the U.S. Treasury. In 1952 a delegation went to Washington to discuss how the tribe planned to spend the money awarded. BIA officials suggested that the per-capita payments might be the first step toward dividing all tribal assets among individual Menominees and relieving the federal government of all responsibility for them. In this proposal, BIA officials reflected changing views on American Indian policy as the major political parties, tired of Depression-era public relief programs, moved to the right.

In the 1952 election Republicans took control of the White House and both houses of Congress. Republicans took a dim view of the New Deal, programs that a Democratic Congress had passed to cope with the Great Depression—and that had enabled the Menominees to gain access to the records on which their legal victory in the claims case rested. The Republicans were not alone in wanting changes, however: the Democratic platform in 1952 also supported revamping Indian affairs. Among the new Republican members elected to the House of Representatives was our congressman, Melvin Laird. When we asked him to introduce a bill providing for per-capita payments from the award, he agreed, and in 1953 the bill passed the House. But many of Laird's Republican colleagues saw our request as an opportunity to overhaul Indian policy. When the bill got to the Senate, the chair of the Committee on Indian Affairs, Senator Arthur B. Watkins of Utah, announced that if the Menominees wanted their money, they would have to agree to termination.

In opposition to the New Deal support of Indian tribes and Native cultures, termination sought to end federal supervision, dissolve reservations, and assimilate individual Indians into the American mainstream. Termination involved abolishing tribal governments, allotting tribal land to individuals, removing the protections of trust status, closing the tribal rolls, and divesting of tribal resources. The National Congress of American Indians went on record as vehemently opposed to this policy, but Senator Watkins was firm. To him, the Menominees appeared to be ideal candidates for termination. Compared to most other Indian tribes, we were prosperous. Our forest and lumber mill had enabled us to support tribal services and build up a financial reserve, which our recent court award had increased substantially. Policymakers failed to understand that tribal sovereignty—the right to govern ourselves—underlay Menominee success. Menominees did not approach management of our forests, labor force, or profits in the same way as private enterprise would. We cut trees selectively so that our forest could renew itself. Our mill employed all Menominee men who needed jobs instead of embracing cost-saving techniques that replaced workers with machines. And we viewed the money in our tribal account as belonging to all our people.

In June 1953 Senator Watkins met with Menominees on the reservation and flatly told us that the only way we would get our money was to accept termination. He insisted that we should run our own affairs independent of the federal government. According to him, Congress had already decided to terminate us in three years, and we would not receive per-capita payments until after then. Tribal leaders expressed doubts about whether the Menominees would be ready to manage their own affairs, and asked why Congress was in such a hurry. Senator Watkins responded, "We want to get out of the bad job we are doing and we don't want to get sued again for $8,500,000." His glib answer did little to reassure the tribe.

Nevertheless, the senator pressed for a Menominee vote on termination. The tally was 169 in favor and 5 opposed, but the vote count did not accurately reflect Menominee views. Only a fraction of the people eligible to vote turned out. Some perhaps could not be bothered to vote, but most followed a time-honored practice of signaling their disapproval by refusing to attend the meeting at all. Unfamiliar with the concept of termination, some of those who showed up did not fully appreciate what the senator meant by the term, so when they voted, they thought the issue at hand was the per-capita payment, not the dissolution of the reservation and an end to the tribe's relationship with the federal government. Furthermore, Watkins refused to permit translation of the proceedings into the Menominee language, which some people understood better than English. As a result, even people who voted in favor of termination were not sure what they voted for.

After the senator's departure, Menominees learned what termination really meant. Some Menominees thought that termination was inevitable but that the time was not right. Others refused to countenance the idea at all. But virtually all Menominees opposed the immediate termination that Senator Watkins demanded. In fact, hundreds of tribal members signed a petition against termination. Tribal officials called another meeting, and those present voted unanimously to give up the settlement the claims court had awarded them if it required termination. This was an extraordinarily difficult decision. Menominees needed access to their money, but they were willing to suffer rather than surrender their reservation and their tribal sovereignty. Senator Watkins refused to accept the legitimacy of this vote and forged ahead with plans to terminate the Menominees.

On the reservation, rumors flew about the senator's motivations. Some Menominees thought that his Mormon faith predisposed him against the Menominees, who were mostly Catholic and, like me, had resisted Mormon proselytizing. Others charged that he was trying to bribe the Menominees with their own money. Later, I realized his attack on the Menominees was part of a much larger agenda. Looking for a guinea pig on which to try out his ideas about Indian policy, he focused on us. He saw himself as emancipating the Menominees from the bondage of federal supervision as the first step in a major reform of Indian relations. In keeping with Republican policy in the 1950s, he championed individual initiative and private enterprise, and he thought that trust status inhibited both. More troubling was his conviction that Menominees—and by implication other Indians—deserved no say in matters crucial to their future. He simply did not care whether or not we opposed termination: our consent to our own termination was not required. And if he managed to terminate the Menominees, he could then restructure Indian policy in such a way as to destroy reservations and tribal sovereignty in general. Indians would legally disappear. I am still appalled at Senator Watkins's disregard not only for treaty rights and tribal sovereignty but also for fundamental democratic principles.

In August 1953 Congress passed House Concurrent Resolution 108, which announced a new Indian policy to "free" specific Indian tribes from federal supervision. The Menominee made the list along with the Flathead, Klamath, Potawatomi, Turtle Mountain Chippewa, and all Indian tribes in California, Florida, New York, and Texas. Congress subsequently passed Public Law 280, which extended state civil and criminal jurisdiction over Indian reservations in California, Nebraska, Minnesota, Oregon, and Wisconsin. President Eisenhower signed the law, although he called it "unchristian," and Eleanor Roosevelt voiced serious misgivings in her "My Day" column. The Menominees requested and received an exemption from PL 280, but the next year the tribe reversed itself and asked an obliging Congress to make Menominees subject to state laws, enforcement, and courts.

In 1954 Congress passed the Menominee Termination Act, which provided for release of our funds as we had requested two years earlier, closed the tribal rolls so that anyone born after the law was signed could not legally be designated Menominee, and mandated that we prepare a plan for ending our status as an Indian tribe by 1958. That meant deciding how to provide schools, health care, social services, and law enforcement; how to pay for those services; and how to manage our tribal assets. Termination became a fact of life for the Menominees. Shawano County officials panicked. The county already was providing some services for Indians but "gifts" from the tribe had helped offset the expense. What would happen when the tribe and tribal assets no longer existed? Indians and whites agreed that they needed more time to prepare for this dramatic change.

In 1954 the reservation was mostly forest, and the majority of Menominee men—including my father and brother Joe—worked in the lumber mill, which actually consisted of a sawmill, planing mill, and lathe mill, as well as a chipper and kilns. The mill also had hydroelectric and steam power plants. Menominees worked in the mill personnel and sales offices, as well in the general merchandise store that served employees. Since its construction, the mill had processed 1.5 billion feet of white pine, hemlock, and hardwood logs, yet the 175,000-acre forest promised to support our tribe indefinitely with careful management. The federal government contributed no more to the reservation financially than it did to white communities; income from the mill supported public services just as local taxes financed similar services beyond the reservation boundaries. The mill and forest, however, had a broader economic impact. A number of individually owned businesses in Neopit—including gas stations, restaurants, and a grocery store—catered to employees of the mill. In Keshena and elsewhere, other establishments, such as "Indian trading posts," depended on tourists who came to enjoy our river and forest and to buy supposedly Indian-made souvenirs to take home. Private enterprise, therefore, also depended on the health of our tribally owned mill and forest. Few if any in the tribe foresaw the impact of termination on the tribe's economy beyond release of the funds from the claim settlement.

The most immediate result of the Termination Act was the distribution of the per-capita payments. The tribe had requested that the payments due to children go to their parents, but unbeknownst to the Menominees, Congress changed those terms. The act specified that the Secretary of the Interior should hold the money for minors until they reached the age of eighteen. My brother Joe and I were old enough to draw our own payments, but our siblings were not. This meant that, since my mother was not entitled to payment, my father's payment was the only one available to provide for the support of the three children still at home. I planned to use my payment for college expenses. Joe announced that he was going to buy a car. I warned him: "You're going to get this car, they're going to get your money, you're going to wreck the car, and you'll have nothing." That is exactly what happened. He had nothing, but I had my education. Like my parents, most Menominees had greater needs and responsibilities than either of us did. They used the money to clothe their children, repair their houses, and buy things their families needed. A single payment of $1,500 could not lift anyone permanently out of poverty, but it could provide some temporary relief from the deprivation that many Menominees suffered.

The BIA played no role in preparing the tribe for termination, but instead left the Menominees to devise their own plan, which Congress ultimately had to approve. Our leaders had little experience developing policies or programs. Until this time, the BIA had set forth policy, and the Menominee government had largely reacted; that is, the Advisory Council negotiated with the agent on the implementation of BIA policy on the reservation, and the General Council approved or vetoed the actions of the Advisory Council. Not knowing exactly how to proceed, the Advisory Council appointed a committee and engaged legal counsel to prepare a plan for terminating our status as an Indian tribe. Most of the leaders of the tribe did not want termination, but they believed it was unavoidable. Nevertheless, they stalled, hoping for a reversal in Washington or, at least, an extension of the deadline.

As Menominees began to comprehend the impending loss of their reservation, they became more critical of their leaders. Some tribal members favored overt resistance instead of the delaying tactics of the tribal government. Although she was not a Menominee, my mother was firmly in the resistance camp. I had just finished my freshman year at the University of Wisconsin when Congress passed the Menominee Termination Act, and throughout my college years, she wrote me frequently about termination, insisting that something had to be done to stop it. She expected me to join the fight. Finally, I had to tell her, "Mom, I am in school. I don't know much. I'm a student and I have to learn a lot more. Eventually I will be able to help, but not right now." Ultimately I did join her, though that time was a long way off. Her example, as well as her words, would inspire me.

My mother joined the growing number of Menominees who opposed termination. She wrote Congress, demanding that the act be repealed, and began to organize her women friends in opposition. Tribal authorities learned of her activism, and in 1957 the hospital fired her from her job as a nurse in retaliation. As a result, we suffered financially because my father's salary was barely adequate, as were the salaries of most of the people who worked in the mill. By the next year, however, she had managed to scrape together seventy-five dollars. She then hitchhiked to Washington, DC. For six weeks, while living at the YWCA, she made the rounds on Capitol Hill, urging repeal of termination. My mother returned to Wisconsin more determined than ever to stop what she insisted was a violation of Menominee rights and sovereignty. Although her lobbying did not achieve her desired results, she made a memorable impression. More than a decade later, as I lobbied for restoration, people heard my name and did a double take. I responded, "Same family, same cause, different Deer."

Both delay and resistance seemed like viable tactics in the late 1950s because attitudes about termination appeared to be shifting. Even the BIA began to have serious doubts about the policy, and in 1958 the new BIA commissioner voiced his opposition. Once set in motion, however, BIA policy stayed in motion, and no one in Washington acted to reverse its course. Powerful members of Congress continued to demand termination, and the president paid little attention to Indians, even after the White House changed administrations in 1961 upon the election of John F. Kennedy. The Menominees did manage to get the deadline for termination extended to 1961. In the meantime, most Menominees lost confidence in the Advisory Council, which seemed unable to come up with a termination plan. This failure meant that the secretary of the interior could step into the breach and appoint a trustee to implement termination.

In desperation, the Advisory Council created a special committee to devise a plan and named as its chair George Kenote, a Menominee who had worked for the BIA on other reservations for years. I remember him as a handsome, well-dressed man who lived in a nice house near Keshena Falls and whose daughters were acquaintances of mine. I formed no particular opinion of him at the time. Even after I became actively involved in the struggle for restoration, which he opposed, I did not personalize my opposition to his political views. Other Menominees (and my mother), however, did. Political factionalism often became personal during this period, further dividing and demoralizing Menominees.

The debates that ensued were bitter, pitting Menominees against one another. People talk about factionalism among Indian tribes, but factionalism is simply one of the ways democracy works. People sometimes don't agree about what course their nation should take. Lots of factors shape their positions—personal experiences, race, ethnicity, class, religion, and education, along with self-interest, altruism, and other motivations. This generalization certainly applies to the Menominees, who are not a homogenous tribe. Almost all Menominees have some European ancestry, but a 1934 congressional act had imposed a "blood quantum" of one-quarter for sharing in an award from stumpage fees, a measure many Menominees still resented since it divided some extended families. Within the tribe, however, "mixed-blood" versus "full-blood" usually reflected cultural orientation rather than a precise blood quantum. Other deep-seated differences gave rise to factions. Religion sometimes divided Catholics from followers of Indigenous religions. Menominees who had money or held managerial positions—people my mother called "upper-crusters"—often espoused views that poorer, blue-collar workers generally opposed. Age, residence, kinship, and a host of other circumstances could shape reactions to particular issues. Nothing quite as serious as termination had confronted anyone on the reservation in a very long time, so it is no wonder that factions arose over the policy and its implementation. However, support for the termination policy gradually dwindled and proposed solutions to the problems it created produced new divisions.

Although my mother was not a tribal member—she called herself a "white-skin"—she had five children who were, and she had spent most of her adult life on the reservation. As a result, she took a central role in the opposition to termination. She began to think, talk, and write about Indians in a way that few people other than scholars and bureaucrats at the time did. In the 1950s, she was arguing that treaties between the Menominees and the United States were agreements reached between two sovereign nations. Neither nation, she insisted, had the right to enact laws doing away with the other. This was the Cold War era, and she saw such violations as analogous to the Soviet Union's annexation of previously independent countries in eastern Europe and central Asia. When the BIA pointed out that a majority of Menominees had voted for termination, she called for a new election, which, of course, the BIA denied. She insisted that tribal leaders demand that the BIA respect and enforce U.S. treaties with the Menominees. Constance Wood Deer was a force to be reckoned with!

My mother made her opinions known in letters to the editor in newspapers, especially, the *Green Bay Press-Gazette*, and at General Council meetings. She did not mince words. In a letter to the governor, published in the *Press-Gazette*, she referred to those who had advised him on the legality of termination as "educated idiots and intellectual imbeciles" because they did not recognize the tribal sovereignty implicit in treaties. The letters sometimes provoked angry responses from other Menominees and from tribal leaders. One letter signed by "A group of Menominee women who are tired of your meddling" urged her to "stay home and clean up your house and mind your goats." My mother had no such intention. She always attended meetings of the General Council as it debated the final plan for termination, and she did not hold her tongue. When the general council limited her speaking time to fifteen minutes, her supporters moved to give her more time, but a voice vote defeated them. Most Menominees had no idea what termination would bring, and the response of many to my mother's warnings was to metaphorically shoot the messenger.

Termination required the resolution of two major issues—how to provide services for Menominees after termination and how to administer the tribe's assets, in particular, the forest and the mill. Both had serious implications for Wisconsin. In 1955 the state established the Menominee Indian Study Committee, which included tribal members as well as state and local officials, to advise the legislature on how to respond to termination. The committee in turn commissioned the University of Wisconsin to study the impact of the dissolution of the Menominee Reservation and tribal government. The more the governor and legislature learned, the more alarmed they became about the effects of termination on the state. Because Wisconsin saw itself as an interested party, the committee and the university became involved in fashioning the termination plan in order to protect state interests. Nevertheless, committee members seemed entirely too interested in the tribe's forest and not interested enough in other issues, such as the implementation of PL 280, which gave the state civil and criminal jurisdiction over the reservation.

Not surprisingly, my mother frequently attended the meetings of the Menominee Indian Study Committee. Menominees Louise Askinette, Gertrude Richmond, and Ernest Neconish often went with her to the meetings in Madison. Mr. Neconish spoke Menominee and one of the women translated. He accused whites of taking Indian land and interfering with Menominee cultural traditions while my mother described termination as a swindle. She also regularly attacked George Kenote, who supported termination, calling him "George the Terminator" and, rather ironically, questioning his Menominee ancestry. By 1960, however, even Mr. Kenote was circulating petitions asking to delay termination. But there would be no delay and, with no viable alternative, tribal members voted apprehensively for the final plan.

Menominee termination became effective on May 1, 1961, the year I graduated with my master's degree in social work. We thought of ourselves as an Indian tribe and as Menominee people, but Congress had taken away our status as Indians without informed consent. Termination left Menominees wondering who they were. It was a period of confusion, despair, and frustration. I remember visiting with a man named Johnson Awanopay, who lived at Zoar. He and my father liked to speak Menominee, and he had been at some of the ceremonies that my father took me to at Zoar. When I came to see him years later, he remembered those experiences. He told me, "You know, it's really strange. One day I'm looking at myself, and I'm an Indian. The next day I'm not. But I'm still me." We knew we were the same, we were still Menominees, but we no longer had legal standing as such. We were merely citizens of Wisconsin and the United States.

My mother was not one to reflect on identity issues or succumb to despair. She and like-minded Menominees promptly organized the Citizens' Association for the Advancement of Menominee People (CAAMP), which engaged a lawyer to file a $15-billion lawsuit against the United States for violation of treaty obligations. CAAMP collected six hundred names on a petition against termination and held a rally in Keshena at which my mother spoke. She charged Congress with "criminally aiding and abetting the abrogation of Menominee rights" and Presidents Eisenhower and Kennedy with being complicit in the crime. She demanded that the salaries of Mr. Kenote, the mill manager, and other high-ranking officials be made public and that the non-Indian mill manager be deported from the Menominee Nation. She directed her ire at him specifically because the mill had shut down for modernization, throwing my father and most of the other employees out of work. Mr. Kenote attended the meeting and admitted that there had been problems with termination. There also were problems with the proposed lawsuit: the attorney the CAAMP had hired estimated litigating the suit would cost $7,000 (more than $56,000 in 2016 dollars), an amount the Menominees would have to raise. That was pretty much the end of the lawsuit.

Termination abolished tribal government, so a group of Menominee men, some of whom had been tribal leaders, organized the Council of Chiefs. In 1962 they got the Menominee Indian Tribe of Wisconsin, Inc., incorporated under Wisconsin law. Through the corporation, the council managed to get some federal assistance to alleviate financial problems, but it had no governing authority. Nevertheless, this entity gave us a nominal tribal identity and the right to file legal claims and suits as a corporation. The corporation also in theory provided us with a collective voice, although very few people ever attended their meetings. Most Menominees were so demoralized that they could do little to improve their situation.

In addition to the Council of Chiefs and the corporation, the people who lived on what had been the reservation still needed governance as well as health care, education, welfare, law enforcement, and road maintenance. County governments in Wisconsin normally were responsible for these services, which taxes supported, but the reservation lay outside any existing county. How do you turn an Indian reservation into a county? The choice was to divide the land among the three adjoining counties or to create a new county that encompassed the land that had been the reservation. The Menominees preferred to be a single county because it kept us together as a people, so the General Council overwhelmingly voted for the creation of Menominee County, which came into being when termination took effect and whose boundaries were contiguous with the reservation.

Immediately upon termination Menominee County became the poorest county in Wisconsin. We had no health care under the Indian Health Service, no assistance to our elderly, no access to scholarships reserved for Indians—and no tribal funds to provide those services. Not only were the citizens poor (80 percent lived below the poverty line) but the county also had a very limited tax base. The population was approximately 3,500, homesteads were small, and tax valuations were low. The only industry was the mill, and the major asset was the forest. State politicians feared that Menominee County would become a financial liability for Wisconsin. Since Menominees lacked the expertise required to create and operate a county government and did not have sufficient population to make the delivery of services affordable, its residents had to depend on the adjoining counties, Oconto and especially Shawano, to provide the services for which Menominee County taxes paid. The state had to make up any deficit.

Education became a compelling issue. Although my siblings and I attended school in Shawano, before termination almost all Menominee children had received their elementary education at a BIA day school or a Catholic school on the reservation. The BIA paid for both the day school and parochial school tuition with funds from the tribe. Now there was no tribe and no BIA presence, so individual families either had to pay tuition, which they could not afford, or send their children to mostly white public schools. At first, the only public schools in the joint school district were in Shawano, where racial animosity seemed to have increased since the days when only a few Menominees, including me, attended high school there. At-large elections for the school board meant that even by 1969 only one of the twelve members of the Shawano School Board was Menominee even though Menominee County made up 25 percent of the combined Menominee-Shawano tax base. Shawano schools had no Indian teachers, no units in the curriculum dealing with Indians, and few books on Indians in their libraries. Even when I was in high school, students learned about Indians only on field trips to the reservation where they gawked at Indians as though we were natural wonders, museum exhibits, or zoo animals. White attitudes toward Indians were often negative, and some teachers openly said that they didn't like Indians. Most Menominee children lived in a largely Menominee world except during their time at school, where they became an ignored and even scorned minority. Not surprisingly, the dropout rate of Menominee students soared to approximately 50 percent.

Menominees also felt the sting of discrimination when it came to law enforcement. The new county appointed six law enforcement officers, but they served as deputies under the Shawano County sheriff. No one in Menominee County was qualified to serve as district attorney, so the Shawano County district attorney and courts served Menominee County as well. Only residents of Shawano County voted for the sheriff and district attorney, which meant that Menominee County residents had no voice in the election of these officeholders under whose jurisdiction they came. As a result, Menominees seemed more likely to be arrested and convicted. So many Menominees landed in the Shawano jail that my brother Joe, who knew what it was like from his own experiences there, called it the "Menominee Motel." Much to Joe's credit, he was his mother's son. While he was in jail, he organized a hunger strike for better treatment.

The only way Menominee County could support its own services and avoid becoming a drain on state funds was to increase its tax base. Before termination, the tribe had not paid taxes on its reservation land, and the BIA had provided services with funds that the tribally owned forest and mill generated. Now the land and the improvements on it, like the mill, became taxable. The termination plan created a private corporation, Menominee Enterprises, Inc. (MEI), to hold the assets—primarily the land and the mill—that formerly belonged to the tribe. Every enrolled Menominee (including minors) received 100 shares of stock in MEI and a $3,000 corporate bond, redeemable in 2000, that paid 4 percent interest. A nine-member board of directors administered MEI. The plan required that four members be Menominees, thereby putting non-Indians in the majority. The Voting Trust, composed of seven members, elected the board of directors. Menominee shareholders elected the Voting Trust, of which four had to be Menominee. In other words, Menominees did not have direct control of their assets but instead elected the Voting Trust, which in turn elected the board of directors. Not surprisingly, few Menominees understood this structure. No doubt most readers of this paragraph are now scratching their heads trying to comprehend MEI's organization. It gets more complicated.

The Voting Trust seriously compromised the Menominees' ability to protect our forest and mill because a second trust, the MEI Assistance Trust, controlled the votes of Menominees who were "incompetent" or under the age of twenty-one. The termination plan authorized a bank, the First Wisconsin Trust Company, to vote the MEI Assistance Trust shares as a block. Like other Menominee parents, my father could not vote the shares of his minor children, Robert and Connie, but instead had to surrender this power to First Wisconsin Trust. Furthermore, the termination plan empowered someone from the BIA to determine who was "incompetent." Instead of limiting the category of those unable to manage their affairs to people with developmental disabilities, mental illness, or dementia, this official decided that people who preferred to speak Menominee were also "incompetent" and assigned their shares to First Wisconsin Trust. As a result, some of the tribe's most distinguished and highly respected elders were disenfranchised. Because First Wisconsin Trust controlled so many shares, they had considerable power in determining who was elected to the Voting Trust. George Kenote, who led development of the termination plan, served as chairman. Although the majority of the Voting Trust had to be Menominees, First Wisconsin Trust tended to support Menominees like Kenote who were likely to agree with the business-oriented white members. They, in turn, elected like-minded Menominees to the board of directors. Consequently, the body that made decisions about the land and the mill did not reflect the views of the vast majority of Menominee people.

One of the early controversies involved the closing of the hospital in Keshena. BIA health standards were not as stringent as those of Wisconsin, so the tribe spent thousands of dollars to modernize the hospital in order that it could remain open when state regulation went into effect. But once the Menominees were terminated, MEI held all tribal assets, and the board refused to appropriate money to operate the upgraded facility. CAAMP demanded that the hospital reopen. They even found a physician who offered to spend his six weeks of vacation at the hospital, but the board declined the offer. That meant Menominees had to use the hospital in Shawano, which, for some, was more than an hour away. In the aftermath of the hospital closing, tuberculosis rates soared. Menominee patients confined to distant sanatoriums could not afford the treatment that the tribe had formerly provided, and MEI refused to pay, insisting that medical care was an individual responsibility. The county appealed to the governor to use the state's emergency funds to cover the $80,000 that Menominees owed. Termination, therefore, seriously compromised basic public services like education, law enforcement, and health care.

When the former Menominee Reservation became the new Menominee County, MEI not only assumed the assets of the tribe, like the mill and hospital, it also became the owner of all the land within the county, including individual homesteads. Because prior to termination reservation land belonged to the tribe and was held in trust by the United States, individual Menominees held only possessory rights to the land, which they had bought or inherited from other Menominees. MEI began surveying the land and offering homesteads for sale with a fee simple title to the Menominees living on them at the value of the vacant acreage. Menominees now had to pay for land on which many had lived for their entire lives. The acreage made available for purchase often did not correspond to that to which the occupants previously had acquired possessory rights. My father had bought 160 acres before he married my mother, but MEI now offered to sell him only twenty acres. He lost all rights to the rest, and MEI retained title.

Menominees had to buy their homes or risk losing them, but many people could not come up with the purchase price. Therefore, MEI agreed to take their bonds in partial payment for their land. These sales relieved MEI of the obligation to pay interest on the bonds while also depriving these Menominees of annual interest payments as well as the $3,000 due in the year 2000 when the bonds matured. More than half of Menominees surrendered their bonds. Since I was not living on what had been the reservation and had no possessory right to land that I now needed to purchase, I was able to hold on to my bond until it matured in 2000 and use the annual interest in the interim. In contrast, Menominees who had no other assets and did live on what had been the reservation had to sacrifice their bonds or lose their homes. My father and brother Joe signed over their bonds to purchase my family's land. Like many Menominees, they fell behind on payments so the bank threatened foreclosure. My brother Robert found out about it, borrowed money, and paid off the bank. Our land was saved, but others who were not as fortunate lost theirs.

By selling land, MEI shifted the property taxes to the purchasers. Menominees had no more experience with property taxes than they did with mortgages. Reservation land had not been taxable because the federal government held it in trust. Once Menominees owned land in fee simple, they owed Menominee County annual real estate taxes in order to support county services. Many people did not understand this, and others simply could not afford to pay. In 1962, the second year of property taxation, only 12 percent of individual property taxes in Menominee County were paid. Although compliance gradually improved, nonpayment of taxes further compromised Menominee County's ability to provide services. The residents were poor, and termination had made them poorer.

Private corporations bought the public utilities that the tribe had owned, with predictable results. My family had only recently gotten electricity in their log cabin, but a rate increase after privatization meant going back to kerosene lamps because my parents no longer could afford the electricity bills. The sale of the tribal telephone company dashed any hope they had of one day getting a phone installed. At least capitalists didn't find a way to privatize the Wolf River. If they had, we probably would have had no water!

The economic situation continued to deteriorate. The mill and forest were virtually the only sources of employment and tax revenue in Menominee County. Yet the board of directors hired managers who had no experience with Menominees or Wisconsin forests but rather came from the Northwest, where forests were larger and clear-cutting was common practice. These managers began implementing measures with which they were familiar and, as a result, made costly mistakes. For example, they bought expensive log haulers that were too big for Menominee roads, and their new methods of calculating how much timber to cut led to waste. As a private corporation, the mill had to operate more efficiently so that it could pay taxes, but its managers also received generous salaries. Modernizing the mill by installing labor-saving devices seemed like a way to generate more income, yet these measures threated the livelihoods of many Menominees. All these decisions made Menominees distrustful of MEI management and led to charges of incompetence and corruption.

In September 1965, four men walked off their jobs at the mill, and most of the 230 or so other workers followed. Mill workers belonged to a union, but this was an impromptu, not an authorized, strike. The next month another wildcat strike took place. Management had reneged on its promise of incentive pay above the base rate, which was simply not enough for most Menominees to live on. George Kenote, by now vice president of MEI, criticized the strikers—after all, they had just received a four-cent-per-hour raise—and announced the mill was closing for repairs, an action he insisted was not a lockout. My mother, of course, weighed in. She attributed the strike to discrimination and to strikers' desire for "some of the financial gravy continually slurping into upper-crust bank accounts." Ultimately the strike was settled and strikers were not fired, but all the labor-saving measures taken at the mill meant that a reduction of the workforce was inevitable.

There were few other jobs in Menominee County. Several years after the strike, Menominee Vern Teller wrote me about his situation in the Menominee community of South Branch. He was an independent trucker with one truck and a hydraulic loader for big logs. He had repeatedly asked for work hauling logs to the mill, but the MEI forester, a white man, always contracted with other whites. Sometimes the white contractor subcontracted jobs to Vern for less than primary contractors were paid. The only difference between them, Vern wrote, was that "it's my timber and my land." He went on, "Why is it that when we went to work, I'm working under him? Is it a lack of confidence in the Indian's ability? Is it because we have outsiders in positions to look out for other outsiders?" Almost all of the other men in South Branch had to work outside Menominee County, most traveling thirty to forty miles each way, because MEI supervisors would not hire them.

The unemployed had little choice but to move away or apply for welfare benefits that the county, with its limited tax base, could ill afford. Furthermore, many Menominees could not qualify for welfare due to their MEI bonds. But people could not eat bonds. Therefore, Menominees began to borrow money using their bonds as collateral, and consequently lost their bonds to banks, lawyers who dealt with their legal problems, and even the State of Wisconsin, which took their bonds as compensation for welfare payments. The state planned to use the bonds to acquire Menominee land and convert it into state forests, a scheme ultimately abandoned following Menominee protests and recognition that such a move would only worsen the tax deficit.

By 1965, 40 percent of Menominee bonds had slipped out of Indian hands. Since the tribe no longer existed and MEI controlled what had been our tribal assets, we could no longer provide essential services to the community. Wisconsin Senator Gaylord Nelson and Congressman Melvin Laird managed to get Congress to pass a four-year appropriation for the Menominees, which was renewed. Congress had intended to end the federal government's financial responsibility for Menominees, however, so everyone understood that this congressional largesse was not permanent. Something had to be done.

Instead of acknowledging that termination was producing an impending disaster for Menominee people, the MEI focused on its own problems. As the major taxpayer in the county, MEI recognized that the growing need for services had dire implications for its bottom line. Wisconsin eased the situation a bit by leasing Menominee land for access to the Wolf River and a campground. Not only did MEI receive an annual payment, but the agreement also removed the land, which now became public, from the tax rolls and MEI liability. Still, the county needed more revenue than MEI and the small number of individual taxpayers could afford to pay. MEI sought to increase profits by diversifying the mill's products, but it could not raise the capital to put the plan into action. MEI then decided that expanding the tax base would ease its tax burden so it focused on attracting new industry. An industrial plant would increase the value of the land, which in turn would increase taxes, and it would employ both current residents and newcomers, who presumably would improve their property and enhance its value. It was a pipe dream: efforts to bring new industry to the county failed dismally.

MEI finally settled on a plan to lure new residents who did not require jobs. The county needed property owners who had assets sufficient to improve their real estate and thereby increase the tax valuation. Summer vacation homes seemed to fit the bill. Menominee County was exceptionally scenic, with its towering forest and crystal clear lakes. MEI decided to exploit that natural beauty. Initially, they leased land to non-Indians for the construction of summer homes, then quietly converted these leases to sales to increase the tax base and shift tax liability. By 1965 plans were afoot to contract with a developer to market lots and construct second homes in Menominee County. By paying taxes, the new owners would augment county coffers, but, because they were not permanent residents, they would not place additional burdens on county services. Much to the horror of many Menominees, this plan meant selling their ancestral land. When the Menominees finally understood what was happening, they were horrified and enraged.

The land, however, no longer belonged to the Menominee tribe but to MEI, which was controlled by people who either were not Menominees or were Menominees who had been cowed into supporting white business interests. Most Menominees knew nothing about the scheme to sell lots until 1967 when MEI called a meeting of shareholders. I was living in Minneapolis at the time, so I was not there, but 253 Menominees did attend. Using terms like "warranty deed," which most Menominees did not understand, the MEI board of directors obscured its real intentions. The shareholders opposed any sale of Menominee land, but through the Voting Trust, the First Wisconsin Trust Company, which favored the plan, voted the shares of minors. The result of the vote was authorization to sell land, but most Menominees who had voted their own shares against the plan did not understand what the vote meant.

Without the knowledge of most of us, MEI subsequently entered into an agreement with a land developer, N. E. Isaacson & Associates, Inc., to form a joint venture that they called Lakes of the Menominees. The plan was to build dams to create lakefront property that could be carved into 2,500 taxable house sites. The developers began hosting big steak dinners in Milwaukee and Chicago to promote Lakes of the Menominees and quietly bringing people to look at the lots. The next thing Menominees knew, MEI was cutting the trees from the banks of one of our most beautiful lakes, Keshena Lake, and selling building lots at what they called Legend Lake. Between 1968 and 1971, MEI sold more than five thousand acres of land to the developer for $150 per acre. By June 30, 1972, Lakes of the Menominees had generated an additional $1,250,000 for MEI.

The developer had no respect for our culture and traditions, nor did the company have any appreciation of us as an Indian people with a recent history of self-sufficiency and sovereignty. This attitude toward the Menominees is all too familiar to Indians throughout the United States, many of whom today continue the struggle to save their land and people. Workers on Lakes of the Menominees thoughtlessly bulldozed an ancient hearth that some Menominees considered sacred. They cut roads, scared away game that had helped feed Menominee families, and destroyed important sources of wild foods, such as berry patches.

They allowed oil that leaked from construction equipment to foul waterways and kill fish, another source of food. In a community where there had been few strangers, outsiders now transformed the landscape and ecosystem in ways that inflicted a severe wound on the tribal psyche.

An unrelated victory in 1968 gave Menominees a shred of hope. Indian men always had hunted and fished to feed their families. We thought that our treaties guaranteed these rights and nothing in the Termination Act restricted them, but Wisconsin insisted that Menominees had become subject to state game laws, which set seasons, imposed game limits, and required licenses. The Council of Chiefs consulted Joseph Preloznik, director of Wisconsin Judicare, a legal aid organization. Joe, who would prove invaluable in the struggle for restoration, put them in touch with a Washington law firm that specialized in Indian law. The Menominee Indian Tribe of Wisconsin, Inc., took the United States to court. The case wound up at the U.S. Supreme Court, which bounced the case to the U.S. Court of Claims. The Court of Claims ruled that there had been no damages since Menominees still held those rights and sent it back to the Supreme Court. In 1968 the Supreme Court agreed that neither the Termination Act nor Public Law 280 nullified the Menominees' hunting and fishing rights. It was a small victory, but one that we welcomed. Unfortunately, many neighboring whites resented what they saw as preferential treatment for Menominees, an attitude that fanned anti-Indian feelings.

As newcomers moved into their vacation homes in the county, the conditions under which Menominees lived further deteriorated. We had long experienced racism in Shawano and other surrounding communities, but now the people living on what had been our reservation, established and guaranteed by treaty, made disparaging remarks about us. They seemed to think that we had dilapidated houses and no jobs by choice, and they found fault with our cultural traditions, which they saw as backward and primitive. Motorboats appeared on our lakes, eroding the banks and disrupting the spawning of fish. New owners chased away people who had hunted and fished on their land for generations. When MEI issued permits that entitled lot purchasers to hunt and fish on any land that MEI owned, the newcomers began to compete directly with us for fish and game. Menominees reported finding deer carcasses left where they fell rather than being butchered and taken home for food. Not only did such waste appall them but recreational hunting and fishing also threatened Menominee subsistence.

Less obvious were the deepening gloom and growing anger among Menominees. In less than a decade, we had seen our tribe dissolved and our future as a people destroyed. We had been self-supporting and self-governing. Our forest and mill provided employment, and tribal income funded education, health care, and social services. Now desperate poverty was widespread, forcing many young people to seek employment elsewhere. And the very land on which our former prosperity had rested was being sold out from under us. For Menominees, this was the last straw.

CHAPTER 4

▪ Working for Justice ▪

I was in college and graduate school while the Menominees were trying to develop a termination plan, and although my mother kept me well informed, my being far away made my tribe's problems seem abstract. Nevertheless, I wanted to go home and try to help. When I graduated from Columbia in 1961, I interviewed for a number of jobs, but none was on the Menominee Reservation. The transformation of the reservation into an impoverished county meant few opportunities existed there, and even if they had, it is unlikely that MEI or tribal officials would have hired Constance Deer's daughter. Since the tribe no longer officially existed and the county that encompassed what had been our reservation could offer little in the way of social services, I had to pursue my profession elsewhere. I decided that although I could not help my tribe, I could help Indians more generally, so I looked for positions in which I could serve Native people. I still had much to learn, but in looking for a job, I quickly realized that Menominees were not alone in being victims of half-baked and destructive federal policies. I was determined to do what I could to achieve justice for Indian people, wherever I was working

Indian policy in the 1950s intended to break up tribes through termination, Public Law 280, and a third corollary, which the BIA called "relocation." Relocation ostensibly provided Indian people with employment opportunities by helping them move from their impoverished reservations to thriving urban areas. Relocation, policymakers hoped, also would sever tribal bonds and force Indians to think of themselves as individual Americans rather than as members of a tribe. On their own initiative, Indians had been moving away from reservations since the nineteenth century—after all, I moved to New York, at least temporarily—but a large-scale effort to assimilate Indians by urbanizing them was new. Many relocated Indians ended up in crowded slums, ignorant of the social services available to them. Reservations were almost exclusively rural, and most transplants found the hustle and bustle of city life disconcerting and unpleasant. Underfunded and understaffed, the relocation program was unable to provide Indians the support they needed and left many families in conditions even more deplorable than those on their reservations. Nevertheless, by 1961 more than thirty-three thousand Indians nationally had left their reservations and moved to cities under the auspices of the federal relocation program. With few opportunities on reservations, countless other Indians joined them without even the meager resources the BIA offered. Most Menominees who relocated went to Milwaukee or Chicago. In 2016 approximately two-thirds of Menominees did not live on the reservation.

■ ■ ■

I had two job possibilities, both with urban Indian populations. One was in Oakland, California. After interviewing there, I decided that California was just too far away. The other was in Minneapolis, Minnesota. I decided on the position as program director at the Edward F. Waite Neighborhood House in Minneapolis, which was relatively close to the Menominee Reservation. Like Wisconsin, Minnesota was in the upper Midwest. It had a substantial Indian population, mostly Sioux and Ojibwe. But what attracted me most to this job was that the Waite House had recognized that their Indian clients had unique problems and perspectives, and they had hired an Ojibwe man, Larry Martin, to work with them full time. This, I thought, was the job for me.

Indian migration to Minneapolis had been going on for some time. People from the White Earth Chippewa Reservation began moving to Minneapolis after the allotment of their tribal lands to individuals at the turn of the twentieth century. Fraud and legal manipulation dispossessed many people, some of whom moved to the city to seek employment and avoid the intense political factionalism on the reservation. The Indian population in Minneapolis grew substantially after World War I as Indians from other tribes moved to the city. Indian organizations subsequently emerged. Some were tribally specific and provided links to home reservations; others were pan-Indian and brought people from disparate tribes together to address common issues. By World War II, many of these early migrants had entered the middle class. The war brought a new wave of Indian migration to the city. Just as my family had moved to Milwaukee, other Indians moved to Minneapolis to work in war industries. After the war, some Indian families went home, but many stayed.

In 1950, Minneapolis became one of the first cities to which Indians were relocated under the new federal policy. BIA employees helped them find employment, housing, and social services, but there was never enough support to make the transition smooth for most migrants. Jobs were not plentiful, especially after the economy went into recession in 1957, and those for which Indians qualified were usually low paying. The census recorded more than six thousand Indians in Minneapolis in 1960, but because of underreporting, the number was probably twice that and represented a sevenfold increase over 1950. Housing was in short supply, especially for Indians coming from reservations, who often had limited means.

Longtime Indian residents of the city struggled to help the newcomers. One longtime resident was Winnie Jourdain from the White Earth Ojibwe Reservation. In the late nineteenth century, the United States had allotted the reservation to individual tribal members. Although they had not been terminated, the Ojibwes had experienced BIA mismanagement of their resources and disregard of their tribal sovereignty. Winnie had grown up on the reservation and spoke Ojibwe, but her family had been forced to sell their home in the aftermath of allotment, which destroyed the reservation as they had known it, and they moved to the city. When I knew her, she was in her sixties. Winnie opened her doors to Indians who had no place to stay, became an advocate for education, and worked with the Waite Neighborhood House to provide opportunities for Indian children in the city. This kind of commitment to helping others made transition to urban living bearable for relocated Indians.

There was a limit to what individuals could do, and the city itself did not recognize an obligation to provide social services for its Indian residents. City officials were not really hostile; they just adopted a "not my problem" attitude because Indians presumably were the business of the federal government. But the BIA provided too little support when it brought people from the reservations and resettled them in the city. Many had no job skills and were poorly prepared for the city's competitive environment. The Department of Indian Work, created by the Minnesota Council of Churches, did the best that it could, but many of those well-meaning people did not have sufficient knowledge of the effects of racism and poverty and the significance of Indian culture. Unemployment, domestic violence, alcohol abuse, juvenile delinquency, and other problems began to plague Indian neighborhoods. White prejudice toward Indians became more pronounced, particularly in the way police harassed and abused young Indian men. These conditions ultimately would give rise to the American Indian Movement (AIM), founded in 1968 in Minneapolis to document and counter police abuse. Ultimately the organization became a major voice in the struggle for Native rights.

The Waite Neighborhood House had opened its doors in 1958, not long before I arrived. It sought to address the social problems of all neighborhood residents, black, white, and Indian. Waite House had deep roots in the settlement house movement that began in England in the nineteenth century with the goal to ameliorate some of the social and economic conditions created by the Industrial Revolution. Settlement houses addressed the problems of the working class structurally and politically as well as individually. By 1900 the movement was well established in the United States, especially in cities like Minneapolis that attracted significant numbers of immigrants. Settlement houses in the United States always served a diverse population, but over time the makeup of their clientele changed as African Americans moved into northern cities, Asian and Hispanic immigration increased, and Indians relocated to cities. Neighborhoods became more divided by race and culture than united by class, so settlement houses came to focus on helping neighborhoods build a sense of community by working to address individual problems. Political and structural issues receded because each group—and even each family—had problems unique to them.

The Waite House staff members organized after-school activities that included young children, teenagers, and intellectually disabled children, as well as programs aimed at specific groups, like Indians. The house itself was an old mansion, which had been very fancy in its former life. It had lots of large rooms where various activities could go on simultaneously, so the house was always full of people. As program director, I supervised all the managers except Irene Marcocini Long, who ran the program for developmentally disabled children and whom the executive director supervised. I enjoyed working with the entire staff. We were a diverse group—whites, Indians, and African Americans—but we had common goals and did our best.

Most programs at the Waite House were for children, but many Indian parents became involved in the neighborhood house and the broader Native community through their children. We encouraged involvement in and service to the community. One of the adult activities I enjoyed most was the Broken Arrow Service

Guild, which actually predated the Waite House but began to meet there when space became available. This was a group of American Indian women who came to the neighborhood house once a week to socialize, sew clothing, and make quilts. They hoped to raise enough money from selling their quilts to provide a college scholarship for an Indian student. Winnie Jourdain was a stalwart member of the Broken Arrow Guild. These little old ladies were relentless in trying to sell me their quilts. Finally I had to tell them, "Ladies, I can't buy any more. I don't have any more room in my closet, and I've given them to all my friends." Even with my numerous purchases, they failed to raise enough money for a scholarship, so they used the income from the quilts to buy eyeglasses for Indian children.

Just before I arrived in Minneapolis in 1961, Indians from a number of tribes organized the Upper Midwest American Indian Center, which met for a while at the Waite House. The center hosted a sewing club, powwows, children's programs, and other events. It later moved into its own space with the help of funding from the Johnson administration's War on Poverty. In the 1970s some of the people who had been involved in the Midwest Center helped found the Minneapolis American Indian Center, which secured funding for the construction of an architecturally distinctive building. Usually Indian centers are in some old wreck of a building that gets badly renovated, but this one was built to reflect Indian tribes and cultures. It is still operating. The center sponsors lots of programs, many of which deal with alcohol and drug problems and child welfare. It also provides a venue for feasts, powwows, art exhibits, and various other gatherings. Both of these urban centers brought together Chippewa (Ojibwe), Sioux, and other Indian people. The Waite House had helped them recognize their commonalities. Living in the city meant that, despite their different tribes and cultures, they shared experiences distinct from those of their families and friends on the reservations. Yet they never forgot where they had come from, and the problems of their rural reservations often followed them even as they faced new urban challenges.

Although the Waite House had many fine programs and a dedicated staff, its mission did not address the fundamental causes of the problems with which we dealt every day. Quilt sales could help a handful of children, but they could not provide the children's parents with jobs that would enable them to support their offspring adequately. Nor could the neighborhood house address the federal policy that sent Indian people scrambling to the city, the labor market that refused them employment or relegated them to minimum-wage jobs, or the racism that denied them opportunity. I wanted to tackle these macro problems, but neither my training nor my job empowered me to do so. I ran programs that helped individuals and families cope with the consequences of bad policies, but I could do little about the causes. Nevertheless, I found satisfaction in small individual victories.

In schools of social work you are told never to give money to your clients, which I always thought sounded reasonable. But not long after I arrived in Minneapolis a Sioux man showed up at the Neighborhood House. He was a sociable guy, a kind of happy-go-lucky ne'er-do-well. He said, "I heard you were here and I wanted to come and meet you." After I had chatted with him for some time, I asked him what he did, and I found out that he was unemployed. He came to the Waite House several times, and I enjoyed talking to him. He seemed like the perfect example of how the relocation policy had failed Indian people. One day he asked, "Can I borrow a dollar?" I knew better, but I gave him the dollar. He was my friend for life—or, at least, for my life in Minneapolis. But he did not abuse our one-dollar friendship. He never asked for money again, and he didn't send a trail of other people to hit me up for money. I didn't feel too bad about violating what I was told in the school of social work. On the other hand, I never saw my dollar again.

They also tell you in social work school that you should not be directive, but sometimes telling people what you think they should do seemed appropriate to me. (I probably got this trait from my mother!) A young Ojibwe man, who had a wife and two or three children, was going to school and came to the neighborhood house regularly. One day he stopped coming. I asked around about him and somebody told me, "He's in jail." I couldn't believe it—he was serving a thirty-day sentence for public drunkenness. Given the propensity of Minneapolis police to arrest Indians who had been drinking, I was not surprised to learn that an Indian was in jail for drunkenness, but I was dumbfounded to find this young man in that situation. So I went down to the jail to see him. I took the social work approach, "You're going to school, you have a job, you have a family, and here you are. Why are you doing this?" He hung his head and didn't really give me a reason. I was irked with him and I let him hear it: "All right. I'm going to come and see you next week and I want you to think about this. Is this the path you're going to take?"

When I came back, he started telling me about the Indian down the hall. It was time, I decided, for me to be more proactive. I said, "No, no, no. I'm not talking about him; I'm talking about you. Now, what have *you* thought about?" He hemmed and hawed and finally said, "I want to ask you something. Why are you trying to help me?" I replied, "First of all, you're a student, a husband, and a father, and you've got responsibilities. Second, you're having problems with drinking and I'm familiar with that. My father's an alcoholic; my brother's an alcoholic; a lot of other Indians I know are alcoholics. I can't help them but I might be able to help you." He looked at me with amazement, but did not respond. I continued, "What are you going to do with your life? You need to get yourself together, stop your drinking, get back in school, get your job back or get another job, and get on with your life." So much for social work school! I certainly recognized the difficulties that Indians faced, both on reservations and in cities, but like all human beings, they have the ability to make choices. As individuals, they can be part of the problem or part of the solution. So I approached him as an individual. I asked how much he drank and told him there were resources that could help him if he took responsibility for his behavior.

When he got out of jail, he showed up at the neighborhood house. I was delighted to learn that he was back with his family and had returned to work and school. I assured him that he could come in to talk to me and that he could call me any time before 11:00 P.M., but only if he was sober. I dealt with his drinking as an individual problem, and I was able to help him because I knew his wife and his little children. The neighborhood house made it possible for me to know individual clients in their social context, so I was able to say to him, "I know your wife, I know your little children, and they are worth a lot." I am happy to report that he straightened out, and I think my direct approach played a role.

Just as my professional training discouraged individual aid and directives, the mission of a neighborhood house limited what it could do, even in regard to a misconceived federal Indian policy that dislocated and impoverished hundreds of its clients. Nevertheless, the Waite House was a kind of incubator for political action because it provided people with contacts, training, opportunities, and experience. People I met at the Waite House went on to make important contributions to Indian affairs.

Leon Cook, a Red Lake Ojibwe, provides a good example. One day Leon just walked in off the street and asked for a job. I told him we didn't have any jobs and asked him if he wanted to volunteer. He replied with a resounding "yes!" Through volunteering, he got to know how a neighborhood house operated, and he learned the importance of an organization that provided an umbrella for community services. In 1969 Commissioner of Indian Affairs Louis R. Bruce Jr. appointed Leon deputy director for economic development at the BIA in Washington. Leon was one of several young Indian activists whom Bruce appointed, a move that bothered career BIA bureaucrats. Leon began agitating within the Interior Department for greater protection of Indian land and resources, which he knew were key to the economic development that would make reservations viable. The career bureaucrats at BIA, who held the purse strings, pushed back in what Leon termed "fiscal genocide." Ultimately, his outspoken advocacy of Indian rights cost him his job, but in 1971 he became president of the National Congress of American Indians, a resounding endorsement of his position on economic development.

Audrey Banks, from the Leech Lake Chippewa Reservation, became an advocate for Indian children. I met her when she enrolled her young son in a summer day camp I ran. Audrey had been sent to boarding school at the age of nine, and as an adult, she settled in Minneapolis. She had given birth to six children, three boys and three girls, but Catholic social workers pressured her to give up the three newborn girls for adoption. She was not alone. The removal of Indian children from their parents, and their frequent adoption by non-Indian parents, became a real scandal, especially in states governed by Public Law 280, which placed Indians under laws that empowered non-Indian officials to terminate parental rights. Audrey's experience later led her to graduate school and a master's degree in social work. She then worked with social service agencies in Minneapolis to ensure compliance with the Indian Child Welfare Act (ICWA), which Congress passed in 1978 to address the problem of Indian children being removed from their birth families. At the time the law as passed, as much as 25 to 35 percent of Indian children were being removed from their birth families and placed for adoption. The law gave tribes jurisdiction over children living on reservations and a voice in the fate of those who came under state jurisdiction. Audrey's work enabled Indian children to grow up in Indian families, even if they lived in Minneapolis or other cities.

I assisted the League of Women Voters to conduct a study of Minnesota Indians, and managed to involve Indians from the neighborhood house in the project. League members knew almost nothing about Indians, so I went to local chapters and conducted "Indians 101"—explaining the histories and cultures of different tribes as well as the role of the BIA and churches—to help them frame the issue. I drafted Yvonne Wynde, a Sisseton woman from the Lake Traverse Sioux Reservation in South Dakota whom I had met at Waite House, for the project. Yvonne was very naïve when she first came to Minneapolis, but she was smart, hardworking, and devoted to her children. She also was artistic and ended up illustrating the League publication *Indians in Minnesota*. (The University of

Minnesota Press published the fifth edition of this important resource in 2006.) Yvonne became an art educator and served as vice president and academic dean of Standing Rock Community College (today Sitting Bull College). President Jimmy Carter later appointed her to the Commission on Presidential Scholars. More recently, she has helped organize commemorative marches to call attention to the injustices suffered by Sioux people, both past and present. I think that the neighborhood house played a role in developing her awareness and commitment.

The Waite House demonstrated that Indians could address their own problems if they had the social and economic resources to do so. Many of the people who came to the Waite House were actively engaged in seeking their own solutions to unemployment, homelessness, child care, education, and health care. The relationship between the neighborhood house and people like Winnie, Audrey, Yvonne, and Leon was reciprocal: individuals helped make the house a success and, in turn, the house helped create a community of people of different ages and from different tribes. By accepting responsibility for themselves, Indian people helped ease some of the suffering that relocation brought about.

I learned two important things at Waite House. First, I did not know enough about Native America to effect broad change. I was well trained as a social worker—even if I did not always follow established protocol—but I knew surprisingly little about tribes other than my own when I arrived in Minneapolis. Columbia University and the School of Social Work faculty were indifferent to and ignorant of Indian issues. They appeared to demean my desire to address the problems that Native people were encountering. I read widely about Indians, and at the Waite House I met people from a number of different tribes, but the knowledge I acquired was anecdotal and random. I needed to know more.

The second thing I learned was that the source of many problems that Indians faced was neither individual nor tribal but U.S. Indian policy. In the upper Midwest, the allotment policy of the late nineteenth century had begun to funnel dispossessed Indians into urban areas, a movement that the Great Depression and World War II accelerated. This trickle swelled to a flood in the 1950s with the relocation and termination policies. Without adequate support from their tribes, the city, the state, or the BIA, people struggled. Social services, churches, and neighborhood houses tried to help, but the needs were overwhelming, and the means available could not address the root causes. We needed to change policy.

When John F. Kennedy had become president in January 1961, many people hoped his "New Frontier" would address Indian issues. On the campaign trail he promised a reorganization of Indian affairs. Once elected, he focused his attention on other issues. My mother overstated the case when she accused his administration of "open contempt for American Indians," but as president, Kennedy delivered little for Native people. Nevertheless, relocation had already begun to grind to a halt after criticism from the General Accounting Office. Kennedy's secretary of the interior, Stuart Udall, created the Task Force on Indian Affairs, which consulted widely with tribal leaders before issuing a report that focused on economic development and more efficient delivery of services by the BIA. The report did not recommend reversal of the termination policy, which was the source of much anguish in Indian Country, but it did counsel less emphasis on termination and greater emphasis on preparing tribes to support and govern themselves.

Udall had intended to appoint an Indian to head the BIA, but his top two picks declined, so he turned to Philleo Nash, a Democrat who had served on the task force and had just lost reelection as lieutenant governor of Wisconsin. Dr. Nash was an anthropologist. He and his wife, Edith, had worked on the Klamath Reservation, which Congress had terminated, and as a result, he opposed termination. But his own incremental approach to policy change, Congress's continuing support of termination, and the White House's lack of interest in Indian affairs, meant that termination continued. Indeed, Menominee termination took effect during the Kennedy administration.

Dr. Nash recognized that many Indians preferred to live on their reservations and be governed by their own tribal officials. Consequently, he advocated economic development on reservations and training of individuals for the jobs that were available there. Nash was comfortable with Indian people, and in an effort to make the BIA more collaborative, he spent much of his time meeting with Indian leaders away from Washington. He not only asked Indians what they thought but he also advocated tackling problems on two levels, structural and individual. As an Indian and a social worker, I heartily approved of his approach, and I wanted very much to talk to him about my experiences with both urban and reservation Indians.

In 1962 I went to Washington, D.C., to attend a social work conference. Although I did not have an appointment, I decided to go see Dr. Nash at the BIA. When I called his office, his secretary told me that he was very busy. I asked her to tell the commissioner that I was a Menominee social worker and that I only needed ten minutes between elevators. The next day, I got exactly that, but it was enough time to discuss the difficulties of urban Indians and the failure of termination. Because of the Menominee experience with termination and the problems that arose from relocation, I had a very negative view of the BIA. Plus, I was not sure how Dr. Nash would receive me since my mother had sent him a number of strongly worded letters about termination. He quickly put me at ease, in part because he looked like Santa Claus with his little round belly, fringe of white hair, and white beard. Dr. Nash also seemed genuinely interested in Indian people and committed to making the BIA work for them. When I started to leave, he opened a door: "Ada, we need people like you working for the BIA. Then perhaps all these problems would not exist." Two years later I walked through that door.

My decision to go to work at the BIA Area Office in Minneapolis in 1964 stemmed in part from my meeting with Dr. Nash, but also from my positive impressions of the area director, Jim Hawkins. Jim had spent much of his adult life in Alaska, where he taught in schools that enrolled mostly Indian and Inuit children. He had served for two years as executive director of the Alaska Rural Development Board before becoming the Juneau area director for BIA programs in Alaska in 1958. In 1962 the bureau moved him to Minneapolis. Unlike most career BIA employees, Jim was determined to hire Indians into positions with significant responsibilities rather than the menial jobs usually reserved for them. Like Dr. Nash, he was committed to helping Indians develop their talents and giving them a chance to make real contributions.

By the time I went to work for the BIA, President Kennedy had been assassinated and Lyndon B. Johnson was in the White House. Building on Kennedy's initiatives, the Johnson administration accelerated social change by tackling two big domestic issues head-on: civil rights and poverty. The first effort focused attention on all minorities in the United States. Indians at last appeared on the national radar screen. For urban Indians, passage of the Civil Rights Act of 1964 promised protection from the discrimination they suffered in cities. For Indians who lived on reservations, however, the argument for integrating minorities into the American mainstream sounded too much like the justification for termination and relocation.

On the other hand, in his 1964 inaugural address President Johnson declared a "War on Poverty" that promised relief to impoverished Americans, including Indians on reservations. Later that year, Congress passed the Economic Opportunity Act. This legislation outlined various programs intended to address poverty through federal aid for education and locally driven economic development. The emphasis on community action projects suggested that Indians might be able to define their own needs and develop ways to address them. In those days before the Vietnam War sapped the nation's zeal for reform, the federal commitment to racial and economic justice drew many idealistic young people like me to government service.

Working for the BIA provided me with the opportunity to serve Indian people not just in Minneapolis but throughout the region since the area office supervised reservations in Wisconsin, Michigan, Iowa, and Minnesota. Nevertheless, when Jim first offered me a job, I declined. I had become increasingly outspoken politically. At a 1963 Indian leadership conference at the University of Wisconsin–Eau Claire, for example, I pointed out that Indians often did not know when their civil rights were being violated and that non-Natives who worked with Indians heard what they wanted to hear rather than what Indians were actually telling them about their circumstances. If I worked for the BIA, such public comments would potentially become violations of the Hatch Act, which Congress passed in 1939 to prevent employees of the executive branch from engaging in partisan politics. I felt strongly about Indian issues, especially termination and relocation, and I had no intention of remaining silent. Jim assured me that I would have complete freedom to speak out on topics about which I was passionate. His assurances and my own curiosity about what went on inside the BIA finally won out over my misgivings about continuing my political activism.

A second reason I hesitated was because at that time one of the main functions of BIA social workers was to take Indian children away from their families and place them with white families. I did not want to do that, so they changed the job, moving it out of the Social Work Department. My new job title was community services coordinator, which made me a liaison between the BIA and tribes, civic and community groups, and nonprofit organizations and associations. I spoke to white organizations not only about issues confronting Indian people, in whom they had become increasingly interested, but also about the importance of helping tribes determine their own futures. With trained leadership and organization, I argued, Indians could begin to plot their own course, even in opposition to BIA policy. I guess this approach made me something of a subversive, but it very much reflected the tenor of the BIA under Dr. Nash's leadership.

After two years of working for the BIA, I submitted a report of my activities. The area office sent it up the chain of command to headquarters, where Dr. Nash read it. He must have been impressed because he decided to send me on a six-month-long training expedition, during which I could go wherever I wanted and meet whomever I wanted. The BIA would pay my expenses as well as my salary while I visited Indians all over the country. To this point, my experience had been limited to tribes in the Midwest, especially Minnesota and Wisconsin. Now I had an opportunity to learn about people who had radically different cultures and histories. At the end, I felt as though I had packed decades of education and experience into those six months.

One of the most interesting things I observed was the implementation of the War on Poverty in Indian Country. The Johnson administration had hired educated, knowledgeable, and highly trained Indians as advisers and had established Indian desks in federal agencies, including the Office of Economic Opportunity (OEO). Community Action Programs (CAPs) empowered communities to identify and address their own problems in ways that made sense to them. In the process, CAPs developed leadership at the local level while providing project funding through OEO. Because the OEO dispersed funds directly to CAP projects rather than channeling them through other agencies, CAPs enabled Indians to bypass the BIA and even their own tribal governments. Leaders of Indian CAPs had the power to make their own decisions, apply directly for federal grants, and decide how to spend funds awarded them. Several of the tribes I visited were demonstrating how successful this approach could be. Among them were the Mississippi Band of Choctaws and the Navajo Nation. These tribes were very different, but both retained much of their traditional culture, including their languages.

In Mississippi, the Choctaws had just succeeded in wresting control of their tribe from an overbearing, patronizing agency superintendent who had tried to keep them in a state of dependency on the BIA. After the superintendent's ouster, the Choctaw council began to identify the tribe's most pressing needs. At that time, unemployment among Mississippi Choctaws was about 80 percent and most people lived in substandard housing. Even BIA-funded houses had no indoor plumbing. Choctaws found Dr. Nash sympathetic, but little support was forthcoming. In 1966, Phillip Martin, whom I met on my visit, left the council chairmanship and became director of the Choctaw Community Action Program. He applied for and received a $15,000 planning grant from OEO to set up tribal departments of human resources, finance, economic development, and planning. Previously, the BIA had managed the tribe, but now the Choctaws began to govern themselves. This was the start of their tribally driven economic development program that ultimately made the Mississippi Choctaws the largest employer in Mississippi.

The Navajos established the Office of Navajo Economic Opportunity (ONEO) with funding from OEO. ONEO secured funding for projects ranging from Head Start to home improvement, all of which addressed needs that Navajos had identified. ONEO also initiated legal services, which soon became a separate entity. New opportunities enticed well-educated Navajos to return to the reservation and accept leadership positions. Among them was Peter MacDonald, whom I met on my visit. MacDonald had worked for Hughes Aircraft in California before returning to the Navajo Reservation, where he became director of ONEO, a position he held until successfully running for tribal chairman in 1970. Another returnee was Peterson Zah. I did not meet him because at that time he was working in Phoenix for Volunteers in Service to America (VISTA), another federal anti-poverty program under OEO. The next year he came home to direct legal services, and in 1990 he became the first president of the Navajo Nation under their newly reorganized tribal government.

The time I spent in Washington was valuable in many ways, but one of the most important was the friendship I formed with LaDonna and Fred Harris. Oklahoma voters first elected Fred to the U.S. Senate in 1964 to complete the term of Robert S. Kerr, who had died, and then reelected him in 1966. LaDonna was a Comanche with boundless energy that she invested in a host of public issues. I got to know her when we both served on the Joint Commission on the Mental Health of Children in 1967–68. LaDonna was already an activist for Indian people in Oklahoma. She had organized Oklahomans for Indian Opportunity, which initially addressed the high rate of school dropouts and moved on to develop programs to build self-esteem among and teach leadership skills to Indian youth.

LaDonna and Fred were Democrats and strong supporters of programs initiated by Presidents Kennedy and Johnson. They became interested in recruiting Indians for the Peace Corps, a Kennedy administration program that recruited Americans to volunteer abroad. LaDonna thought that North American Indians would have special rapport with Indigenous peoples elsewhere in the world, especially those in Mexico and Central and South America. At the same time, the Peace Corps offered Indian young people an opportunity to acquire leadership skills useful to their tribes. In 1968 I signed on for one summer to help train the recruits for Project Peace Pipe, as the program was called, in Puerto Rico. OEO funded it for three years, long enough to train two groups of volunteers, but only two volunteers finished their overseas assignments. Despite this disappointing outcome, LaDonna and Fred did not give up, and by 1970 LaDonna had founded Americans for Indian Opportunity to take her ideas about leadership training nationwide. I served on the board from 1970 to 1983 and enjoyed every minute of working with these young Indian people who ultimately made a difference in their tribes and in national Indian affairs.

The War on Poverty provided unprecedented leadership training for individuals and some financial autonomy for tribes. Bypassing the BIA empowered tribes in ways that often made BIA officials nervous and even resentful. Suddenly Indians were thinking and acting for themselves. Dr. Nash certainly recognized and appreciated the role that the OEO played in empowering tribes, but career BIA bureaucrats were not always as supportive. In some cases, I imagine, this led to suspicion and resentment of the Indian employees in the bureau and of the Indians who tried to circumvent the BIA. LaDonna, for example, had to do an end run around the BIA to get funds to support Americans for Indian Opportunity.

By the time I returned to Minneapolis, Dr. Nash had left his position as commissioner of Indian affairs. Interior Secretary Udall had become dissatisfied with the slow pace of the consultations that Dr. Nash used to build relationships with tribes and shape policy. Hoping for quick results from the top down, Udall named Robert L. Bennett, an Oneida, to replace Dr. Nash. Subsequent staff changes reached into the area offices as well. The BIA transferred Jim Hawkins, who had recruited me, to the Pacific islands that the United States holds in trust and appointed his assistant, Paul Winsor, as the new area director. Winsor abolished my job and reassigned me to a position as an employment counselor. Everything I had learned seemed to be inconsequential for that job. My supervisors, all of whom were non-Indians, had no interest in what I had to say and largely ignored me. This BIA was far removed from the BIA Dr. Nash had envisioned. After six months, I quit.

The war in Vietnam had begun to redirect the attention and energy of the Johnson administration away from the problems of poverty and of racial and ethnic minorities in the United States. At the same time, many American people began to lose interest in marginalized peoples, and the radicalization of reform movements made many recoil from the changes sweeping society. In their minds, people of color moved from worthy but oppressed victims to suspicious, irrelevant, or dangerous pests. The attitude in the Minneapolis area office of the BIA reflected this change, but leaving the BIA did not enable me to escape it.

I accepted a job at the University of Minnesota Training Center for Community Programs. The center had a number of missions, one of which was training Indians in how to administer OEO programs. It also produced reports on subjects like employment, housing, and education in Minnesota. I accompanied the director on visits to Minnesota Indian reservations and helped prepare a report on Indian education that was quite critical of current practices. By the time I completed it, she had resigned and the new administration was not concerned about Indians. The new director took issue with the report, which he thought was too critical although he knew little about Indians. He had no interest in what I thought and isolated me. As a result, my time at the Training Center was brief.

Compounding the growing disinterest in Native issues, hostility toward Indian people in Minneapolis was increasing. Young men, many of whom were Vietnam veterans, bore the brunt of the backlash. Every weekend, police raided Indian bars and arrested 150–200 Indians for public drunkenness. Jail sentences meant lost jobs and impoverished families. By 1968 the Indian community had resolved to do something about police harassment. A group of activists met in a church basement and decided to offer the community some protection by setting up patrols and documenting police brutality. Among them was George Mitchell, a boarding school–educated Ojibwe whom I had met at the Waite House. This was the founding of AIM. What began as a local organization in Minneapolis ultimately attracted members throughout the United States. As it did so, AIM became more radical and violent. I do not approve of AIM's methods, but I certainly understand the circumstances that led to them. I was not aware of AIM at the time, but in 1968 I felt a bit of the powerlessness that motivated some of its members to take a course different from mine. I believed in working within the system, a belief that often brought me frustration, but I held to it.

After leaving the Training Center for Community Programs, I took a position as a social worker with the Minneapolis public schools. I was interested in education, especially public education, which had served me well. I asked for an assignment in a school with Indian students but ended up working in a junior high school with virtually no Indians. Nevertheless, I threw myself into my new job. I made home visits and got acquainted with parents. Mothers started calling me when their children were sick so that I could report them as excused and keep them off the truancy rolls. But I felt like I was beating my head against a wall. The students lacked even the most basic skills, and teachers seemed to be doing little to help them. They simply blamed someone else—usually elementary schools and parents—and took few steps to rectify the situation, whatever its cause. Even more disturbing was school administrators' attitude toward troubled students. Rather than receiving counseling or other kinds of help, students ended up expelled or shipped off to "alternative" schools that were little more than holding pens. I finished the year, but I did not go back.

My experiences in Minneapolis deepened my commitment to young people and drew me into unlikely organizations. In particular, I served on the national board of directors for the Girl Scouts of the U.S.A. I had never been a girl scout and I knew nothing about girl scouts, but the woman who called me told me that the national organization wanted to become more inclusive. She didn't use the word "Indians" but that is what she meant. I resisted. Finally, she said, "Ada Deer, if you don't do this and help us, who will?" Bingo. I told her that I would give it a try, but I would not wear a girl scout uniform since I had never been a girl scout. I attended board meetings in New York two or three times a year and went to the national conference, which drew thousands of girls, almost all of them white. I met interesting people, including First Lady Pat Nixon. Like all first ladies, Mrs. Nixon served as honorary girl scout president. I was present when she was installed in the office. A lifelong Democrat, I tried to hide in the back of the room. But I am tall and, in a sea of white faces, likely to stand out. I was dragged up to meet Mrs. Nixon, which in retrospect, I am very happy about. But at the time I was mortified.

The first American Indian girl scout troop had organized in 1921, but even in the late 1960s most members of the national organization continued to be white. I was surprised at how few people of color were at the 1969 convention, where the organization made a commitment to change things. Inspired by the civil rights movement and Dr. Martin Luther King, the Girl Scouts organization launched "Action 70," a program intended to combat racism and make the organization more diverse. In 1975, they selected Dr. Gloria Randle Scott as their first African American president, but progress was slow. Under Dr. Scott's leadership, the national organization held conferences on recruiting young blacks, Hispanics, and Indians. They evaluated their written materials, brochures, and calendars to make them more inclusive. Although this effort was commendable, it was not likely to expand scouting into inner cities or onto Indian reservations where people were very poor and troop leaders could not afford to volunteer the way more affluent women could. I suggested that leaders be paid, but that idea got little support. Nevertheless, I was pleased to serve on the board for six years, during which time the Girl Scouts formally committed to diversity and social justice.

A senior girl scout troop in Wisconsin Rapids took outreach seriously and applied for a grant from *Reader's Digest* to fund a weeklong Girl Scout Day Camp for Indians. Lasting six hours a day, the camp provided transportation and lunch. I conducted a sensitivity training workshop for the teenage girls who acted as counselors. All of them were white, of course, and I reminded them that Indian and rural children were often left out of scouting because they didn't have the money to pay dues or buy uniforms. The counselors worked hard to stretch their budget of $600 and to lead activities appropriate for children who never had experienced scouting. In the end, everyone agreed that the experience had been worthwhile.

My time in Minneapolis ended just as I began to serve on the board of the Girl Scouts. In 1969, I got an opportunity to go home—or nearly home. I received a call from Bob Powless, an Oneida whom I had met when we were both students at the University of Wisconsin–Madison. After he completed his undergraduate and master's degrees there, Bob went on to obtain a PhD in educational administration from the University of Minnesota. University of Wisconsin–Stevens Point had just hired him as director of its new Program for Recognizing Individual Determination through Education, or PRIDE, and he offered me a job heading Upward Bound. I accepted Bob's offer.

Another campaign in the Johnson administration's War on Poverty, Upward Bound sought to encourage high school students whose parents had not been to college to seek higher education. In practice, it targeted students from minority groups and rural areas, populations underrepresented on most college campuses. Upward Bound at UW–Steven's Point exposed reservation-based Indian students in Wisconsin to the college experience. The chancellor and administration were enthusiastic and eager to host the program.

Upward Bound brought students to campus for a six-week summer session during which participants took a range of courses focusing on basic skills in math and reading but also including enrichment courses in art, drama, and music. We offered courses on American Indian history and culture, the first time these students had ever thought of their own tribes as deserving of serious study. College students acted as tutors. One year, LaDonna and Fred Harris's daughter, Kathy, and Bruce Froehlke, son of prominent Wisconsin Republican and U.S. Secretary of the Army Robert Froehlke, served together as tutors. We continued tutoring and provided other support for participants throughout the academic year.

One of the great benefits of this program was that it gave students confidence in themselves—they learned that they *could* do it. For Indian participants, it instilled pride in themselves and their people. To foster this pride, I hired a largely Indian staff. Among them was artist Truman Lowe, who went on to become chair of the art department at UW–Madison and curator of contemporary art at the National Museum of the American Indian. Learning what was possible—what they *could* achieve—improved these students' chances of succeeding in college.

I invited prominent Indian leaders to address the Upward Bound Convocation. I particularly remember hosting the Osage ballerina Maria Tallchief, who was a supporter of Americans for Indian Opportunity. She talked about living in a world without racial prejudice, the arts world: "I never asked my dance partner before I leaped into his arms if he was black or yellow or white." She also told the students about falling onstage, picking herself up, going on, and pretending it never happened. Her message that racism is not inevitable and that people cannot let setbacks stop them was one that the students found very inspiring. Joseph Preloznik, executive director of Wisconsin Judicare, also spoke. Although not an Indian, Joe had been working for CAAMP, and he explained about treaties and tribal sovereignty as well as the legal aid available through his organization, which was an OEO program.

Upward Bound tried to fill the gap in knowledge about Native histories and cultures that existed in the curricula of many reservation and public schools. Professor David Wrone, who taught Native American history at UW–Stevens Point and introduced the study of the Menominee language there, spoke to the students. At the time, he was working on a collection of documents about relations between Indians and whites, which was published in 1973 as *Who's the Savage? A Documentary History of the Mistreatment of the Native North Americans.* We also took students on field trips to the Stand Rock Indian Ceremonial at Wisconsin Dells, sponsored by the Ho-Chunks, and to the Wisconsin Historical Society, where they saw the material culture of their peoples' pasts.

I enjoyed working with all these promising young people so, when Bob Powless returned to graduate school in 1970, I became acting director of PRIDE. UW–Stevens Point made a real effort to reach out to Indian students. Every Wednesday a group of college student volunteers tutored about sixty Indian high school students at Wisconsin Rapid's Howe School. PRIDE-sponsored tutoring also took place in four Indian communities, including Neopit and Keshena. These sessions gave Indians and non-Indians opportunities to interact with each other. For many participants this was the first time they had talked with someone of a different race and background. Thus, in addition to academic help, this experience fostered understanding. Getting to know college students made college seem more attainable, and for Indian students who decided to give postsecondary education a try, PRIDE offered "Ease-In," a program to help them adjust. But attracting Indians to college and keeping them there was no easy task. In 1970 UW–Stevens Point had twenty-five Indian students, the most of any college in Wisconsin. UW–Madison was next with fifteen.

Equally distressing was the general attitude in American schools and universities toward Indians and their histories and cultural experiences. For that reason, I was delighted to have a chance to participate in the first meeting of the National Indian Education Association in 1970. About six hundred people, two-thirds of whom were Indians, attended. LaDonna Harris spoke about the contributions Indians have made to American society, but the panels and workshops focused on the problems Native students encounter. I summarized the conclusions of the panel I chaired as follows: "The existing educational system is a racist structure which does not meet the needs of the community." Because of growing unrest on Indian reservations across the country, many educational institutions had instituted "Indian Week" or some such thing, but teachers generally lacked sufficient knowledge to do anything more than perpetuate stereotypes. Furthermore, colleges in particular often seemed more interested in learning about dead Indians than in knowing and supporting living Indian people.

My experiences at UW–Stevens Point led me to reconsider my own life and what I wanted to accomplish. They strengthened my determination to improve the situation of Native people—for my own tribe, tribes in my state, and those throughout the United States. Everywhere I had worked before Upward Bound, my supervisors had missed the point: to have a major impact on people's lives, we needed to focus on the sources of their problems, which were often institutional and legal. We had to make the whole system more just if we were ever to obtain justice for individuals. I made a decision to go in a different direction. For ten years, I had wanted to go to law school, in part perhaps because of my mother's obsession with the illegality of termination and the rights that Indians retained under their treaties.

In 1971 I applied to and was accepted at UW-Madison. At thirty-five years old I was about to become a student again. I spent that summer in the two-month American Indian Law Program at the University of New Mexico, created to prepare Indians to enter law school. I arrived in Madison in the fall, excited to be back on a campus that held so many happy memories. I looked forward to the future, which I thought I had all planned. Boy, was I wrong! The future held challenges and triumphs that, in the fall of 1971, I could not even imagine.

CHAPTER 5

▪ Joining the Struggle ▪

M y mother no doubt sparked my interest in law school because she regarded it as a way for me to be useful to my people. Her opposition to termination was partly moral and religious but mostly it rested on legal grounds. She firmly believed that treaties with the United States recognized Menominee sovereignty—the right of the tribe to govern itself—and that Congress could not unilaterally enact legislation that destroyed the Menominee Nation. Her solution was for Congress to repeal the Termination Act, respect the tribe's sovereign status, and return the reservation land to the tribe. Such a course offered an obvious answer, one that I feared my graduate courses and work experiences did not prepare me to help achieve. In 1969 I did not see how social work could solve Menominee problems. I had moved back to Wisconsin in 1969 to take the job at UW–Stevens Point in part because it was only a couple of hours from the Menominees, who were facing a crisis over the Legend Lake development. Land sales promised to increase the tax base for the impoverished county, MEI claimed, but landowners who registered to vote also jeopardized Menominee control over their county and over the way those taxes were spent. Something needed to be done.

My mother had been speaking out about termination for nearly two decades, so much so that local newspapers called her a "loudmouth" and claimed she had appeared before more Wisconsin legislative committees than any other citizen. But my mother was not the only person in my family who was upset about the situation. My sister Connie, a student at the University of Wisconsin, and brother Robert, who also lived in Madison, were outraged, especially at MEI and its relationship with the land developer. At the shareholder meeting in December 1969, Connie demanded a financial accounting of the project, only to be put off. When she and Robert turned up at MEI headquarters asking to see financial records, officials told them that they did not have that right. I had delayed getting involved in the fight against termination ever since my mother had asked me to do something when I was a freshman in college. Now was the time. Connie and Robert needed a lawyer, so I called Joseph Preloznik, the director of Wisconsin Judicare, who had previously been involved in several legal issues for our tribe. Preloznik filed suit and forced MEI to open its books.

MEI often had shareholder meetings off the reservation. After the land sale scheme was announced, I started going to them and sitting right up front. Some other Indians attended the meetings, but whites did most of the talking. The governing structure set up at termination was so complicated that I didn't understand much of what they were talking about. So I stood up and said, "I would like for someone to explain this." They would try to justify the sale of our land to wealthy white people for vacation homes, but in language so garbled that it was hard to follow. So I asked, "Why don't you have more meetings on the reservation?" When they answered that few Indians would attend, I replied, "I don't agree with that." After one meeting, a white guy asked what my profession was and then told me, "Miss Deer, you are so articulate. You really should come back to the reservation and help your people." His paternalism got to me. I replied that if I came back, it would not be as a social worker in the usual sense. I would return in a position of power and *really* make a difference.

I decided I had to know more about what was going on, so I arranged to talk with Preloznik. The first time we tried to meet, we missed each other—I went to Madison and he went to Stevens Point. We must have passed each other on the highway. But we connected on the second try. Being a lawyer who already was involved in Menominee affairs, Preloznik had a really good grasp of the termination policy and its disastrous impact on Menominee people. I said, "All right now, I need to understand exactly what this is about." He was very patient with me in explaining the Menominee Termination Act. I was stunned. Here I was, a well-educated Menominee, and for the first time I really understood what termination meant. Not only had termination converted our reservation into a county and turned our resources over to MEI, which had become a state corporation, but it had also taken away our status as Indians. I guess I just had not paid enough attention to my mother! The more I understood, the angrier I got. "We have to change this," I blurted out. Joe replied, "You have to get a law through the Congress." I responded, "Well, Congress did this and they need to undo it." But lots of work had to be done before Congress would listen. Menominees had to believe that they could change things, and then they had to unite in opposition to land sales, MEI, and the Voting and Assistance Trusts.

The civil rights and antiwar movements of the 1960s provided models of activism, but Indian problems were different in fundamental ways. In December 1969, Vine Deloria Jr. published an article, "The War between the Redskins and the Feds," in the *New York Times*; it addressed Menominee termination in the context of the dispossession of other Indian people and their efforts to reclaim their land and resources. The federal policy of termination applied to only a few tribes, but across the country Indians were suffering loss of water and mineral rights along with discrimination, appalling poverty, social and political dysfunction, police brutality, poor health, and inferior education. The chief source of these problems, Deloria argued, was the federal administration of Indian affairs. Most politicians in Washington understood and cared little about Indians, but they thought they knew what was best for them. Termination certainly fit the bill. As Menominees were realizing, legislators often enacted policies with little consultation or explanation and usually in total ignorance of the principle of tribal sovereignty.

Most Menominees shared Deloria's anger without reading the *New York Times*. They were incensed and dismayed that their land had passed into the hands of non-Indians who were destroying its natural beauty. Like me, most Menominees who had left the reservation in the 1950s and 1960s retained a sense of tribal identity and community and stayed informed about what was going on at home. Tribal members living in Chicago, Milwaukee, and elsewhere began to search for a way to save their homeland. Menominees were not alone in their anger and despair. Indians all over the country began to press the federal government to acknowledge and address their many problems. In 1968 AIM quickly came to protest all kinds of injustice—poor health care, poverty, conditions on reservations, and lack of opportunity in the cities. The next year another group, Indians of All Tribes, took over Alcatraz Island in San Francisco Bay, the site of a closed prison, and occupied it for eighteen months. They demanded that the federal government sign the land over to the Indians under the terms of an 1868 treaty pledging return of federal property that the government no longer used. An AIM delegation visited, as did a host of celebrities including Jane Fonda and Marlon Brando. The occupiers did not get the island, but they did attract a lot of attention to Indian problems.

Someone in Washington must have been paying attention. President Richard

Jim White (Washinawatok) demanding that First Wisconsin Trust surrender
Menominee proxies, April 26, 1971. *Wisconsin Historical Society, image WHi-35256.*

Nixon's July 1970 message to Congress signaled a change: "The time has come
to break decisively with the past and to create the conditions for a new era in
which the Indian future is determined by Indian acts and Indian decisions."
Then in September two small Chippewa tribes in Wisconsin, Red Cliff and Bad
River, managed to hold on to their land after a decade of pressure to sell it to the
National Park Service for the Apostle Islands National Lakeshore. Protest and
resistance seemed to be paying off, and Indians across the country, even those
opposed to radical action, were taking stock of their situations.

Menominees were a long way from stopping the Legend Lake development,
but they were beginning to organize. In the spring of 1970 I started contacting
everyone I could think of to publicize the crisis facing the tribe. Jim White (later
called James Washinawatok), who worked in an alcohol treatment program in
Chicago, had organized a group of Menominees living there, so I went to find
out what they were doing. They were learning as much as they could about the
situation and mobilizing opposition. People like Jim and me were not dependent

on MEI and could be more vocal than local people, who often were afraid of retribution, in particular, of losing their jobs. Jim and his group were determined to bring pressure to bear. I did not always agree with Jim's confrontational style, but I admired his charisma and passion. He was a rousing public speaker, and he returned to Wisconsin almost every weekend to raise awareness. I found his engagement with Menominees on the issues that confronted them inspiring.

Professor Wrone, the historian at UW–Stevens Point who had worked with Upward Bound students, told me, "Whenever there is a crisis in your tribe, leadership emerges and it gets resolved." I thought about this. In the nineteenth century, the United States had tried to force the Menominees to move farther west, but Chief Oshkosh insisted that their land on the Wolf River was better than that offered them in Minnesota. He signed a treaty in 1854 that guaranteed them their reservation. Furthermore, the Menominees were the only Indians in Wisconsin who did not accept allotment in the 1880s and continued to hold their land in common. Surely we could resist termination and restore our tribe. We had lots of potential leaders, and many of them rose to the challenge.

Milwaukee had a large Menominee population, so I went down to meet, educate, and organize them. John Gauthier, a university student and artist who put his considerable talent to work for the cause, helped contact people, and we arranged to meet at the home of my friend Nancy Oestreich Lurie, a professor of anthropology at UW–Milwaukee. People were so eager for information that we soon outgrew Nancy's living room. There was no real communication coming from MEI or the Voting Trust, so we had to reply on what people had heard. I shared what I had learned from Preloznik. It was the first time that many of them understood what termination meant and how the bizarre governing system established by termination was destroying their homeland. They formally organized and chose Lloyd Powless as their president.

Soon the Chicago and Milwaukee groups linked up and decided to form an organization to address the problems confronting the Menominees. Meeting together to discuss strategy, they elected Jim White president. The first issue on the agenda was to come up with a name. It had to have the word "Menominee" in it, of course, and it had to express the purpose of the organization. The name also had to be easy for people to recognize and remember. Although she was finishing college and subsequently working as a nurse in Madison, my sister Connie was very involved in the opposition to termination and was present at this meeting. She is the one who finally came up with a name: Determination of Rights and Unity for Menominee Shareholders, or DRUMS. Everyone agreed it was perfect. Then we needed a term for what we hoped to accomplish. I suggested "restoration" and everyone agreed. What we wanted to do was restore our sovereign status and reclaim our land and resources.

The more people knew about what was going on, the angrier they became. Lo and behold, by midsummer Menominees were demonstrating against MEI! When about fifty members of the Menominee Action Group picketed the sales office, George Kenote filed a complaint against seven of them and had them arrested. Preloznik arranged representation for them through the American Civil Liberties Union. The next week DRUMS sponsored a rally where people voiced their frustrations against specific issues—tribal rolls had been closed since 1954 so that children born since then were not officially Menominee; MEI was undemocratic, corrupt, and nearly bankrupt; poverty was so severe that some people had to haul water five miles; taverns had proliferated. The sheriff deputized twenty-five mill hands, supposedly to keep the peace, but DRUMS was not what endangered law and order. After the rally, two of the "Menominee Seven," who had been arrested earlier, found death threats tucked under their windshield wipers, and three men, including at least one deputy, attacked a cameraman and a producer from National Educational Television who were filming the rally. Not to be cowed, demonstrators kept protesting every weekend at the developer's sales office and the visitor's center, as well as at the Milwaukee bank that managed the Assistance Trust. They also targeted restaurants in Milwaukee, Appleton, Green Bay, and other cities where the developer hosted steak dinners for potential buyers. In October the Cree singer Buffy St. Marie joined demonstrators and urged all Menominees to get involved in the fight against termination.

My mother was in the thick of the fight. She and her best friends, Mary Blumreich, Louise Fowler, and Genevieve Otradovec, pitched in to help wherever they could. They brought food to events and held meetings in their houses. They also got their children involved. Lloyd Powless, Shirley Fowler Daly, and Sylvia Otradovec Wilber were active in DRUMS, as were my sister Connie and brother Robert. (Ferial was living with her husband and children in South Dakota. Joe was vulnerable because he worked at the mill.) Lloyd was president of the Milwaukee chapter of DRUMS until his untimely death in 1973, and Laurel Otradovec was president of the Menominee County chapter. Lloyd, Sylvia, and Robert won seats on MEI's board of directors in 1972, and Sylvia ultimately became chairwoman of the board. Shirley and Sylvia served with me on the Menominee Restoration Committee, the group charged with organizing a tribal government after restoration in 1973. Sometimes the children of my mother's friends did not participate voluntarily. During a visit with her family, Franciscan Sister Verna Fowler declined to join a demonstration because she thought her nun's habit might attract negative attention to her order. Her mother produced shorts and a T-shirt and said, "Let's go!" She went. Ultimately, Sister Verna would take leave from her order, enroll in courses at Catholic University, and help me lobby in Washington.

At first I was hesitant to join the demonstrations because I was planning to go to law school, and I was leery about getting arrested, which would have complicated my plans. Plus the sheriff's special deputies were not averse to using force. At one march I did join, the deputies, who were well armed with billy clubs, nearly outnumbered the protestors. I thought to myself, "What is this? We are only going from Keshena to Legend Lake!" Plus, we were a jovial group, laughing and talking as we walked. We certainly posed no physical threat. I began to look closely at the deputies, and I recognized some of them as Menominees who worked at the mill. So I smiled and said, "Well, hello! Hello, Bruce! Hello, so-and-so!" I knew that they were there because MEI ordered them to be, but I was still nervous. When you confront the power structure, the response sometimes goes way out of bounds.

MEI tried to get an injunction against the demonstrators, but Preloznik got it thrown out of court. He also filed lawsuits on behalf of DRUMS that called into question the legality of both the Voting Trust and the Assistance Trust. Menominee shareholders elected the Voting Trust, which elected the MEI board of directors, but the Assistance Trust, managed by the First Wisconsin Trust Company, voted the shares of minors and "incompetents." In the early 1970s, the Assistance Trust held approximately 16 to 20 percent of the votes, a share that becomes really significant when one considers that many Menominees did not vote at all. Confusion and a lack of understanding of the governing structure, as well as despondency and distress over their situation, kept many from the polls. Voter turnout soon became a major concern.

According to the termination plan, Menominee shareholders had the right every ten years to vote on whether to dissolve the Voting Trust. That vote was coming up in December 1970, and DRUMS was determined to prevent renewal. The catch was that getting rid of the Voting Trust required a 51 percent majority of the shares, not 51 percent of the votes. Preloznik filed suit asking that a simple majority of voters prevail. MEI board chairman George Kenote offered to add four members to the Voting Trust and ensure greater Menominee participation, but he argued against doing away with it because he believed that Menominees could not handle their own affairs. Confronted with the enormous task of educating voters, DRUMS sued to postpone the vote until April 1971. DRUMS won this battle, but lost lawsuits to alter the 51 percent shareholder requirement and to abolish the Assistance Trust. Making good on his promise, however, Kenote called a special election in March to add two of the four new members of the Voting Trust. I was elected along with Georgianna Ignace, another DRUMS member. She was an advocate for Indian health, and three years later she and her husband, a physician, would establish an urban Indian health center in Milwaukee, where they worked.

This was a small victory compared with the battle to come. DRUMS had to get the word out about the vote to abolish the trust altogether. We got our hands on an old-fashioned mimeograph machine and, with the help of a couple of VISTA people, went to work publishing a newsletter. We began educating Menominees about how to read the ballot. MEI had posed the question as, "Shall the Voting Trust be terminated?" This meant that a "no" vote was not a vote *against* the Voting Trust but *for* it. We contacted Menominees across the nation and asked them for their proxies. In Chicago and Milwaukee members went door-to-door trying to convince Menominees to sign over their proxies to DRUMS. Most of them did, but in the end, it simply was not enough. We got more than half the votes cast but not the 51 percent of shares that the termination plan specified and the court confirmed. We had lost, but far more Menominees were aware of our situation and the changes that needed to be made, and we did have two DRUMS members on the Voting Trust.

In June, DRUMS sent a delegation to Washington to present testimony before the U.S. Senate Committee on Interior and Insular Affairs about the effects of termination on the Menominees. The Senate committee was considering Resolution 26, which would repudiate termination. As the spokesperson I presented DRUMS's case. I pointed out how disastrous termination had been for the Menominees: it had impoverished them and robbed them of their land and resources. I urged restoration of the tribe and its trust relationship with the federal government. Mr. Kenote also spoke. By now, even he was ready to admit that termination had not worked, although he insisted it had failed only because it had been implemented too quickly. The resolution passed.

By the time I testified, I was attending the summer program in Indian law at the University of New Mexico, and in the fall I enrolled in law school at UW–Madison. I had barely arrived when I was reelected to the Voting Trust along with Georgianna. DRUMS members John Gautier and Carol Dodge won the two other seats Mr. Kenote had pledged. These were talented people. Carol, who had a graduate

Ada Deer, ca. 1972.

degree in education, taught elementary school in Keshena but soon joined the faculty of UW–Stevens Point to direct the Indian Teacher Corps Project, and John served on the state's Menominee Indian Study Committee as the representative from the Department of Industry, Labor, and Human Resources. DRUMS now had control of the trust, and in December I was elected chair. I had hoped that I could use a law degree to help achieve restoration, but the Menominees needed help *now*, not in three years. Plus, I really did not like law school. I took a leave of absence, came home, and devoted myself full time to the struggle. I never looked back.

Things had gotten ugly. The developers got an injunction barring seven DRUMS leaders from protesting at the sales office. The leaders defied the injunction. People from the Chicago Indian Village, which had occupied a Wrigley Field parking lot, and La Causa, a Chicano organization, joined DRUMS in Keshena, where leaders spoke and a rock band played. Then they all marched a half mile to the sales office, where a group of potential white buyers and their children were touring the lake on a paddlewheel boat. I was not there, but apparently the crowd became increasingly unruly. According to newspaper coverage, some protesters demanded a boat ride, then occupied the deck of the sales office, and eventually moved inside where the sales staff and clients had taken refuge. Efforts by Laurel Otradovec, president of Menominee County DRUMS; Lloyd Powless, president of Milwaukee DRUMS; and John Gauthier to disperse them failed, until Lloyd began to beat his drum and lead the protesters to a nearby field. As they were leaving, he supposedly held up his weasel-skin medicine bag and asked the spirits to make the developer's "warriors fall in battle, their women barren, and their children turn their backs on their elders." Despite Lloyd's and Laurel's efforts to control the crowd, deputies arrested them and they spent a week in jail.

Seizing the opportunity for sensationalistic journalism, Wisconsin newspapers portrayed participants in DRUMS protests as outside agitators. I don't know whether they meant the Menominees from Chicago or the more radical groups that sometimes participated in DRUMS demonstrations but were not members. They also charged that communists were involved, but, to my knowledge, I never encountered any communists. What had become clear was that the Menominees were not going to back down. Many non-Indians in Wisconsin found that unnerving, and local press coverage heightened their anxiety. The national press was more favorable to our movement, but DRUMS needed to do something to win over Wisconsin, especially Wisconsin voters and politicians.

In September 1971 Jim and Lloyd began to organize a march, not the usual march from Keshena to the Legend Lake sales office but a "March for Justice" from Keshena to Madison, where they hoped to meet with Governor Patrick Lucey. The purpose of the march was to win friends and influence people as well as to protest. On October 2, I joined about a hundred other Menominees at Legend Lake to begin the march. I walked only ten miles, but there were Menominees who walked the entire 220 miles. Support vehicles followed with food and water, and churches and community centers opened their doors to people at night. As the marchers neared Madison, people began to join us—Menominees, Indians from other tribes, whites, blacks, Chicanos. Social justice groups from all over the country sent representatives. The marchers were friendly and well behaved, totally unlike how the newspapers described them.

On October 14, marchers held a rally and paraded down State Street to the capitol, where Governor Lucey met us. Jim presented a list of things that Menominees wanted: the governor's support in our struggle against termination; investigations of the Legend Lake development and of discrimination in the schools; a medical center and alcohol treatment facility; and compensation for the bonds that had been turned over to the state in payment for social services, economic development, and housing programs for Menominees. He also requested that the governor tour Menominee County. Within a month, Governor Lucey visited us and pledged his support. That gubernatorial visit along with the DRUMS election victories in December consolidated support for restoration, nominally bringing in groups like the Council of Chiefs that had opposed our efforts. The naysayers became few and far between.

Having consolidated support for restoration, we needed a bill to present to Congress. In the midst of all this, someone from Senator Edward Kennedy's office called and said the senator wanted to meet with us in Milwaukee. I am not sure why he was there—it was not for a public event—but he may have been visiting his disabled sister Rosemary, who lived in a convent close to Milwaukee. The DRUMS people plus Preloznik headed to Milwaukee. We made our case for restoration and told him that we were in the process of drafting a bill to restore our trust relationship with the federal government. It turned out to be a very worthwhile meeting. Senator Kennedy joined Preloznik and me in requesting help from the Native American Rights Fund (NARF), headquartered in Boulder, Colorado.

David Getches, previously with California Indian Legal Services, and John Echohawk, who had just become the first graduate of the University of New Mexico's Indian law program, founded NARF in 1970 with financial support from the Ford Foundation. The organization's whole focus was providing legal assistance to Indian people and Indian tribes. NARF established five priorities for cases: preserving tribal existence, protecting the natural resources of tribes, promoting the human rights of Native people, holding state and federal governments accountable to Indians, and developing Indian law and educating people about it. We met several of these priorities, especially the first, so NARF assigned Charles Wilkinson and Yvonne Knight to our case. We were very fortunate to have these high-caliber lawyers working with us. Having received his law degree from Stanford in 1966, Charles had worked at law firms in Phoenix and San Francisco. Yvonne had just graduated from the University of New Mexico, the first woman to complete the Indian law program. They met regularly with us, explained every step, and offered us support and encouragement. They also provided some humor, especially after Charles showed up late for a meeting because he had gotten lost in Keshena, a town of less than a thousand. "How's he going to get us restored," Menominees chuckled, "when he can't even find his way around Keshena?" Fortunately, he could find his way around a law library.

Then, all of a sudden, we had unsolicited help coming from another direction. Senator William Proxmire and Congressman David Obey, both of Wisconsin

Ada discussing restoration with Senator Ted Kennedy.

and seemingly sympathetic to Indians, sent a draft bill to DRUMS and MEI, which DRUMS now controlled. In January 1972 the General Council debated it. The council decided that the bill was not specific enough, and resolved that the Menominees would work with Judicare and NARF to draft their own bill. Preloznik had remained the on-the-ground guy after NARF entered the picture, but neither of us had ever been involved in drafting a bill. Furthermore, Preloznik had other Judicare duties. I asked Yvonne and Charles, "What do we do, and how do we do it?" They said that first of all, we needed to decide the purposes and goals of the bill.

To do that, we had meetings with Menominee people. Jim White managed to get enough money from the Akbar Foundation in Chicago to buy a car, which we used to transport people to meetings. We had at least twenty people at every meeting. Many of them were suspicious at first and wondered, "What are these agitators and troublemakers doing?" We explained that we needed to write a bill and get Congress to pass it. People had never been given this type of information. We wanted them to understand the issues because what we were doing affected all Menominees. We asked, "What are your ideas?" At first, the response was surprise. Many attendees did not realize that they had a voice in this process and that we were listening. We hoped they would recognize that restoration was their responsibility and take part. These meetings were a way to empower Menominee people, who decided that the bill had to provide for the democratization of our tribal corporation, abolish the two trusts, return control of MEI to the original shareholders, and place all land and assets in federal trust.

Once we had a bill, we needed to get it through Congress. Somebody had to go to Washington to lobby for this bill, so I asked, "Who's going to go to Washington?" I waited to see if anybody raised a hand. No one did. Most of them, of course, had other responsibilities—families, jobs, and so on—or they were intimidated by the idea of talking to senators and congressmen. I agreed to do it, and everyone seemed surprised and relieved. I had both the training and the experience to be a lobbyist. Part of being a social worker, after all, is being sociable and able to talk to people. So off I went to Washington. Other Menominees, including Sylvia Wilber, came to Washington from time to time and accompanied me on my rounds of congressional offices, but I was there for the duration.

Working for restoration was a full-time job, but I had not had a paying position since I left UW–Stevens Point in spring 1971. My position as chair of the Voting Trust, which began in December 1971, paid $500 a month, but that didn't go far in Washington. Plus, I traveled back and forth to Wisconsin frequently to stay in touch with DRUMS. We did receive contributions, the largest of which Jim got from the Akbar Foundation. Vine Deloria Jr., Nancy Lurie, and other non-Menominees donated, as did various nonprofits including the Center for Community Change in Washington, D.C., the first project of the Robert F. Kennedy Memorial Foundation. A lot of Menominees also slipped us a few dollars from time to time to help with expenses. One of the biggest contributions from a Menominee came from Reginald House, who had lived right down the road from us when he was growing up. He was the son of Judge Rhoda House, the first woman to serve as a Menominee tribal judge. Reginald was in the military and stationed out in California, but he cared about his people back in Wisconsin. He had some money, so he gave us five hundred dollars. I was just astounded. It was nice to see a revival of pride and participation among lots of Menominee people.

In Washington, I usually saved money on hotels by staying with friends. Grace Thorpe, a member of the Sac and Fox tribe and daughter of Olympian Jim Thorpe, lent me her apartment for a while. She was a legislative aide and had been involved in the occupation of Alcatraz. Other people I met in Washington also put me up. I spent most of my time, however, with Oklahoma Senator Fred Harris and his wife LaDonna, president of Americans for Indian Opportunity. They not only opened their home to me, but also provided invaluable coaching about how Washington worked. Fred helped me on Capitol Hill when he could. He had already established himself as a champion of Native rights and self-determination by leading the successful struggle in Congress to restore land that included the sacred Blue Lake to Taos Pueblo.

When I arrived in Washington, I needed a place to work as well as sleep. I went to the office of the National Congress of American Indians where I ran into Executive Director Charles Trimble. I had first met him in 1956 when we both participated in the Encampment for Citizenship. He went on to become a prominent journalist. He said, "Ada! What are you doing here?" I told him that the Menominees had been terminated, which he already knew, and that we were now working for restoration. He generously offered me a desk. I thought it was so cool that all these connections and circles in my life were coming together. Sister Verna Fowler, the Menominee nun who subsequently served as the first president of the College of the Menominee Nation, helped me in the office, taking care of correspondence and making phone calls.

My mother had been writing letters to politicians about termination for years, so the Deer name was not unknown to some of them or, at least, to their staffs. I targeted committee members first because the bills dealing with Indians get referred to the House and Senate Committees on Interior and Insular Affairs and then to the respective Subcommittees on Indian Affairs, but I saw everyone I could. I made appointments, showed up, and said the same thing to almost everybody: "Hello, I'm Ada Deer, member of the Menominee Indian Tribe, and I'm here to talk about Menominee termination and the Menominee restoration bill." I then summarized the bill. Most members of Congress didn't know what in the world I was talking about. Indians were not on anyone's radar screen. Their ignorance astonished and angered me. Indians were here before they were, but these people knew nothing about us except the stereotypes—the Indian on the nickel or Plains Indians in feathers on horseback. Menominees do not fit those stereotypes. They are a forest tribe that once lived in small groups and hunted, fished, and gathered wild rice. Now they work in their forest and mill or in their homes, although they still hunt and fish. Most politicians also knew nothing about termination. Presumably they were more knowledgeable about other pending legislation. I was angry, and I didn't let anybody shunt me aside.

Sometimes it was hard to get past the gatekeepers. Democrat David Obey had been the Menominees' congressman before redistricting and, along with Senator Proxmire, had sent us the draft bill. He was in his second term in Congress when I tried to get an appointment with him. (He did not retire until 2011.) I think that we probably were the first Indians ever to call on him, although he clearly had been monitoring the Menominee situation. After a number of tries, our lawyers, several other Menominees, and I finally got in to see him. After we made our case, he assured us, "I believe in your cause." Before he could think about it further, I replied, "Great! So that means you'll introduce our bill?" He agreed. Interestingly, he did not think introduction of the Menominee Restoration Act in the House of Representatives was important enough to earn a mention in his autobiography, *Raising Hell for Justice.* But at the time, his willingness to help was crucial for us.

There were far tougher nuts to crack, most notably the Menominees' own congressman, Harold Froehlich, a Republican from Appleton, Wisconsin. He had bought a lot on former Menominee land, and he saw himself as the defender of white property owners rather than his Indian constituents. He kept throwing up roadblocks, such as trying to amend the bill to delay federal trust status, protect the property rights of white owners of Legend Lake lots, and guarantee hunting and fishing rights to whites. We could not wear him down and finally agreed to compromise on the issues of property rights and hunting and fishing so that we would not have to delay restoration.

And then there was Democratic Congressman Wayne Aspinall of Colorado. He was a bear: he was rude, disrespectful, and practically hostile. I am afraid I just maligned bears. The chair of the House Interior and Insular Affairs Committee, he had supported termination. He had an appalling environmental record and no interest in Indians who could not help him. When Charles Wilkinson and I called on him, he sent his aide Lewis Sigler to talk to us. Sigler suggested that, in order to avoid offending Aspinall, we drop the word "restoration" from the bill, which he then predicted might come up for a vote in twenty years. I didn't get anywhere with Aspinall, but in 1972 he was defeated in the Democratic primary, so I thankfully did not have to deal with him anymore.

Our senators, Gaylord Nelson and William Proxmire, both Democrats, were more supportive. I made it a point to become friends with their staffs. When

I called, the secretaries immediately assigned me a staff member with whom I met. My staff contact in Senator Proxmire's office was Don Chambliss and in Senator Nelson's office was Ronald Way. Both took a real interest in Menominee restoration. They understood the importance of the bill and recognized that it was a historic reversal of Indian policy. Passage of the Menominee Restoration Act would signal that Congress had recognized and rectified a mistake and that Indians had asserted control of their own destiny.

The press had begun to pay a bit of attention to the issue, and even early on reporters occasionally talked to me. One day I made an offhand comment about Senator Nelson that the press interpreted as meaning he was noncommittal on the issue of restoration. I was uncertain about his support because he had introduced the bill to create the Apostles Island National Lakeshore, which would have taken land on Lake Superior belonging to two Chippewa bands. I had not had an in-depth conversation with him because I realized that the senators were extremely busy, and they could not meet everybody who came into their offices. Plus I was working directly with Ron Way. Senator Nelson saw the article in the paper and asked, "What's this? Doesn't Ada know I'm supporting her?" Ron replied, "Actually, no. You never told her that." I was greatly relieved when Ron told me how the senator had responded.

When DRUMS had met earlier with Senator Kennedy in Milwaukee, he had invited me to come to his office when I got to Washington. That is one of the first things I did. I told the receptionist that I was Ada Deer, I was working on Menominee restoration, and I had met with Senator Kennedy in Milwaukee. I immediately was referred to his legislative director. The senator remembered the meeting and took a special interest in our efforts from the very beginning. One time I was having a small reception to promote the bill. Somehow he heard about it, and a member of his staff called me up. "May the senator come?" the staffer asked. Almost dumbfounded, I answered, "Well, of course!" So he came and gave a wonderful speech about how we were all working for social justice. It was very moving.

I used several tools in my lobbying. One was the book *Freedom with Reservation: The Menominee Struggle to Save Their Land and People*, by Deborah Shames, a student at UW–Madison. One of her anthropology professors told her that people should not just study about Indians, but should try to help Indians. So she asked, "Where do I go and what do I do?" He sent her to Judicare, and Preloznik sent her to me. I told her that we needed a publication that told the Menominees' story and, with help from Preloznik and others, she produced a very comprehensive, readable account of termination. The cover features a painting of Chief Oshkosh, who led the Menominees in the first half of the nineteenth century, done by Menominee artist and DRUMS member John Gauthier. Oshkosh is wearing a beaded leather vest, a black topcoat, a stovetop hat with tribal ribbons of varying colors, and a presidential medal. The National Committee to Save the Menominee People and Forest, which was the name of our office in Washington, had the book printed, and DRUMS sold copies for $2.50 each, with the income going to support our lobbying efforts. I carried copies with me wherever I went.

My second indispensable tool was my briefcase, which was plastered with stickers promoting restoration and filled with copies of *Freedom with Reservation*. I carried it on my many trips back and forth to Wisconsin and between buildings and offices in D.C. If anyone asked me about it, I'd say, "Oh, you want to know about this? Well, I can tell you. Do you have time?" Next thing I know they're shelling out money, buying my book, and agreeing to write to their representative or senator. I gave away some too: "Now if you'll read it, I'll give this to you." I got invited to a lot of receptions—Washington loves receptions—and I always took along copies of the book. I seized every opportunity to educate people about restoration. I was relentless in getting this act through Congress. I think people really appreciated the Menominees' persistence, and as a result, their admiration and respect for the tribe grew.

I was on an airplane once when I recognized Michigan congressman John Conyers, a founder of the Congressional Black Caucus. The Black Caucus was on my list of groups to contact. He was up in first class and I was in coach, but that did not stop me! I left my briefcase in coach and went striding up into first class. I don't remember, but I probably took a copy of the book with me. He was sitting next to a beautiful woman and having a drink. I said, "Excuse me, Congressman Conyers. Could I have two minutes of your time?" What's he going to do? He's strapped in an airplane thirty thousand feet in the air. Even so, I did not give him time to respond: "I'm Ada Deer, member of the Menominee Indian Tribe of Wisconsin. I'm working on the repeal of termination. This is the Menominee Restoration Act and it is as important to Menominees and to Indians nationwide as *Brown v. Board of Education* was to you." I am not sure whether he took a sip of his drink at that point, but I am sure he wanted to. "Come to my office," he said. I replied, "Thank you. And who should I see?" He answered, "Just come and see me." He probably thought it was the quickest way to get rid of me! I did go to his office, and the Black Caucus supported the bill. Most people would have been reluctant to disturb a congressman in first class. Not me.

I went to the BIA first, of course, because its support was essential. The commissioner of Indian affairs was Louis Bruce, a Mohawk from New York. Most Indians called him "Uncle Louie." He was a kind, affable, and compassionate man. The assistant commissioner was Ernest Stevens Sr., an Oneida. The Oneida Reservation is very close to the Menominee land, and there is a lot of intermarriage and interaction. Most informed Oneidas know that they are living on what was originally Menominee land, and we remind them of that periodically. Both men were reformers, committed to self-determination, but they had their work cut out for them facing the BIA's entrenched bureaucracy.

I needed to see someone in the solicitor's office at the BIA. The first lawyer they sent me to was somewhat officious. I thought, "Oh, gee. Why do I have to start with him?" I told him why I was there. He immediately tried to discourage me. "Well, that's not going to work." He clearly wanted to be rid of me, but I was not putting up with that. I asked him who his supervisor was, and he gave me the man's name. Night-and-day difference! The supervisor was a kindly, courtly, gray-haired gentleman who not only was receptive and supportive, but also immediately grasped the significance of what we were trying to do. I was enormously relieved.

I also met with the congressional liaison at the BIA, who had been talking to the lawyers in Interior. I asked him why he was discussing restoration with them. He replied, "We were talking about amend. . . ." I almost shouted, "Whoa! Stop right there." My mother always thought compromise was overrated, and she passed that belief on to me. I might have to compromise with a congressional representative, but I was not compromising with the BIA. He stared at me. "You said 'amend'?" I almost shouted. "No, no, no, no, no! Let me explain this. English is my first language. I am a graduate of UW–Madison, and I have a master's degree from Columbia University. I know the difference between 'amend,' which means you're tinkering around the edges, and 'repeal'!" I found his unconscious racism lamentably common among bureaucrats. They think Indians can barely put one foot in front of the other. "Okay, Ada, okay," he said, "Repeal." If I had not been the person I am, I would have thought, "Well, the lawyers said 'amend' and let it go forward." The Menominees already had decided that "amend" was not what they wanted, and he was not going to undermine their will so long as I was on duty. We weren't asking for the moon. We were asking for restoration of our land and tribe.

The BIA, both in Washington and in the tribal agencies, was full of longtime bureaucrats who doubted the wisdom of self-determination. They continued to believe that assimilation was the best policy. Running all these programs to assimilate Indians kept them employed with good federal salaries and benefits, whereas self-determination meant turning programs like health care, education, and economic development over to the tribes. Such recalcitrance stoked the anger that was growing in Native America, especially among young Indians to whom AIM appealed. In September 1971 a group of AIM members led by Russell Means, an Oglala Sioux, pushed their way into the BIA building, purportedly to make a citizens' arrest of Deputy Commissioner John O. Crowe, an Oklahoma Cherokee, whom they held responsible for replacing some of Commissioner Bruce's progressive appointments with people from the old guard. Security officers arrested twenty-six of them, but the Interior Department requested their release. At the same time, the National Tribal Chairmen's Association was meeting, and the members expressed some of the same concerns about the BIA as AIM had, although in a more decorous way.

I understood exactly why both groups were upset, especially after I learned about Assistant Secretary of the Interior for Public Lands Harrison Loesch's attitude toward restoration. He must have been the most negative person in the BIA. After Nixon fired him for refusing to help cover up Watergate, he became the counsel for the Senate Committee for Interior and Insular Affairs. He handled a number of Indian issues, including land claims. He announced to everyone who would listen that the Menominee Restoration Act was going nowhere. I never even talked with him, but he would tell other people what he thought, and then eventually the news would get to me. There were other people who I'm sure were not happy about this situation. On the other hand, Commissioner Bruce and his staff worked very hard for restoration, no doubt widening the breach between progressives and conservatives at the BIA.

Just when I thought things were going pretty well, the bill got held up at the White House. I worked with two White House staffers, Brad Patterson and Len Garment. Brad knew who I was because I had worked with his wife on the President's Conference on Children and Youth. I had two meetings with them. They wanted to know whether the struggle for restoration was a fly-by-night thing or if we were serious. I got really irked with them. It was, after all, their boss, Richard Nixon, who had given us hope in 1970 that termination might be reversed. I couldn't sit around waiting on the White House, I thought, so I'm going to call Melvin Laird. He was our former congressman and was now secretary of defense. I called up his office at the Pentagon and said, "I am from Wisconsin. I'm a member of the Menominee Tribe. Secretary Laird was our congressman, he is very familiar with our tribe, and he knows the issues confronting us. I need him to call the White House and get them to move on our restoration bill." A week or so later, I called back. The woman I spoke to assured me Laird had done what I asked. So then I called the White House. Brad said, "Hello, Ada Deer! When are you coming to see us?" I went over there. Smiling, they asked, "What did you do?" I confessed, "I called Mr. Laird." They were incredulous: "You called the secretary of defense?" By now I was enjoying myself: "Of course. This is an important bill. We've got to get moving on this." They were amazed, first, that I would have the chutzpah to call Secretary Laird and, second, that I could get the secretary of defense to call them.

The Menominee Restoration Act was introduced in both houses on April 20, 1972, but it was an election year, and no one in Washington seemed focused on pending legislation. Recesses for presidential nominating conventions and adjournment before the November election meant that the Menominee Restoration Act was dead, at least for the Ninety-Second Congress. One more year.

The inattention of Congress did not mean that I could go home. I had been a registered Democrat since 1969, and I supported George McGovern, but I attended both the Democratic and Republican conventions. Menominee Shirley Daly, who was also working for restoration, was a delegate to the Democratic Convention. We talked to anyone we could about Menominee restoration. President Nixon, who was running for reelection as a Republican, had voiced his support for tribal self-determination in 1970. Democrats had majorities in both houses in the Ninety-Second (1971–1973) and Ninety-Third (1973–1975) Congresses, and I had worked hard to get powerful Democrats like Senator Henry Jackson and Congressman Lloyd Meeds, both from Washington, on board. Nevertheless, the Republican platform was clear about who was to blame for the slow pace of reform: "The opposition Congress, by inaction on most of the President's proposals, has thwarted Indian rights and opportunities." I was determined to get a plank pledging my party's support for self-determination. Ultimately, Democrats committed themselves: "We strongly oppose the policy of termination." Much to my disappointment, McGovern lost, but prospects for Menominee restoration in the next Congress looked good.

The week before the election, however, AIM occupied the BIA building. The takeover came at the end of the Trail of Broken Treaties Caravan, a protest sponsored by a number of Indian groups including NARF. Leaving several points on the West Coast in early October, the caravan grew as it made its way east and arrived in Washington. Harrison Loesch was supposed to provide housing and arrange meetings with BIA officials to discuss a list of twenty demands. But when the caravan arrived, he reneged on his promises—hardly a surprise to those who had dealt with him before. Several hundred participants ended up barricading themselves in the BIA building, occupying it for seven days, then trashing it before they vacated it. I was afraid that this protest would derail the Menominee Restoration Act. A friend of mine, however, pointed out that AIM probably did us a favor. Congress and the White House might be more willing to work with the Menominees now that they had seen an alternative method of advocating for Indian rights. In any event, the AIM takeover of the BIA did not seem to have any negative effect on the Congress that convened in 1973.

Senators Nelson and Proxmire and Congressmen Obey and Froehlich simultaneously reintroduced the Menominee Restoration Act on May 2, 1973. I persuaded Congressman Meeds, chair of the Indian Affairs subcommittee, to hold hearings in Menominee County. He presided and Congressmen Obey and Froehlich attended. The day before the hearing, I chaired an informational meeting for Menominees to prepare them for the hearing, which lasted a day and a half. Congressman Froehlich had added a provision for a two-year delay before the United States took Menominee land in trust. Sylvia Wilbur, chair of MEI, countered that proposal by pointing out that MEI would be bankrupt by then. Other Menominees who spoke at the hearing were unanimous in their support of the Menominee Restoration Act as originally written and opposed Congressman Froehlich's amendment. Both DRUMS and the Menominee chapter of AIM opposed the delay. Two representatives of the Menominee County Property Owners Association spoke in opposition to restoration, and two Wisconsin legislators wanted the state to mandate the kind of government Menominees could have. I couldn't believe it! The wind went out of their sails when a letter arrived from the state's Menominee Study Committee endorsing the Menominee Restoration Act. Congressman Meeds promised quick action.

Hearings in Washington followed. The House Subcommittee on Indian Affairs and the Committee on Interior and Insular Affairs heard testimony in May and June. I, my brother Robert, Shirley Daly, Sylvia Wilbur, Jim White, and several other Menominees appeared before the committee. Most of us were DRUMS members, but others like George Kenote were not. Jerome Grignon conveyed the support of the Menominee Council of Chiefs, which originally had opposed DRUMS. Non-Menominees, including Vine Deloria, Nancy Lurie, and Philleo Nash, testified. The League of Women Voters, AIM, the National Congress of American Indians, the Great Lakes Inter-Tribal Council, Chippewa Indians from

Jane Neconish, Ernest Blackhorse Neconish, Ada Deer, and Senator Gaylord Nelson in Washington, D.C., for the official restoration of Menominee tribal status, April 1975.

Minnesota, and various state and federal departments sent people to speak while other organizations sent letters of support. Hearings before the corresponding Senate committees followed on September 17 and 26. The most memorable moment of these hearings was Ernest Neconish's statement in the Menominee language, which Louise Fowler translated. He began, "I want to tell you folks that I love my lands and my waters, and I don't like the idea of the non-Indians coming into our land and building homes." Mr. Neconish had cast one of the five votes in opposition to termination, but because he did not speak English the Assistance Trust determined him to be "incompetent" and took control of his shares. Now here he was, testifying before a Senate committee.

The House of Representatives conducted a roll-call vote on October 16. I was in the gallery, and the lights kept going and going and going and going as members electronically cast their votes. I could hardly sit still. Under my breath I was saying, "Oh, wow! That's great. That's great." And then finally it was over: 404 in favor and 3 against. On December 7, the Senate passed the bill, and on December 22,

President Nixon signed the Menominee Restoration Act into law. There was no signing ceremony because by this time the president was hunkered down in the White House trying to deal with the Watergate burglary. It really didn't matter to me: I didn't even know that important bills had signing ceremonies.

This left one more issue to be resolved before true restoration of our sovereignty: we had to figure out how to get rid of Public Law 280, which gave the state jurisdiction over the Menominee Reservation. We had omitted any reference to PL 280 in the Restoration Act. Since it applied to tribes in other states, an attempt to repeal it would have stirred up a hornets' nest. But the Menominees wanted to get out from under it. I was discussing this problem one day with a couple of NARF lawyers and a wonderful attorney from Green Bay, Steven Cohen. Someone suggested that we get the state legislature to act, but the legislature was not likely to do anything that we wanted, especially retrocede jurisdiction. Steve piped up, "I was in law school with Attorney General Bronson La Follette; I can ask him to approach the governor about retroceding jurisdiction." This confirmed my view that lawyers can be really crafty—they figure out how to do things. It turned out that the governor was amenable, and he restored our ability to enforce our own laws over our reservation.

We could hardly believe it. A small tribe in Wisconsin had persuaded the United States to reverse its Indian policy. Our success, however, turned out to be only part of a major restructuring that brought Indian tribes self-determination. The Self-Determination and Education Act (1975) enabled tribes to control their own affairs, including contracting for services rather than depending on the BIA. The Indian Child Welfare Act (1978) empowered tribal courts to decide custody cases involving tribally enrolled children. Also in 1978 Congress passed the American Indian Religious Freedom Act, which legalized Native religious practices, including the use of peyote. Enacting laws, however, was only the first step. Indians had to make them work. With that understanding, we Menominees went home to Wisconsin and our restored reservation.

CHAPTER 6

■ Restoration ■

Reestablishing the Menominee Nation proved to be at least as challenging
as getting the Restoration Act through Congress. For many, apprehension
replaced the elation that had followed the victory in Washington. Menominees
still suffered from termination, and they continue to do so in some respects. A
whole generation had grown up without a tribe. Their parents and grandparents
had lost their government, their schools, their hospital, their power plant, their
phone company, and their control of their forest and mill. Many also had lost
their jobs and homes. This demoralization could not be rectified overnight.
Nevertheless, Menominees had to pull themselves together, decide what kind
of government they wanted, then convert their ideas into a constitution. As
for me, I was planning to go back to law school, but that was not to be. Lots of
people insisted that I stay to help because I was more familiar with the bill than
anyone else. So I did.

The Menominee Restoration Act repealed termination and called for a general
council to elect members of the Menominee Restoration Committee (MRC),
whose job it would be to draft a new constitution and act as the tribal government until the Menominees ratified the document. It also provided for the tribal
enrollment of children who were at least one-fourth Menominee and were born
after termination closed the tribal rolls in 1954. I supported this provision but
with mixed feelings. My nieces and nephews would not be eligible for enrollment
since my siblings had not married Menominees. The expanded tribal membership
would elect a government under the new constitution. The act authorized the

Secretary of the Interior to accept tribal assets in trust, but Menominees had a right to incorporate for the purpose of managing their economic activities. Menominees could retain privately owned land if they wished, and if they did so, the land became subject to taxation; those who placed their land in trust no longer owed taxes on it. The act also protected the property as well as hunting and fishing rights of whites who had bought land in Menominee County.

The Menominee Restoration Act had taken a long time to pass, and the many delays had taken a toll on the Menominees. I count my own family among the casualties. My brother Joe's drinking worsened. One day he showed up at my mother's house and forced her to go with him to Keshena to buy him more wine. When they got home, he threatened her and shot toward her with a shotgun. My father's abusive alcoholic behavior also worsened, so much so that in 1974, my mother left him for good. Both men had serious drinking problems before MEI started selling off assets and the movement for restoration began, but the tension surrounding these events probably made both their drinking and their propensity for violence worse.

Ironically, just as we achieved passage of the Restoration Act, fissures began to develop among Menominees. Like any group of people, Menominees held a variety of opinions about most things. By now, unity existed on the general principle of restoration, but not everyone agreed with all the provisions of the act. People would stop me and say, "You didn't get my point in the Restoration Act," and I replied, "Well, we couldn't put everything in." Even before final passage of the bill, people began to raise objections. Some thought that placing our assets in federal trust was a bad idea because it would subject us to the BIA; others thought the assets were being transferred too soon or not soon enough. Many people, including my mother, were upset that there was no provision to recover land that had already been sold to whites, a concession we had to make to secure Congressman Froehlich's support. Some objected to the extension of hunting and fishing rights to whites. Factions promoting a host of ideas began to form, though none succeeded in derailing the act.

From my perspective, there seemed to be little rhyme or reason to many of the factional choices people made. Some high-profile leaders of DRUMS left the organization. Among them was former president Jim White. I was in Washington at the time, but perhaps he had developed philosophical differences with DRUMS. Rumors flew, including speculation DRUMS had asked him to resign his office after he appropriated the DRUMS car for personal use and disrupted negotiations with developers for the purchase of land. Inexplicably to me, he became a member of the Committee for Independent Menominees (CIM), which included disaffected people who had worked for Menominee County and for MEI before DRUMS took over the board.

Other factions as well as individuals contested DRUMS leadership in the restoration process, with even more confrontational groups yet to come. AIM organized in Menominee County in 1972. Lew Boyd, a student at UW–Green Bay and brother of former MEI vice-president Ted Boyd, was very active in AIM early on and led the Menominee chapter in protesting discrimination against Indians in the Shawano schools. AIM demanded the firing of the principal, vice principal, and teacher Mary Louise Kenote. Mrs. Kenote, a white woman, was wife of George Kenote, former chairman of the board of MEI. Theresa Jacobs, a community counselor for the Indian Student Advocacy Program funded under the federal Indian Education Act, was a local leader of AIM. A former secretary of DRUMS, she had marched to Madison and testified before the House Committee on Interior and Insular Affairs. But she also was a supporter of the right-wing American Party, which had backed George Wallace's presidential bid.

Despite this dissent, implementation of the Menominee Restoration Act went forward. The Menominees could not really function as a tribe until they established a government. About 250 Menominees attended the general council, as specified in the act. They nominated forty-nine people, including me, to stand for election to the nine seats on the MRC, which would serve as an interim government until we could approve a new constitution. DRUMS put forward a slate of six candidates. The opposition CIM, the group dissatisfied with DRUMS leadership, nominated nine people, most of whom were associated with the Menominee County government or had been defeated for election to the MEI board of directors. When the votes were counted, the six people nominated by DRUMS, two people on the CIM slate, and two independents had won. (One of the winning candidates, Carol Dodge, was on both the DRUMS and CIM slates.) I had the highest number of votes, which made me chair of the MRC.

The most immediate problem we faced was lack of funds. To get us off the ground, MEI loaned MRC $10,000. We immediately applied for $239,000 from the BIA, but four months later, we had received only $12,000. The people who had been elected to the MRC received no salary and had to pay their own expenses for attending meetings, making phone calls, and so on. None of us was rich, and we had jobs and families, so this was a real sacrifice. The MRC appointed several subcommittees. The contracting subcommittee applied for grants from the Indian Health Service (IHS), Tribal Government Development Program,

Comprehensive Education and Training Act, and Relief to Needy Indian Persons Program. In the meantime, we were in a financial bind because MEI's assets had not yet been taken into trust, which meant that the company was still responsible for the lion's share of the county taxes. Finally in November 1974, Congress appropriated $2.7 million to support education, housing, economic development, road construction, and various social services.

The enrollment subcommittee, which was responsible for drawing up a new tribal roll, needed to send out enrollment forms, but that could not be done until guidelines from the BIA arrived. Then the subcommittee had to try to determine which persons on the roll in 1954 had died so that their names could be removed. We estimated that there were five or six hundred deceased members. The subcommittee also had to locate people who had been born in the twenty years since termination closed the roll and decide whether or not they met the one-quarter blood requirement. Since many Menominees had moved away from the reservation, this was a laborious task.

The constitution subcommittee had to write a new constitution, since at that point in the process, almost no one thought we should go back to the 1924 constitution. We wanted far less BIA presence and oversight than we had had under that constitution. We took tribal sovereignty, referring to our right to govern ourselves, and self-determination seriously, and we intended to write a constitution that reflected our commitment to those principles. The governing documents of lots of other tribes dated to the Indian Reorganization Act of 1934, when the BIA just churned them out thinking one size would fit all. Many tribes are still struggling with the inadequacies of those constitutions. Although we had outside help, we were determined to write a constitution that was right for the Menominees. Charles Wilkinson, Yvonne Knight, and Joe Preloznik helped us, but we worked most closely with Yvonne. I think NARF lawyers enjoyed working with us because we made a real effort to involve the Menominee people in the process and create the government that they wanted.

As we were drafting the document, we encouraged all Menominees to attend our meetings and voice their opinions. The whole committee convened once a week, and the subcommittees often met three or four times a week. We assembled in the major Menominee settlements of Keshena, Neopit, Zoar, and South Branch. Attendance varied, but everyone who wanted to offer suggestions had a chance to speak. Usually the MRC or one of the subcommittees presented something in writing, ideally in advance, so that people would have something to react to. In any event, we did none of our work in secret.

In October 1974 an opposition group formed under the auspices of the Council of Chiefs and called itself the Menominee Indian Tribe Advisory Council. The chair was Kenneth Fish, a candidate for Menominee County sheriff, and Jim White was among the members. The ignorance and recalcitrance of some members of this Advisory Council were unbelievable. They were unhappy with how long it was taking to write the constitution, update the roll, and obtain financial benefits for tribal members. They questioned the advisability of placing tribal assets in federal trust, and if we did so, they demanded thirty dollars per share be paid to shareholders rather than the one dollar per share the federal government had agreed to. That would have left the Menominees footing the bill for the twenty-nine-dollar difference. The old constitution, a few maintained, was good enough. Apparently, they did not understand that under the 1924 constitution, actions of the Menominee General Council were only advisory to the BIA. The new constitution would make them binding. I am not sure what planet the Menominee Indian Tribe Advisory Council had been on, because they also demanded that we keep the tribe informed. Although there were some older members on the Advisory Council, most of those objecting to the MRC were young people who could not remember when the Menominees had been a tribe. They had gotten used to protesting termination over the years that it had taken to get restoration enacted, and they did not seem to be able to shift gears.

Political factions were only one of the challenges that Menominees faced. More troubling was the increase of violence in the county. On Thanksgiving Day 1974, someone murdered a Catholic priest, Marcellus Cabo, in Neopit while trying to steal money from the rectory. A Menominee man, John Mark Latender, turned himself in to the sheriff and was charged with the priest's murder. Then he insisted that he could not be tried in state court because he was a Menominee. Public Law 280 had transferred jurisdiction over reservation Indians to named states, including Wisconsin, in 1953, but the Menominees had no reservation in 1974 because their land had not been transferred back into federal trust. With termination, Menominees had become citizens of the state, which did not retrocede jurisdiction to the federal government until March 1, 1976. At that time Menominees once again came under the Major Crimes Act, which gave the federal government jurisdiction in cases involving serious crimes. That is why Latender stood trial for second-degree murder in state court, where he was found guilty and sentenced to twenty-two years in prison. Violence escalated from there, with the burning of a house owned by MEI, a bomb threat at the Neopit school, a series of telephone threats, firebombings, and shots fired through windows. I publicly denounced the perpetrators as degenerates, social misfits, school dropouts, and people outside tribal life.

In the midst of all this violence, we faced a critical decision because the deadline for placing our assets in trust loomed. The decision on whether or not to do so rested with MEI shareholders, who met in December to vote on a plan and elect members of the MEI board of directors. The Menominee Indian Tribe Advisory Council put forth three candidates for the board, as did DRUMS. The DRUMS candidates won, but the Advisory Council managed to delay the submission of a plan to the federal government for taking our assets into trust. Jim White threatened to delay the vote even further if I did not apologize for supposedly slandering young Menominees, which I refused to do. Finally, just before Christmas, the issue came to a vote. Shareholders overwhelmingly endorsed the transfer of lands held by MEI to the federal government as trustee and acceptance of one dollar in payment for each share. This was a vote of confidence in the MRC—the best Christmas present I ever received. My euphoria, unfortunately, did not last long.

On New Year's Day 1975, about forty-five well-armed Indians calling themselves the Menominee Warrior Society took over the vacant Alexian Brothers novitiate in Shawano County, about six miles from the Menominee County line. The Alexian Brothers had received the estate, which encompassed two hundred acres, a sixty-four-room mansion, and outbuildings, as a gift to be used as a facility for training priests. In 1968 the order closed the facility, leaving only a caretaker on the property. Michael Sturdevant, who led the takeover, styled himself "the general." At least half the men, including Michael, were Vietnam veterans. There also were women and children among the occupiers. The Warriors fired their guns; took the caretaker, his family, and two visitors hostage; and demanded that the Catholic brothers turn over the building to the tribe for a hospital. I could not believe it! The novitiate was not on Menominee land, and seizing it struck me as not terribly different from whites taking Indian land. Plus, this happened just as restoration was in progress and threatened to really muck up the works.

After a couple of hours, the Alexian Brothers agreed to send a negotiator, and the Warriors released the hostages. One of the leaders called me and asked me, as chair of the MRC, to meet with the so-called Warriors. The only body with legal authority to act for the tribe was the MRC, and any sort of negotiation with the Warriors would imply that they had comparable standing. I consulted with other MRC members, and they agreed we should not intervene. The novitiate was not in Menominee County and, therefore, did not really involve the tribe, only some individual tribal members. At the time, I was really angry with the Warriors because these people were not well informed. They had made no effort to come to meetings or understand what was going on. Nevertheless, I thought that the less said or done about the takeover the better. So much for the opinion of the head of Menominee tribal government.

The next thing I knew, the Shawano County sheriff had called in the FBI, and deputies from several counties, the state patrol, and federal marshals, armed with high-powered rifles, blockaded the novitiate. Shots rang out occasionally, mostly from inside the novitiate. Law enforcement officials refused to allow anyone to enter or leave, which meant no food could get in, and disconnected the telephone lines, cutting off communication. For a while, they turned off the electricity on which the building depended for heat—remember, this was Wisconsin in January—and the pipes froze. The FBI closed the Shawano airport, created a no-fly zone over the novitiate, and evacuated nearby white residents. None of these bozos bothered to contact the MRC, which was the tribe's legal government, to ask for advice. Ultimately Governor Lucey called in two hundred members of the Wisconsin National Guard, which sent in food and eased the tension a bit. Even the Warriors wondered why all these officials got involved since they considered it to be a matter between them and the Alexian Brothers.

By now the Menominee Warrior Society could not decide whether they wanted the property to be a hospital, housing, a rehabilitation center, a recreational facility, or a school. Little did they know that the Alexian Brothers had already been negotiating with the Wisconsin Indian Task Force to turn the building into an alcohol and drug rehabilitation center when, on the spur of the moment, the Warriors decided to take it over. Neil Hawpetoss, who had permission to go back and forth to the novitiate as a mediator in the early days of the occupation, told reporters that when those inside first called some of their friends and urged them to join the warriors in the novitiate, they thought it was a joke. AIM soon became involved, and what perhaps started as a protest in search of a cause found one. AIM leader Russell Means, an Oglala, proclaimed that the novitiate occupation would be the Menominees' Wounded Knee.

That is just what many people feared. In 1973, heavily armed AIM and Oglala Sioux tribal members had seized the small community of Wounded Knee on the Pine Ridge Reservation in South Dakota. They held it for seventy-one days in protest against reservation president Dick Wilson's corruption, his private police force's abuse, the U.S. failure to fulfill its treaty obligations, the heavy hand of the BIA, and violence against Indians in white towns bordering the reservation.

Public figures, ranging from musician Johnny Cash and actress Jane Fonda to communist/black power activist Angela Davis and lawyer William Kunstler, offered their support for the protest. U.S. marshals, the FBI, and the National Guard responded with helicopters, armored personnel carriers, and all sorts of armament. The militarization of the Wounded Knee occupation had tragic consequences: two Indian men and maybe more dead, an African American activist presumably killed, and a U.S. marshal paralyzed. Dick Wilson remained in power, and violence on the reservation intensified. Now the Menominee Warrior Society seemed to have blundered into its own Wounded Knee.

Menominees attributed the takeover to a variety of factors. Supporters of the Warrior Society claimed that the young people inside the novitiate lashed out because they lacked influence in tribal affairs. I wanted to shout, "People! All meetings are open to whoever wants to attend. Participate in the process." Others suggested that passage of the Menominee Restoration Act had raised expectations and the young people wanted change immediately. That might be true, but constructive change takes time. Because restoration was a process, they became impatient. We had had twenty years of incompetence, deprivation, and neglect under termination. These young people had never known tribal life or the working out of differences through negotiation. What they did know was discrimination in Shawano schools, lack of economic opportunities, substandard housing and medical care, and constant fear that the Menominees would lose what little they had left. The rhetoric of political factions such as the Menominee Indian Tribe Advisory Council made them even more impatient for change. But my sympathy had limits. They clearly had too much time on their hands and could have funneled their energy into more constructive activities. In any event, what resulted was a mess.

The national press showed up. Indian militants fed national stereotypes of bloodthirsty savages, and efforts by the press to get human-interest stories, interviews with leaders, and photographs of the estate heightened tensions. A couple of reporters even hired a small plane to fly over the novitiate in violation of the no-fly zone. It is a wonder they weren't shot down. One reporter who did get inside was thrown out when he refused to pay for interviews. Others who later gained access had their film seized. The press did find an accommodating source in my mother, now seventy years old, who was not at the novitiate but was happy to voice her support for the takeover. She cited the seven treaties between the Menominees and the United States and asserted that, according to the U.S. Constitution, they were the law of the land. "Those treaties say the police have no rights inside that land," she told a reporter. "The Indian people were and are the landowners here. All others are not landowners here until they pay the Indians for their land." Good grief! As if I didn't have enough problems already. But it was true to form for my mother, whose independent spirit I have always admired, even now.

Where the press went, AIM leaders were sure to follow. Russell Means, Ojibwe Dennis Banks, and Oneida Herbert Powless arrived and wanted to be involved in negotiations. Then actor Marlon Brando showed up to support the Warrior Society. Everybody, including the U.S. Civil Rights Commission, seemed to want to negotiate. By now the MRC had offered to try to resolve the dispute, but we did not want outsiders, Indian or white, involved. These people should have stayed home and taken care of their own communities. If the novitiate became a facility for Indians, we maintained, the state and federal governments had to operate it since we did not have the money, and it was not on what would soon become the Menominee Reservation. We were willing to accept the goal—expanded services for Menominees—but we were not going to condone the Warrior Society's forcible seizure of the novitiate.

A group calling itself the Menominee People's Committee organized and opened negotiations with the Warrior Society, which should have been easy because the People's Committee members were sympathetic to the Warriors and the occupation. They began to hold rallies in Keshena. At that point, other factors contributing to the takeover began to emerge. Virtually all the people supporting the Warrior Society had tried to scuttle the trust agreement in December and had supported the losing candidates in the MEI board election.

Then a new ultimatum arrived from those inside the novitiate: the Warrior Society demanded my resignation from the MRC. They accused me of poor leadership, particularly in terms of economic development. I don't know exactly what they had expected me to do in a year when the MRC was busy writing a constitution and bylaws, placing tribal assets in trust, and securing funds to operate schools, health care, and social services, and to repair infrastructure. I was a social worker, after all, not a magician. Circuit Court Judge Gordon Myse, who had tried to negotiate with the Warriors just after the takeover, now revealed that in the night he spent with them, no one ever mentioned turning the novitiate into a hospital. He had concluded that the Warriors were trying to save face after their election loss and enhance their political position. I agreed.

The Menominee People's Committee called for the resignations of MRC members Sylvia Wilber and Shirley Daly as well as me. Their reason, according to Ted Boyd, was that "the chief is always regarded as a male. I don't know if there is a term to describe a female chief." Other Menominee dissidents accused men of deserting their appropriate role as leaders and becoming followers. They urged men to reassert themselves and take command, which they thought was culturally appropriate for them to do. As one woman member of the People's Committee put it, "It's not tribal tradition for skirts to lead our tribe." The democratically cast ballots, of course, told a different story: the vast majority of Menominees were supportive of our leadership, even if we were women.

Growing hostility against the Warriors among whites in Shawano County exacerbated the situation. Early in the siege a caravan of white residents went to Madison to demand that Governor Lucey put an end to the occupation. At a rally in Shawano, one man opined, "They ought to be shot. That is what we do to white students who take over buildings." Snowmobilers taunted the occupiers by slipping past the barricades, buzzing the building, and exchanging fire with the people inside. One Warrior and one snowmobiler were wounded. It is a wonder no one was killed. An unidentified snowmobiler wearing a red, white, and blue helmet planted a sign with offensive, anti-Indian language next to a Shawano service station. It was signed "American White Movement." So was an ad in the Shawano newspaper that asked the governor, "Where is justice for Shawano County?" Because the Alexian Brothers were negotiating with the Warrior Society, several white Catholic parishioners in Shawano asked to have their names removed from church rolls.

The National Guard became concerned about the growing antagonism of whites toward the Warrior Society. They brought in additional personnel, increasing their total to 825 heavily armed men along with armored personnel carriers and even a tank. The Warrior Society interpreted the buildup as evidence of an impending attack. On January 18, some women and all the children evacuated the estate, and the remaining men prepared for the National Guard to storm the building. The real reason for the reinforcements, however, was to prevent white snowmobilers who were in town for a rally from straying too close to the novitiate, intentionally or unintentionally, and getting shot by the Warriors. Instead of attacking the building, the National Guard sent in a substantial amount of food, including fifty pounds of venison, in hopes of greasing the skids for an agreement. The Menominee People's Committee continued to negotiate, and finally on February 2, the Menominee Warrior Society agreed to accept an offer from the Alexian Brothers to sell the estate to the tribe, after restoration of its reservation status, for one dollar on the condition that the tribe make a good faith effort to pay a fair price in the future.

The next day, about fifty men, women, and teenagers vacated the novitiate, leaving it in shambles. They had held the estate for thirty-four days. The Shawano County sheriff arrested them, loaded them in buses, and took them to the county jail. Michael Sturdevant and four others, John Waubanascum Jr., Robert Chevalier, John Perote, and Doreen Dixon, were charged with armed robbery, armed burglary, false imprisonment, and other felonies and held under $50,000 bond. Others faced lesser charges and bonds. The judge bound those under eighteen over to juvenile court. Most were soon out on bail. By the time the five leaders went on trial in 1976, Waubanascum had been murdered and Robert Chevalier had jumped bail. John Perote pleaded guilty, and the judge sentenced him to serve five years. Doreen Dixon, who had two small children, got eighteen months' probation. When Chevalier was caught eight months later, he was acquitted but served thirty days for resisting arrest. A jury found Michael Sturdevant guilty, and he received an eight-year sentence. At thirty, Sturdevant was the oldest of the Warriors. I strongly disapproved of what they had done, but I also recognized that these young people were all victims of termination.

Then there was the issue of the estate. The Warriors and law enforcement together had destroyed the beautiful novitiate. The MRC had not been party to negotiations, but the Alexian Brothers had committed to sell the property to the Menominees, for whom we were the governing authority. In my view, it was a white elephant. The estate was not located on what would become the Menominee Reservation, and Gresham, the town it was in, had zoned most of the land residential. A physician who looked over the mansion concluded that it was not suitable for a health-care facility. It was too far from the reservation to be easily accessible as a school or social services center. Renovations promised to be prohibitively expensive—$250,000 for plumbing alone. The Alexians told us that annual operating expenses ran about $40,000 when the buildings were in good shape. The most important factor for me, however, was that the Alexians had made the offer under duress as the result of criminal behavior. I was not going to have my name on any such deal. Sylvia Wilber and Shirley Daly agreed with me, and we announced our intention to resign rather than accept the deed for the property. When the MRC backed us, the Alexians terminated the sale agreement.

The end of the occupation ushered in a period of even more violence. It was so bad that Joe Preloznik insisted I have bodyguards. Someone firebombed a clinic and newspaper office in Shawano, fired shots into a home for Indian juvenile delinquents near Gresham, and shot into MRC member Shirley Daly's house. Warrior Neil Hawpetoss's cousin was shot in the head and his body left along a roadside. Then things calmed down a bit until the Alexians canceled the agreement for transfer of the novitiate property. That incited firebombings of the Keshena elementary school, two cottages, a railroad bridge, the former Legend Lake sales office, and the Little Papoose Restaurant. The white woman who ran the restaurant reported that two young Menominee men ate at the restaurant just before the bombing and apologized to her as they left, saying she was on their list. The Warrior Society denied responsibility. By the end of 1975, there had been three more murders, with a fourteen-year-old boy charged in one of them.

The Menominee People's Committee had been busy in other ways. Jim White, a spokesman for the group, accused me of promoting totalitarianism in the tribe and insisted that the takeover of the novitiate was to protest tribal government rather than white oppression. Ted Boyd, Jim White, and Gordon Dickie organized a visit to Washington where they lobbied our congressional delegation to sponsor legislation that would force a new election for the MRC. Hoping for a different outcome, they tried to get a new vote on the restoration plan that Menominees had approved in December 1974, and they filed a frivolous lawsuit against me for mismanagement of tribal funds. They got nowhere.

At an MRC meeting in April, a person endorsed by the MRC for an open seat on the committee defeated the candidate supported by the People's Committee. The People's Committee then made a motion to elect a chair for the meeting, something they clearly had no right to do since this was an MRC informational meeting and I was the MRC chair. Nevertheless, the motion passed, and the MRC members, including me, began to leave the room. Then a young woman physically attacked me, struck me in the head, and knocked off my glasses. A scuffle broke out, but the bodyguards intervened and the MRC members managed to leave. The dissidents who remained voted to reestablish the General Council as the governing body of the tribe, dissolve the Voting Trust, hold a new election for the MRC, and fire tribal attorney Joe Preloznik. This was all hot air since MRC was the legitimate governing body, the Menominees had elected MRC members in a democratic election, and no self-appointed committee could usurp its authority. They could hold all the meetings they wanted, but those facts were not about to change.

What had to change in the face of all the violence was law enforcement. Restoration officially took place in April 1975 when the secretary of the interior signed the trust agreement, and Menominees attending an MRC meeting voted unanimously to govern ourselves and enforce our own laws. PL 280 had assigned law enforcement on Indian reservations in Wisconsin to the state, but both the tribe and the Interior Department agreed that, after passage of the Restoration Act, this law did not apply to Menominees. The state and the Justice Department disagreed. The Menominee County sheriff, who was Menominee, had just resigned between scheduled elections, so Governor Lucey appointed Ken Fish, another Menominee, sheriff with the power to arrest Indians and whites.

In the midst of all this chaos, the MRC was making real progress. A Trust and Management Agreement turned control of the forest and mill over to the tribe, but management rested with Menominee Tribal Enterprises (MTE), an entity that would be independent of the tribal legislature as soon as we approved a constitution. In September more than seven hundred Menominee children enrolled in the tribal school system. We had concrete plans for a Menominee health center, under control of the tribe, with construction to begin in 1976. And the MRC was hard at work on the constitution and tribal roll.

In February 1976, we faced another crisis. Sheriff Fish and a deputy had responded to a domestic dispute at the home of John Waubanascum, one of the Warriors indicted for the novitiate takeover and freed on bond. He and two friends had been holding a drinking party for two days, and his wife asked for help because she feared for the safety of her children. When Waubanascum pointed a gun at the deputy, Fish shot him. One of his friends, Arlin Pamanet, came out of the house with a gun and the sheriff shot him, too. Both died.

There had already been criticism of Fish for being gun-happy; now there were calls for the governor to dismiss him. Lawyer Mary Kay Baum, a wannabe Indian who had become involved with Michael Sturdevant, filed a formal complaint alleging that Fish was not qualified to be sheriff. She had sat next to me in law school, and I was just astonished when she showed up. Two hundred people marched on the state capitol in protest of Fish, and about ninety refused to leave the building. Michael Sturdevant was there, of course, but most of the demonstrators were not Menominee. I agreed with one elderly Menominee woman who said that these people should keep their noses out of our business. Although we had not appointed Fish, the MRC stood by him because we believed we should await the outcome of the investigation of the incident, which ultimately exonerated Sheriff Fish.

At the end of the month, Governor Lucey handed responsibility for law enforcement on the reservation over to the federal government. From then on, Indians charged with traffic and misdemeanor cases appeared before a three-judge tribal court while the U.S. District Court in Milwaukee became responsible for Indians accused of serious crimes. The whites who lived in the county remained under the jurisdiction of state courts. The MRC had to work out arrangements with the BIA for its own police force, but due to whites having purchased land during termination, the reservation did not encompass all the land in Menominee County, so there also had to be a sheriff. In May, the Wisconsin Council on Criminal Justice awarded the MRC a grant of $220,000 to pay for eight patrol officers, a lieutenant, and a captain. Ultimately, they would be cross-deputized with county officers. Like all transitions, there were some hiccups with this one. The federal court was slow in bringing to trial a number of Menominees arrested for assaulting federal officers, possessing illegal weapons, and carrying concealed weapons. Since many were out on bail, this failure probably added to the violence on the reservation.

Despite the progress we were making, the dissident faction refused to give up. This really irked me. Mary Kay Baum filed suit to have Fish's office investigated because several deputies had criminal records and many were not qualified. I agreed that these were problems, and some deputies had not received proper training, in large part because they could not take time off to complete it in the face of all the violence we were experiencing. Furthermore, many of the crimes for which deputies had been convicted were fairly minor or had taken place when the deputies were teenagers. Those affected asked the governor for pardons, but he granted only one. When Fish kept them on the payroll, a state court judge held him in contempt. In the November election, Fish lost to one of his deputies, but the harping continued. Gordon Dickie and his buddies organized the Menominee General Council, which began investigating the grants the MRC had received for law enforcement.

Nevertheless, the MRC kept plugging along. The enrollment subcommittee headed by Sarah Skubitz accepted applications between May 16 and August 13, 1975, at offices in Keshena, Milwaukee, and Chicago. Staff members didn't just sit around waiting for people to come in—they really beat the bushes to get young people enrolled. They also worked through the Department of Family and Children's Services to reach adoptees and foster children in non-Menominee households. Then they had to verify that the people applying for enrollment were at least one-fourth Menominee and were not enrolled in another tribe. The roll had to be submitted to the secretary of the interior for his certification, and then sixty days later we could vote on the constitution.

The constitution subcommittee, which I chaired, had a draft ready by the end of the year. We began to educate the Menominee people about it and ask for their recommendations. Because a subcommittee had drafted the constitution, some people accused us of writing it in secret, but we had to have something written down for people to react to. Some Menominees insisted that we would be better off staying with the old constitution. I wanted to shout, "People! That constitution denies tribal sovereignty!" Others objected to the requirement that tribal members be at least one-quarter Menominee because, they feared, intermarriage with whites would make the tribe extinct. Still others thought that there was insufficient protection of Menominee rights. Clearly, some Menominees were going to be dissatisfied with anything the MRC did. In an effort to inform people fully, we arranged for Professor James Clifton of UW–Green Bay to teach a three-credit-hour seminar on the constitution at the Menominee Community School in Keshena. Threats of violence forced cancelation of the course, which would have given people an opportunity to make an *informed* decision on the constitution.

Despite the opposition, the MRC once again held regular meetings in the major settlements. We set up a hotline that people could call to ask questions, offer recommendations, and request meetings about the constitution. We also began broadcasting a weekly program from a radio station in Shawano and published a series of newspaper articles to help people understand the issues. We began the series by asking, "What is a constitution?" We explained that we needed a new constitution because the 1924 document permitted the tribal government to make *recommendations* to the BIA, not enact legislation to govern ourselves. We urged Menominees to contact us to get more information or make suggestions.

After the secretary of the interior approved the roll, enrolled members had until October 20 to register to vote on whether or not to approve the constitution. Voters received their ballots by registered mail and returned them to the BIA office in Minneapolis. The deadline for the return of ballots was November 12. I found the level of participation disappointing. Of the 3,270 Menominees eligible to vote, only 1,308 registered and a mere 894 actually cast ballots. The result was 468 in favor of approving the constitution and 426 against.

The Menominee Restoration Act had given us the right to govern ourselves. The purpose of the constitution was to establish how we would go about governing ourselves. The act promised sovereignty; the constitution was sovereignty in action. The constitution gave tribal citizens the responsibility for the land and people within the boundaries of the reservation. We could write and enforce our own laws, tax ourselves, and assume responsibility for education and health care. The constitution provided for a tribal legislature of nine members with three members elected each year to three-year terms, and no one could serve more than two terms. Legislators had to be no younger than twenty-five years old, and at least seven of the members of the legislature had to live on the reservation. People convicted of major crimes were ineligible unless the Tribal Court declared them rehabilitated. The legislature had to meet at least four times a year, and the meetings had to be open to the public. The constitution gave tribal members the right to present their own ordinances or request repeal of laws to the legislature. Following Menominee tradition, the legislature had to call a General Council of all Menominees at least once a year, and the General Council elected its own chair. The legislature appointed judges to the tribal supreme court and trial courts. The constitution prohibited the sale of tribal land without the consent of a majority of voters and charged the legislature with developing a comprehensive land-use plan.

Menominees were set to govern ourselves. Most Indian tribes had constitutions written by white government lawyers, but we had developed our own constitution with legal assistance from NARF. As soon as the secretary of the interior signed off on the vote, I resigned from the MRC and announced that I would not stand for election to the legislature. Menominee Restoration had dominated my life for more than five years. I had seen my tribe wracked by dissension and violence, and I had endured verbal and physical attacks. But I also had witnessed Indian people coming together to take control of their own future. Self-determination was no longer merely a president's promise or an Indian's pipe dream. The Menominees had made it a reality. All the time, all the anguish, all the labor was worth it. Menominee restoration became the most satisfying chapter of my life.

CHAPTER 7

▪ On the National Stage ▪

As the struggle for restoration ended, I wondered what lay ahead for me. As it turned out, I became more deeply involved with national issues than I had ever been before, either in Minneapolis or in Wisconsin. I brought to these issues experiences with urban Indians, reservations, self-determination, the BIA, and federal Indian policy, but I also had learned much about economic inequality, racism, and the American political system. I wanted to share these lessons with a broader audience and work to make our society more just. One way to do this was through education, particularly training people how to go about solving social problems. Another was through political activism; that is, serving in government and on political commissions as well as running for political office. A third was working for and with nongovernmental agencies that advocated for the poor and the disenfranchised, both Indian and non-Indian. These kinds of opportunities had already been coming my way, but now I focused my attention on them. They brought me onto a national stage.

By now, I had landed on all sorts of boards, usually as a result of my various contacts. In 1974, LaDonna Harris asked me if I was willing to stand for election to the board of Common Cause, founded by John Gardner in 1970. LaDonna was giving up her seat on the board because her schedule was too tight to permit her to attend the meetings regularly. Gardner had served as secretary of health, education, and welfare in Lyndon Johnson's administration. He started Common Cause as a nonpartisan organization dedicated to making public institutions, in his words, "responsive and accountable." LaDonna took me to a Common Cause reception in Washington, introduced me to Gardner, and told him I was a candidate for the board. "Where's the ballot box?" he joked. "We have to start stuffing the ballot box." Of course, we all cracked up at this. Even without stuffing the ballot box, I got on the board of Common Cause, which he chaired. I got to know him pretty well, and I found him to be a very open, receptive person. I really liked and admired him, as did almost everyone, including Republicans.

In 1975, the Senate Select Committee on Indian Affairs appointed me to the American Indian Policy Review Commission whose purpose was not just to review Indian policy but also to make recommendations for change. Senator James Abourezk of South Dakota was the chair and Congressman Lloyd Meeds of Washington the co-chair. On the committee were three senators, three congress-men and, since there were no Indians in Congress, five Indians. I already knew the members from my days lobbying Congress. The commission recognized that not all Indians have the same histories and circumstances, and the appointees reflected that diversity. Three of us were from federally recognized tribes. John Borbridge, a Tlingit-Haida from Alaska, was president of the Sealaska Corpora-tion, one of the Native corporations established under the Alaska Native Claims Settlement Act (1971) that extinguished Native title and vested ownership of resources in twelve corporations, not unlike Menominee Tribal Enterprises. Jake Whitecrow, an enrolled Quapaw and Seneca-Cayuga, had been Quapaw Tribal Chairman and later became director of the National Indian Health Board. Louis Bruce, Mohawk and Oglala Sioux, had served as commissioner of Indian affairs. He represented urban Indians. Adolph Dial, a Lumbee who was a professor at Pembroke State University in North Carolina, spoke for tribes that did not have federal recognition. Nearly half the staff was also Indian.

My position on the American Indian Policy Review Commission was not a full-time job. There were eleven investigative task forces—I served on the education task force—but the staff did the research. Members met periodically to review and discuss staff findings and formulate recommendations. In the mid-1970s, the federal government recognized 287 tribal governments, and perhaps that many additional tribes had state, local, or historical recognition. So this was a complicated task. One of the first things the commission acknowledged was that there is no one-size-fits-all in Indian Country. We set forth two fundamental principles as a guide for future Indian policy: tribal sovereignty and the trust relationship. The commitment to tribal sovereignty meant that the commission signed on to self-determination for Indian tribes and a recognition that the trust relationship meant the United States must acknowledge its obligations to tribes. We advocated policies that would help Indians achieve self-sufficiency and economic independence.

On the education task force, we examined ways in which the current approach to education had failed Indian children. The average educational level of American Indians was eighth grade. We found that Indian education focused on preparing students for blue-collar jobs. The few Indians who went on to college enrolled in education programs, and a handful became lawyers. These professions were important to tribal communities, but they did not create additional jobs on reservations. Few Indians went into fields like engineering or business that had the potential to generate jobs for tribal members who had less education. Nor did many Indians train as administrators, health-care professionals, or technical experts to fill jobs already available on reservations but often filled by non-Indians. For Indian children enrolled in schools off-reservation, drop-out rates were very high, largely because of racism and discrimination in the majority-white schools they attended. These children also failed to acquire skills that would make them employable. Therefore, problems in Indian education contributed substantially to the economic problems on many reservations and in non-reservation Indian communities.

The commission had far too little time to do its work adequately because Congress had demanded a report by 1977, but I am proud of what we did accomplish. We repudiated termination and called for the expansion of federal services to reservation and non-reservation Indians. We called for the extension of federal funds available under the Johnson-O'Malley Act (1934) to the schools urban Indians attended, and we recommended a process under which tribes that lacked official recognition could seek federal acknowledgment. Not surprisingly, our findings did not please everyone. Congressman Meeds was so upset with the recommendations calling for the expansion of federal services that he wrote a minority opinion. He saw the federal government's trust responsibility for Indian people as antithetical to tribal sovereignty. Many Indians, on the other hand, were unhappy that we made no recommendations to enable tribes to regain lands lost under treaties. Many non-Indians resented our failure to limit the exercise of tribal authority on reservations to Indians, a goal ultimately achieved not by congressional action but by the U.S. Supreme Court decision in *Oliphant v. Suquamish Indian Tribe* (1978).

Serving on the commission was not a job, although it did pay my travel expenses to meetings and a small stipend. Therefore, when I stepped down as chair of the Voting Trust, which had paid me a small salary, I was unemployed. Just about the time I resigned, however, University of Wisconsin–Madison Chancellor Edwin Young, his wife, and Truman Lowe, a Ho-Chunk who coordinated the American Indian Program and taught art at the university, showed up on the rez. I didn't really understand why they had come. I thought they were just stopping by on their way somewhere else, since people always seem to find their way to my door. The upshot of this visit, however, was that they had come to invite me to join the faculty. I said, "Wow! That's very flattering, and I am honored to be invited, but I don't have a PhD. Furthermore, I have no intention of writing or doing research. I'm busy doing something about the problems in society." I liked being a social worker involved directly with people. Dr. Young assured me, "All you have to do is come down, teach a course, and then do whatever else you want." I finally decided that it was an offer I couldn't refuse, and I agreed to start in January 1977.

I had no place to live. My brother Robert and his wife, Ginni, who lived in Madison, urged me to come stay with them, but they had two children, and living there seemed like an imposition. I said I would get an apartment. But then Robert and Joe Preloznik urged me to quit being a vagabond and buy a house. I didn't think I had enough money. I had saved my Policy Review Commission stipend, but that was not enough for a down payment on a house in Madison. Then I found out that I could borrow money from two insurance policies that I had taken out. So I bought a small house, surrounded by fields, on the outskirts of Madison. That is where I still live, although the fields are disappearing. Over the years it also has been home to two nephews and a niece as well as several friends.

I arrived in Madison in December 1976. I went over to the university and stopped by American Indian Studies. Nobody was there. I showed up at the School of Social Work, where my academic appointment was. Once again, nobody. Of course, it was Christmas break! University life was going to take some getting used to. I had to teach this course, but I had never taught anything. When the chancellor talked to me about teaching a course, I thought, "Well, I really don't know that much about teaching a course, but I probably can figure it out." Someone in the School of Social Work called me in the fall and told me that I was free to develop whatever course I wanted to. We decided to call it Current Issues in American Indian Affairs. I really appreciated the freedom to do whatever I wanted at the wonderful University of Wisconsin, but I was hoping to get a little guidance or, at least, a little consultation.

As it turned out, developing a course was not rocket science. But I don't think people understand just how hard it is. If you are going to teach a course, you can't just bop in and start talking. You have to decide on reading assignments and means of evaluation. You must prepare a syllabus outlining what topics you will cover. If you're using videos or any other kind of auxiliary information, you have to locate and preview them. Preparing to teach this course was a lot of work. Fortunately, I was able to draw on what I had learned while serving on the Policy Review Commission. I tried to cram everything that the average citizen should know about American Indian policy into the course. I also tried to demonstrate to social work students how they could utilize the social work value system and methodology in working with American Indians.

First of all, the students needed to know something about the history of Indian affairs in this country. I devoted two or three sessions to bringing them up to speed with a brief discussion of treaty rights, the reservation system, allotment, the IRA, termination, and self-determination. I also discovered—a wonderful discovery—that there were video machines available, so I managed to find relevant videos. This was before DVDs, much less computers (which I still haven't mastered), but videos were within my technological ability. Because this was a social work course, I included topics on Indian health, Indian tribal government, Indian education, and other issues of current interest. I spent one session on the Menominees to discuss termination and restoration. So they got an appreciation and a basic understanding of American Indian history, issues, and problems and of what it meant to be a social worker.

I introduced the students to social work methodology by using specific examples. As a trained social worker, one assesses the problem, whether it's at the individual client level, the group level, the community level, or the policy level. Then one decides what kind of intervention should occur and actually undertakes it. This is what I like about being a social worker. You can't just theoretically hypothesize and consider yourself done. Social work is a doing profession. This was the first time that a course using social work methodology to address Indian issues had been offered on the campus. People in the School of Social Work were mildly curious about what I was doing, but nobody ever called me in to discuss my course syllabus or came to observe me. I thought, "Wow! This is amazing!" Who knows what I could have been teaching there? Nevertheless, students enrolled, and eventually others from outside the School of Social Work also took the course.

I was supposed to spend half my time in the School of Social Work and half my time in the American Indian Studies (AIS) Program, but my office was in the Educational Sciences Building where AIS was located. Coordinator Truman Lowe took me over there. He said, "Well, here we are. We are the American Indian Studies Program." There were only two faculty members, Truman and me. Plus AIS had what was probably the smallest office on campus. It was in the middle of the building and didn't have any windows. I said, "What? This is not where I'm going to spend most of my time!" But I did. I never got a clear explanation of what "the program" was. "What is this program?" I asked. "What are we supposed to do?" It turned out that there was almost no AIS program. I decided to go around campus and see if I could find any other Indians. There was a small group of American Indian students and an Indian student organization called Wunk Sheek, a Ho-Chunk (Winnebago) word meaning "Native People." But there was very little else going on.

I decided to broaden my own mission beyond American Indians through field placements for students to work directly with minority populations. I went to the field director and asked, "Do we have any people in the neighborhood houses and the Urban League and so on?" When he told me that we didn't, I asked, "Why not?" He failed to give me a satisfactory answer, so I said, "Well, it seems to me that the School of Social Work should have interns in places like that." He told me to investigate and bring in a list of possibilities. The first place I went was the Urban League of Greater Madison, where I met with Executive Director Betty Franklin-Hammonds. I always want to learn about people, so I asked her about herself. She was originally from Florida and she had worked in corrections. She had quite an extensive background. I had just returned to Madison and did not know it at the time, but she was a beloved member of the community. She told me that they did not have any social work interns, but that she would welcome them and serve as their supervisor.

I went around to other places, investigating the possibilities for placements. Not all of the sites were as well run as the Urban League, and I was afraid they would not provide a good learning experience for the students. But I came up with a list and gave it to the field director. "You can't just give me this list," he said. "Now you have to do it." That meant organizing a fieldwork seminar that would provide supervision and structure for the interns. I decided to name the course Advocacy in Multicultural Settings, which it was. This was not a course in clinical social work, which focuses on individuals with serious problems such as drug abuse or mental illness, usually in an institutional setting. Instead it focused on how to help people organize so that they can address problems in their communities and make changes. We met once a week to talk about various cases and issues that had come up in their placements.

I agreed to create this course because, being a social worker and an Indian, I was very concerned to have UW–Madison students, who were mostly white and middle class, learn about people whose experiences were different from theirs. I turned to agencies that dealt primarily with African Americans, Hispanics, and poor people. Many of these organizations needed help. I went to Centro Hispano, a hole-in-the-wall that offered English lessons to Hispanic people. Ilda Thomas Contreras, a nurse from Uruguay, had started it because no one in Madison was serving Hispanics. She was willing to accept interns in order that the agency could expand its efforts. Some people, however, were hesitant about interns. The person I met with at the Salvation Army had had a poor experience with an intern, and she was not exactly jumping out of her seat with enthusiasm when I showed up. I told her about the student who was particularly interested in a placement there. The student was from Korea, and she was trying to understand American poverty and programs to alleviate it. The Salvation Army, of course, is on the front lines of combating poverty. I knew and liked the Salvation Army woman, so after my pitch, she said, "I wouldn't ordinarily do this, but for you, Ada, I'll do it."

Several leaves of absence punctuated my years on the faculty at UW–Madison. I had barely started at the university when I got a call from the Institute of Politics at Harvard, inviting me to become a fellow. This was the third time they had called me. Previously, I had told them, "I am working on my tribal government, and I don't have time to come to Harvard." I no longer had that excuse. I asked the School of Social Work if I could have a leave of absence. They approved the leave, so I went to Harvard for the fall semester of 1977. After I got there, I didn't understand why they had spent all this energy trying to get me to become a fellow because the only requirement was that you had to show up at five o'clock for sherry.

I had looked forward to getting to know the other fellows and learning about what they were doing. The first time we met, I went around shaking hands saying, "Hello! We're fellows!" I thought we would be an interactive group. Wrong! Everybody had his or her own project. They were a pretty unsociable group, and some of them were a bit self-important. Every now and then the fellows program would have a speaker, and one of the speakers was Senator Ted Kennedy. He requested in advance that I sit next to him. That impressed the others. I was surprised that he remembered me since it had been four years since restoration, but he did. I enjoyed seeing him again, and I *really* enjoyed the reaction of the other fellows.

There were eight of us, but I had little contact with most of them. My favorite was Tom Roeser, a Republican lobbyist for Quaker Oats, who ultimately became vice president of the company. He was a big teddy bear of a guy, and he was so happy to be a fellow. He had held a number of government positions of which the most interesting, as far as I was concerned, was director of public affairs for the Peace Corps. He had worked for various newspapers, mostly writing op-eds. I enjoyed getting to know Manuel Carballo, who had been in the administration of New York City Mayor John Lindsay. I had heard about him before Harvard because, for the two years prior to the fellowship, he had headed the Wisconsin Department of Health and Social Services, but I never met him when he was in that position. I had several good conversations with Martin Nolan, Washington Bureau chief for the *Boston Globe*. The only other woman was Patricia Goldman, executive director of the House Wednesday Group composed of moderate Republican members of Congress. Her husband was Republican Senator Charles Goodell of New York. We had several cordial conversations, but we were hardly buddies. Ray Price had been Richard's Nixon's speechwriter and had just published a book, *With Nixon*. He appeared to be so busy that he barely had time to say hello. I have no memories of Terry Goggin, a Democratic member of the California legislature, or of the Pulitzer Prize–winning investigative reporter Jack Anderson.

I don't know what the other fellows did, but it was clear that I was not going to see much of them. I decided that I would find the other Indians, who were mostly in the Harvard Graduate School of Education. I think I met all of them that semester—there were not many. They were a little lonely, and I think they were glad to see another Indian. The program had been founded in 1970 to bring together faculty who taught about or did research on Indians and to recruit Indians to the university, especially to the graduate program in education. I asked students about their educational backgrounds, how they got in, and so on. I got vague answers. Apparently Indians could get into the graduate program without a college education, something I thought was a real disservice to them because it cheapened their degrees.

Having met the Indians, I looked around for something else to do, and I learned that I could audit two courses. I ended up attending James Q. Wilson's course on government. Although I did not agree with him on many issues, I learned a lot from him. He was quite conservative and had just published a book, *Thinking about Crime*, in which he argued that long prison sentences reduced crime. Then I took a course from psychiatrist Robert Coles, author of *Children of Crisis: A Study of Courage and Fear*, a series of five books that began with the impact of desegregation on black children in the South and went on to discuss other groups of children in America, including Indians. In their lectures, both of these professors cited all kinds of data and statistics without using any notes. It was a joy to listen to them.

My semester at Harvard was the first time since I was fourteen years old that I didn't have to work, so I decided to take yoga. I knew nothing about it, but I ended up in this Hatha Yoga class, which is the first level of yoga. It's not this meditation stuff. It's physical yoga where they teach you certain postures and stretches. I decided that I could do this. I really liked that course, but you have to take an hour out of your day every day in order to go through all these postures and bends and stretches, so I didn't keep it up. Nevertheless, I have this great admiration for yoga. So I had my two courses, the yoga class, and the five o'clock sherry.

Since I wasn't going to do much socializing in Boston, every weekend I went somewhere. It was the twenty-fifth anniversary of Queen Elizabeth's ascension to the throne so I called up my friend Kahn-Tineta Horn, a Mohawk activist who lived in Ottawa, Canada, to see what was going on there. Kahn-Tineta said, "Come on up. It's the Queen's Jubilee." The queen was in town to celebrate. So I took along some dress clothes, and Kahn-Tineta got us invitations to a gala in the queen's honor at the National Arts Center. The concert featured Canadian performers from three major groups—Plains Cree singer Buffy St. Marie, Québécois composer and pianist André Gagnon, and the Canadian Brass quintet from Toronto. At the end of the program, the announcer said, "Her Majesty and the Duke of Edinburgh will take their leave." The queen walked slowly down each level from the top of the building, smiling and nodding regally to people as she passed. Prince Philip walked dutifully behind her. It was a memorable evening.

Another weekend I went to Washington for a meeting of the President's Commission on White House Fellowships. As I was just settling into my new job in Madison, John Gardner had called: "Ada Deer, what are you doing in May?" I replied, "Whatever it is, the answer is, 'Yes, John.'" He laughed, then he told me about the Commission on White House Fellowships, which he chaired. Gardner had proposed this program to President Johnson, who established it by executive order. The purpose was to develop dedicated public servants by providing a select group of young people the opportunity to work for a year with senior administration officials. They also attended weekly seminars, often with guest speakers, and took domestic and foreign policy study trips. On John's recommendation, President Jimmy Carter appointed me to the commission, and when my term ended, President Ronald Reagan reappointed me. One of the commissioners' responsibilities was to choose each new group of fellows. At my first meeting, I started looking at the criteria and then the applications that had come in. Almost all of them were white liberals with great educations but little in the way of community or public service. I suggested that we should amend the criteria to include service, and the other members agreed. I really enjoyed this group and the people I met through my membership on the commission.

One of my most memorable experiences while serving on the commission took place at a sit-down dinner in the Supreme Court. We were all standing around before dinner with our little drink glasses when suddenly it came to me: "Whoa! I am in the Supreme Court, and we're having dinner here!" Then Chief Justice Warren Burger came walking up, greeted me, and introduced himself with, "Hello. Glad to see you. I am Warren Burger." I caught myself just before I said, "That's *Justice* Burger!" This happened while I was a fellow at Harvard. I would have loved to tell someone at Harvard that I had been to Ottawa for the Queen's Jubilee and to Washington where I met the Chief Justice and had dinner at the Supreme Court, but no one asked anyone else what they were doing.

I was happy to get back to Madison at the end of my stint at Harvard. Edwin Young, who hired me, had become president of the University of Wisconsin System. Lots of people criticized him for his firm stand against antiwar demonstrators during the Vietnam War, but I liked him personally. He was warm and supportive, and he had a wonderful sense of humor. I found out that he had decided to mentor me. That meant invitations to lots of functions where I met interesting people from across the university, including the famous geneticist James Crow. Just after I returned to campus, I saw President Young at one of these events. "Where have you been?" he asked. "Well, I was gone for a semester. I was a fellow at the Institute of Politics at Harvard." I told him that they had been calling me for several years. I had finally thought it might be possible for me to go, so I asked the School of Social Work for a leave of absence, and they gave it to me. "What?" he said laughing. "They don't give lecturers leaves of absence." Nobody had told me that, of course. I asked for it and they gave it to me.

I returned to Madison with an even keener interest in American politics. I had registered to vote in Wisconsin in 1957, but I was in graduate school in New York City for my first presidential election. In those days in New York, you had to be a resident and at least age twenty-one, present identification, and register by party. I took my Badger red diploma as identification. The registrars, who were nice Brooklyn ladies, were astonished: they had never seen a college diploma, much less one from the University of Wisconsin. We all had a good laugh. When I returned to Wisconsin in 1969, I registered as a Democrat. I was living in Stevens

Point and working at UW–Stevens Point as director of Indian Upward Bound. I attended a campaign event for Congressman David Obey in 1970 when he was running for reelection. Oklahoma Senator Fred Harris, who was then chair of the Democratic National Committee (DNC), flew out from Washington to address a rally. He was a fabulous speaker. Then Obey spoke, and I thought, "Wow, this is for me." So I started going to Democratic Party functions.

I decided I would try to get Indian people more involved in the Democratic Party. I called down to the party headquarters in Madison and told them I would like somebody to come up to the Menominee Reservation and talk about the Democratic Party. So who comes up but Secretary of State Doug La Follette. I didn't know who he was. The name "La Follette" was familiar, of course, and I later learned that Doug was distantly related to Republican governor and senator as well as Progressive presidential candidate Robert M. La Follette. Doug was an environmentalist and an organizer of the first Earth Day in Wisconsin. He was very earnest in his description of the party and its principles, and I was impressed that he would drive all the way up from Madison to talk to a group of Indian people.

Nothing ever came of that particular effort to spark enthusiasm for the Democratic Party, but I didn't give up. I just put the idea on the back burner. Restoration took over my life, so it was only after my move to Madison that I began to think seriously about state and national politics again. Lobbying for Menominee restoration had given me a nuts-and-bolts introduction to getting things done in Washington. Professor Wilson's class at Harvard provided me an intellectual and philosophical perspective on government. And the Commission on White House Fellowships exposed me to the opportunities available in government for people who wanted to make a difference. I decided once again to try to motivate Menominees to become active in state and national politics.

In 1978 I went to talk to Sue Ellen Albrecht, the Wisconsin member of the DNC. I told her that I was from the Menominee Tribe and I wanted to discuss how to get more Indian participation in the Democratic Party. She said, "Oh, we're not going to talk about that. I want to talk about you." She thought I should run for public office. This was the first time I had ever seen this woman. I was astounded: "What? Me? Run for public office? What office?" She replied, "Secretary of state," and I asked, "Why?" She said, "Because it's vacant." Doug La Follette had decided to run for lieutenant governor. I gasped, "But you don't even know me." "Oh yes, we do," she assured me. "We're aware of you, Ada Deer, and we want you to do this." She didn't even say "think about it." She was giving me instructions. At that point, I wasn't even sure what the secretary of state's job involved. But run I did.

I had a wonderful time campaigning. I went all over the state. I especially enjoyed going up to northern Wisconsin. I would go into some of the newspaper offices up there and introduce myself: "Hello, I'm Ada Deer, and I'm running for secretary of state." You could see their reactions on their faces. What? An Indian woman running for secretary of state? Then I said, "Are you aware of the duties of the secretary of state?" They were not, of course, so quite earnestly I said, "One of the most important duties is to maintain the seal of the great state of Wisconsin." Some of them saw the humor in this and were willing to laugh with me. I then went on to tell them about the more consequential things that the secretary of state did, such as chartering corporations. The most important duty, however, involved lobbyists. The legislature recently had passed stricter regulations on lobbyists, and the secretary of state had the responsibility for supervising their conduct.

Since I actually had been a lobbyist, I thought I brought experience to the position. Seven other Democrats entered the primary. A problem arose with balloting, however: voting machines could accommodate only five names, so three names had to appear in a separate location. We drew straws to see who those three would be, and I was one of them. Some people told me they looked for my name and could not find it, but I did not challenge the vote because I was confident that it was a fair election. Vel Phillips, an African American civil rights activist and attorney from Milwaukee, won. If I had to lose, I am glad it was to another woman of color. I joked that if my name had been Ada Deer La Follette, I would have been in, but maybe not—Doug lost his race for lieutenant governor. I ran again in 1982 and came in second in a field of four.

With the 1978 election over, I settled into my job at the University of Wisconsin. One day the phone rang. This was in the days before email and text messages, neither of which I have mastered. John Echohawk of NARF, which had provided legal assistance for Menominee restoration, asked me to come to Washington to serve as a legislative liaison. So I took another leave of absence from 1979 to 1981 and went to Washington. NARF had a very congenial office, and I met some interesting people, especially the two lawyers.

Lawrence Aschenbrenner, or "Lare" as everyone called him, had been practicing law in Oregon in the 1960s when he volunteered to go to Mississippi for a month as a volunteer lawyer for the civil rights movement. He was so appalled by the racism he encountered in the courts that he accepted a job as chief counsel for the state office of the Lawyers Committee for Civil Rights Under Law and moved with his wife and children to Mississippi. Even before his sojourn in Mississippi, he had worked on Indian water rights, and when he left the South, he became assistant solicitor in the Interior Department Division of Indian Affairs. In the late 1970s, he joined NARF, where he focused on tribes in the Northwest.

Arlinda Locklear, a Lumbee, was also memorable, very knowledgeable and dynamic. She had gone to work for NARF just after she graduated from Duke University Law School in 1976, and in 1984, she became the first Indian woman to argue a case before the U.S. Supreme Court. She won the case for the Cheyenne River Sioux, which had challenged South Dakota's prosecution of a tribal member for conduct on the reservation.

I worked with a number of different tribes. The first thing I did was go to the Shinnecock Nation on Long Island. The federal government had not formally recognized their nation, and NARF thought that my explaining the steps the Menominees took to secure their restoration might encourage them. Lare Aschenbrenner wrote their application, but it was not until 2010 that the United States officially acknowledged them as a sovereign tribe and made them eligible for federal services.

I also worked briefly on the New York Oneidas' land claims case with Arlinda. *Oneida Indian Nation of New York v. County of Oneida* ended up before the U.S. Supreme Court in 1984. The 1985 decision in this case recognized the right of tribes to sue in federal courts on the basis of aboriginal land title. Although my part in the case was very small, I am proud to have had an association with it. I also spent some time lobbying Congress. I helped NARF stop a bill introduced by Republican Congressman Gary Lee of New York to extinguish Indian land claims. We also worked to extend the time allowed for Indians to seek legislative action regarding land claims.

Most of what I did, though, focused on housing issues. The BIA and the Department of Housing and Urban Development (HUD) had failed miserably to provide decent housing on reservations. Thousands of Indians lived in unsafe and unsanitary houses, and NARF's Washington Advocacy Project was trying to remedy that situation. But the remedy was not easy. Roads had to be constructed, which was up to the BIA. Then HUD built the houses, and the IHS connected water and sewer service. So at least three government agencies were involved. NARF sought to simplify the situation by revising Indian housing regulations and creating a Federal Office of Indian Housing. Nongovernmental agencies were also involved. I spent a lot of time working with the Housing Assistance

Council, which collaborates with nonprofits to provide affordable housing in rural areas, including Indian reservations. I also met with people at the National American Indian Housing Council, an advocacy group. We were particularly concerned with impending federal budget cuts. Urban Indians often depended on public housing, but Ronald Reagan's administration planned to eliminate public housing. Anticipated budget cuts also threatened reservation housing, which already was way short of meeting needs. I often felt like I was swimming against a strong current. Even today, the National Congress of American Indians reports that 14 percent of reservation houses are substandard and 16 percent have no indoor plumbing.

I did not intend to make the pages of the *Washington Post* while I worked for NARF, but I did. I was mugged. I was walking home about eight o'clock one night when two men confronted me. One of them ripped my purse off my shoulder, and they both ran. At first I was startled, but then I became really angry. They had taken my keys, cash, and credit cards. I am basically a fighter, and I was not just going to stand there wringing my hands. I took off after them, yelling, "Give me my purse back!" I chased them for several blocks then lost sight of them. I asked two guys standing at a corner if they had seen them. They told me that the purse snatchers had gotten on a passing bus. I spotted a police car and flagged it down. I got in and told the officers what had happened. We took off in pursuit. Several blocks later, they pulled the bus over. A young man jumped out and ran into a building, but the police pursued and caught him, and arrested him for robbery. When I saw him, he had blood on his face, which the officers said resulted from a fall he had taken. He really needed medical attention. As I looked at this young man, the social worker in me thought that he probably had no education, skills, or chance in life. But then the Menominee thought, "I don't let people walk on me. I fight back!" The police found my purse minus only the cash.

I was excited to work for NARF because they had done such a wonderful job for the Menominees, but my position didn't work out the way I expected. Soon after John appointed me, he hired Suzan Harjo, a Cheyenne and Arapaho tribal citizen also of Muscogee descent. I had met her in New York years earlier when I was working on Menominee restoration. I remember that I had felt sad for her because she and her husband, Frank, looked very bedraggled. We had a conversation, but I kept thinking, in my social worker mode, "Wow, they have a lot of problems and they need help." Her father had been in the military, and she had grown up on a number of different bases, including ones in Hawaii and Italy. Although she had lots of relatives in Oklahoma, she did not grow up in an Indian community. I found it very difficult to develop a cooperative relationship with her; she seemed to be trying to compete with me. I felt like she was undercutting my work on the Hill, and I thought, "This makes no sense. Why do we have two people with very different approaches and views up there representing NARF?" After two years at NARF, I finally spoke with John Echohawk about the problem. His response was, "I'm not going to be involved in two Indian women fighting." I couldn't believe it! I have enormous respect for John and I like him personally, but this was an appallingly sexist comment. So I quit.

My friendship with John Echohawk and his extended family has endured. I continue to be very supportive of NARF, and I subsequently have served on their board, including a stint as chair, but I just could not work with Suzan. Even though we were incompatible, I respect her accomplishments. She has gone on to serve as executive director of the National Congress for American Indians, author of fine articles in *Indian Country Today*, curator at the National Museum of the American Indian, and president of the Morningstar Institute, which has led the fight against Indian mascots. As for me, I went back to Madison and resumed my position at the university.

While I was in Washington working for NARF, the Democratic Party asked me to serve on a commission to revise convention rules. This move came out of the bitter primary fight between incumbent President Jimmy Carter and Senator Ted Kennedy in the 1980 election. Just before the convention, Kennedy urged delegates pledged to Carter to abandon their candidate, who was leading, and vote for him. The delegates, however, honored their commitment to the people who selected them, and the party nominated Carter. The rancor and turmoil divided the party. Kennedy supporters' lack of enthusiasm for and even hostility to Carter, who won the nomination, contributed to his defeat in November.

One of the perceived problems at the 1980 convention was the absence of many party leaders, including members of Congress. Because the presidential primaries were so acrimonious, many politicians hesitated to endorse either Carter or Kennedy. Many candidates running for Congress or state offices declined to serve as delegates to the Democratic National Convention. They feared that pledging their support to either Carter or Kennedy would alienate the supporters of the other Democratic presidential candidate and lead to a Republican victory in the general election. Many delegates to the convention, therefore, were not party regulars but people more passionately committed to their particular candidate than to the Democratic Party. Following the election, party leaders decided that greater convention representation by delegates who put the party first might prevent future debacles like the one they had just experienced. Therefore, they established a commission of sixty-nine Democrats chaired by Governor Jim Hunt of North Carolina.

The Hunt Commission enacted a number of changes, but the most significant and controversial one was the creation of so-called "superdelegates." These delegates were Democratic officeholders whose loyalty to the party superseded that to candidates. The National Organization for Women (NOW) opposed this move because it threatened to reduce the number of delegates who were women. The commission ultimately agreed that, henceforth, half the convention delegates would be women and that the party also would seek greater racial diversity. Many African American leaders remained dubious, and Reverend Jesse Jackson later criticized the scheme openly, but it remains in place today (2018). The Republican Party is not organized in this way, a circumstance that helped Donald Trump win the nomination despite opposition from most party leaders. Superdelegates made the nomination of former Secretary of State Hillary Clinton more likely, but they certainly have not resolved the problem of factionalism within the Democratic Party, as her primary battle with Senator Bernie Sanders demonstrated.

In September 1981, I attended a meeting of the Hunt Commission in Des Moines, Iowa, that coincided with the DNC's first National Training Academy. The purpose of the academy was to prepare campaign managers and potential candidates to challenge Republicans in the 1982 election. There I met Lydia Bickford and her soon-to-be husband, Jon Holtshopple, who were attending the academy as the managers of Tony Earl's ultimately successful campaign for governor of Wisconsin. We became fast friends. Although they were working for Earl, I depended on their advice when I decided in 1982 to run once again for secretary of state. Vel Phillips sought reelection, and former Secretary of State Doug La Follette, who had lost the lieutenant governor's race in 1978, also decided to run. Once again, I lost, but this time Doug won instead of Vel, who came in third. After that I shelved my political ambitions for the moment.

I remained active in Democratic Party politics, and in 1984, I served as an at-large delegate to the convention, which met in San Francisco. At that time, Wisconsin had a primary but it was only advisory. Congressional district cau-cuses selected delegates, who then caucused to choose fifty-three delegates to the convention, and those delegates selected an additional thirty-six delegates. Every state had its own system, and if you are confused about what Wisconsin's was, you are not alone. I was a pledged delegate for Walter Mondale, who had served as President Carter's vice president. At the convention 3,882 delegates voted; 544 were the superdelegates, the party officials provided for by the Hunt Commission. The final tally at the convention was 58 percent for Vice President Walter Mondale, 30 percent for Senator Gary Hart, 10 percent for Reverend Jesse Jackson, and 2 percent uncommitted.

Mondale chose Congresswoman Geraldine Ferraro of New York as his running mate. I was thrilled that the Democrats became the first major party to nominate a woman for vice president. She delivered a memorable acceptance speech. The daughter of an immigrant from Italy, she had worked her way through law school at night. Her speech reflected the love of country her father instilled in her, but she criticized the disparity between what women and men earned, the Republican threats to student loans and Social Security, and the nuclear arms race. I was enormously impressed.

I was less impressed with the number of Indian delegates at the convention. There were only thirty-two of us, so we got together and appointed an unofficial committee to meet with party leaders about increasing our representation. We also pressed the platform committee to add a plank referring to Indians, the first since the Republican platform of 1972. The platform ultimately promised to address Indian poverty, resource claims, and problems at the BIA. One of the results of these complaints may have been my appointment as vice chair of the Mondale-Ferraro national campaign. I was delighted to help and enjoyed campaigning for the ticket. Unfortunately, President Reagan was reelected.

I experienced a far greater loss a month after the Democratic convention: my mother died. She had left my father and the cabin on the Wolf River in the early 1970s and had moved to a house in rural Shawano County near the reservation. By the early 1980s, she could no longer live alone, so she moved to Madison to live with my sister Connie. My brother Robert and I both lived in Madison, so we could help Connie care for her. Doctors ultimately diagnosed my mother with pancreatic cancer, and in her final months she moved to a nursing home. We visited her together the week before she died. I think she loved having all of us there with her because she smiled most of the time we were in her room. She died on August 23, 1984. I still miss her. I don't think I ever have met anyone with her clear sense of justice and her determination to achieve it.

I appreciated having most of my family close. Connie had earned a bachelor of science in nursing from the University of Wisconsin. After a couple of years working as a nurse, she decided that it was not the career for her. She had been at the forefront of the Menominee struggle for restoration, so it seemed logical to pursue a degree in law. In 1979, she graduated from the University of Wisconsin

School of Law, becoming the first Menominee to earn a law degree. She recently retired from a distinguished career working at Legal Action of Wisconsin. My brother Robert received master's degrees in water resources management and urban and regional planning, and he did the coursework for a PhD but did not finish his dissertation. He worked for the Wisconsin Department of Natural Resources. (Robert died on Thanksgiving Day, November 27, 2014, of esophageal cancer.) Joe did not go to college, but he sought advanced training in lumber grading, worked at the Menominee mill and at other local mills, and lived on the reservation. Ferial was still living in South Dakota. She had graduated from the University of Wisconsin and studied dance at Julliard. After she married and moved to South Dakota, she earned her EdD in educational psychology and counseling. She has published a short book on the Menominees and several articles in scholarly journals. After she and her husband divorced, she returned to the reservation, where she worked in the tribal school. Most teachers on the reservation are white, so it was important, I think, to have such a highly educated Menominee as a psychologist and counselor. We are now all retired.

I enjoyed my nieces and nephews as well. Joe's son, Joe III, lived with me one summer and repaired my roof. Robert's son Rob, who was a handful, also moved in after he and his father had a row. They were in their late teens, so I thought I could leave them alone and take a trip to Alaska. When I returned home, there was a girl living there, too! Rob tried to explain that she had nowhere else to live, a dubious excuse that did not cut the mustard with me. No way was I having a teenage girl living there with these two guys. It was a small house, and there was barely room for the three of us. So she left. Even with their hijinks, I liked having them around. My niece Wenonah Skye, Ferial's daughter, is currently living with me while she looks for her own place. I have helped other nieces and nephews with college and even medical school tuition, and I consider it money well spent. I am enormously proud of them and count a physician and a Coast Guard captain among their number. I also get pleasure from my friends' children and grandchildren, but I do not regret having no children of my own. My life has been full and rich, and my time has gone to trying to make this country a better place for all children.

In 1992 I decided to make another run myself, this time for Congress. In 1990, Republican upstart Scott Klug unexpectedly defeated Democratic Congressman Robert Kastenmeier, who had served in that office since 1959. I had met Congressman Kastenmeier in the 1960s, when I was in Washington. I just went up to his office said, "Hello, I'm from Wisconsin, I graduated from the University of

Wisconsin, and I would like to meet the congressman." He was very warm and thanked me for coming in. I met him again several times when I was lobbying for restoration, and he ended up being one of the cosponsors of the Menominee Restoration Act. Like other Democrats, I was crushed by his defeat. Wisconsin Democrats hoped Scott Klug would be a one-term congressman.

Lydia and Jon started bugging me to run against him. They weren't the only people, but they were the ringleaders. I happened to go to a meeting in Washington, and I decided to talk to John Gardner. I told him that I had been asked to run for Congress but I was not sure about it. I summarized my two previous races and explained how I really enjoyed campaigning. Furthermore, I was no stranger to elective office. I had been the chair of the tribe through restoration and writing the tribal constitution. John asked me if I would regret not doing it. That was a new question, so I thought about it. I recalled all the people that I had met while I was lobbying for restoration. I remembered wondering at the time, "These people are running the government?" I concluded that I could do a better job, so I decided to run.

First I had to win the Democratic primary. My chief opponent was David Clarenbach, who had served nine terms in the Wisconsin legislature, beginning at the age of twenty-one. He was Congressman Kastenmeier's heir apparent, which made him the front-runner according to the pundits. Because he had been planning this run and making connections to people with deep pockets for a very long time, he was very well funded. He also was a good guy, and I never put him down. His mother was Kathryn Clarenbach, a founder and the first chairwoman of NOW. Because of this, many women in Wisconsin felt conflicted, and those who came out publicly for me before the primary vote had a lot of courage. NOW split its endorsement in the primary. But I did have support from several well-known women, including *Ms.* magazine cofounder Gloria Steinem, Congresswoman Maxine Waters, and Cherokee Chief Wilma Mankiller.

Jon and Lydia mapped out the campaign, and we generated some publicity, although not much to start with. The press didn't even cover the announcement of my candidacy, which took place on the steps of the Wisconsin Historical Society. Former UW–Madison Chancellor Edwin Young was there along with my fourth-grade teacher, Mildred Raasch, who was in her nineties. I lost one opportunity for lots of publicity. I had adopted the campaign slogan "Nothing Runs Like a Deer," a parody of the John Deere farm equipment slogan. John Deere threatened to sue. Lydia and Jon said, "Please do." They thought that a huge multinational company suing an American Indian's congressional campaign could only help us.

Gloria Steinem, Ada Deer, and Wilma Mankiller
during Ada's congressional campaign, 1992.

Apparently John Deere thought so too, because they promptly withdrew the threat.

Jon and Lydia had a clear strategy that was very different from David's. He ran a "rose garden" campaign and appeared primarily at major events, but I ran a "main street" campaign, going everywhere and talking to everybody. At a parade, for example, David was likely to be sitting on the grandstand—if he appeared at all—while I was working the crowd. His funding came mostly from big donors, many of them lobbyists; I raised funds in people's living rooms over coffee. He depended on paid campaign staff, and volunteers had to present résumés; I ended up with people coming out of the woodwork to volunteer, and I welcomed all of them.

I knew a campaign was hectic and time-consuming—fifteen hours a day, seven days a week—but I have a lot of energy and stamina. I went to Rotary Club meetings where I joined in singing hymns and patriotic songs. I traipsed from business to business in small towns, introducing myself to whoever was there. I called on the editors of weekly newspapers, who always needed to fill their columns. I visited senior centers, but never while the residents were eating because old people do not like their meals interrupted. I had a booth every

Saturday at the farmers' market at the state capitol. Every time a radio or TV reporter interviewed me, it was on the street or at an event where lots of people were milling about. I was busy all the time. I went to a school once to visit a fourth-grade class. I asked them what they wanted to be when they grew up. The little boys said things like fireman or policeman, and the little girls said teacher or nurse. Then one little girl piped up, "I want to be president!" It was the perfect opening for me to explain about elections. I told them that I was running for election to Congress and that the president also had to be elected. Then I said, "You all can help her. You can sign up to work on her campaign."

I was a real believer in involving as many people in the campaign as possible. We ended up with more than four hundred volunteers. One of my favorite volunteers was a fifteen-year-old named Anika, who originally was from Quito, Ecuador. She came down to our headquarters every afternoon, and we often took her to campaign events. We invited her to our primary victory dinner where we presented our volunteers with "Worker Bee" T-shirts. She was thrilled. One of our best volunteers was Dylan Abraham, a young man with schizophrenia. As a result of medications and the Program for Assertive Community Treatment, he was doing well. His mother, Nancy, one of the founders of the National Alliance on Mental Illness, also volunteered, and we were pleased to have people knowledgeable about and devoted to the treatment of mental illness with our campaign. We also had a group of kids with developmental disabilities. I gave them a list of names and addresses and put them to work addressing envelopes for mailings. Sometimes our volunteers filled needs we didn't even know we had. A young woman called one day and asked, "To whom should I speak about joining the press group?" There was no press group, so she alone ended up dealing with the press. We welcomed people with small children as volunteers. We also encouraged them to bring kids to our events. Years later I ran into one of those kids at a fund-raiser in Middleton, and he said, "Ada Deer, you don't remember me, but my mother took me up to one of your events when I was in grade school. That was the first political event I ever attended, and I was so impressed with you." He currently is a political staffer in the Capitol.

I had to depend on volunteers because, upon the advice of my auto mechanic, I decided not to accept funds from lobbyists or political action committees (PACs). My campaign office was in a rather dilapidated building several miles from the capitol. Just to afford that, I had to spend a lot of time raising funds. Gloria Steinem gave me $1,000 when I first announced my candidacy, and there were some other large donations, but most contributions were very small. One fund-raiser stands out. On my birthday, which is in August, a group of Menominees came down from the reservation to hold a fund-raiser with me. It was raining cats and dogs, but we had reserved a shelter at Madison's Westmorland Park so everyone crowded inside. The group included dancers and drummers, and they did an honor dance for me. I was enormously pleased. They did not live in my district, of course, but they attracted a lot of attention, and we were able to raise some money. I very much appreciated the support of my people.

Among the most gratifying things about running for office were the notes that often came with small contributions. One woman wrote, "Although I am not in your district, I'd like to help you out as an SHS [Shawano High School] grad who looks up to you in your quest for justice and equality." A man sent a $75 check with the note, "Two days ago we sent $75—but my wife argues that we should double it! We are doing so." From a woman in Idaho came $30 and this note: "My state of Idaho is rather far from Wisconsin, but you sound to me to be good for our country." A woman from California wrote, "I manage to pay my bills and eat well. $25 is all I can afford. I do hope it will help."

Out on the campaign trail I met all sorts of people. Two of the funniest experiences took place in the rural area of the district and involved gasoline. I was driving along an empty highway when I spotted a car parked on the shoulder. I stopped to see if I could help, and out stepped Peter Peshek, who was in charge of Wisconsin's environmental affairs. He apparently had taken fuel conservation too far because he had run out of gas! I said, "Hop in, Peter," and I gave him a ride to the nearest station. On another day at a different gas station, a man came up and asked if I remembered him. I didn't. He said, "When I was twelve years old, a bear treed me"—but he called it a "bar"—"and you chased the bear away and got me down out of the tree." I guess I was becoming a legend in my own time!

As the campaign progressed, I began to get more attention. The Madison press wanted interviews, and more people came to my events. We started slow, but by August we were on a roll. Finally, Lydia felt the "thump" that she claimed to get before a winning campaign. Even I started thinking that I might squeak by. Imagine how surprised I was when precincts began to report, and I was leading. When the final tally came in, I was stunned. I had won the Democratic nomination for Congress by 20 percent! I came out to address my supporters and the press. I said, "Friends, I've been waiting all my life to say this: Me nominee." They roared.

By the time I woke up the next morning, my campaign people already had sent three or four hundred letters to raise money. We had only seven or eight weeks until the general election. I did get a boost on the day of the primary with an endorsement from EMILY's List, an advocacy group founded in 1988 to support Democratic women seeking elective office. They had held off endorsing me, perhaps in deference to Kathryn Clarenbach. Also the dominant view in the organization was that women candidates had to be tougher than men—tough on crime, tough on defense, and so on—in order to win. That was just not me. I had never held those positions and I was not going to change my views because someone thought it expedient. Instead I campaigned on a platform of using the "peace dividend," the funds that became available when the Iraq War ended, for job creation and health care. I also supported racial and gender equity in our political system. At the time, only 6 percent of Congress was female whereas women were 51 percent of the population. I supported the efforts of EMILY's List to change that, and I appreciated their endorsement, even if it came very late in the primary.

My Republican opponent in the general election was one-term congressman Scott Klug, a handsome former newscaster. He was well educated, with master's degrees from both Northwestern University and the University of Wisconsin, and was accustomed to dealing with the media. He also was a moderate Republican who was pro-choice and favored family leave. He had gained national prominence as a member of the Gang of Seven that exposed the House banking scandal in which members of Congress had long-standing overdrafts with the House bank. So he came across as a reformer although he toed the Republican line on most issues, including using the peace dividend to reduce the federal deficit that the Republicans had run up through the arms race and Iraq War. Klug did not run a rose garden campaign. Because his family had not moved to Washington when he was elected in 1990, he came back to Madison every weekend and made good use of his time attending picnics, parades, and other events. Furthermore, he had been a local television newscaster, so he had both face and name recognition. He was much better funded than I was. I continued to refuse to take donations from PACs, unless you consider EMILY's List a PAC, but he rolled in the dough. The final tally put his donations at $868,065, with $225,000 coming from PACs, while my total was only $428,710.

We had a series of debates, where he did much better than I did. He knew how to play to the camera, and he excelled at spouting off facts and figures and speaking in sound bites. I was better at finding ways to bring people together to solve problems rather than simply describing problems. I also had a firmer grasp of urban issues than farm policy, which proved to be a problem because the congressional district included rural areas in addition to Madison. Dairy farming was just not my thing. I ran one television commercial, but we were not able to get more time because it was a presidential election year and a Wisconsin Senate seat was open. We did air one commercial that had me looking at a television, slightly askance, and saying, "Boy, he's slick." It really made Klug mad. But generally the campaign was not mean-spirited or extremely partisan. As in my earlier campaigns, I enjoyed it.

My platform was basically that of the Democratic Party, but my own experiences shaped my message. I supported reproductive rights because I had seen what happens when women have too many children too close together. My mother had six children in thirteen years, and she struggled to keep the five of us she raised clothed and fed. Many other women on the Menominee Reservation had similar stories. I supported national health care because I had seen what happens when health care was not available: during termination the Menominees lost access to health care when their reservation hospital closed. I supported environmentalism because I had lived on the banks of the Wolf River and I belonged to an Indian tribe that practiced sustainable-yield forestry. I supported jobs programs and campaign finance reform because I had seen what happened when MEI reduced its workforce to increase its profits and manipulated what was supposed to be a democratic system of governance to sell tribal land. I encouraged people to vote because I had seen what citizens could do when they decided to take back their government from special interests. Sometimes I wasn't as well informed as people wanted me to be, but you can't be an expert on everything all the time. I might not have had all the facts and figures. But I had experience.

The DNC gave me its support. New Jersey Senator Bill Bradley campaigned for me, as did California Congresswoman Maxine Waters. Harriet Woods, a Democrat who had served as lieutenant governor of Missouri under Republican John Ashcroft, came to support me in her role as president of the National Women's Political Caucus. Reverend Jesse Jackson endorsed me when he was in Madison for his voter registration drive. His rally at the university fieldhouse drew 8,500 people. When we walked in together, they all cheered and clapped. What a thrill! He introduced me, and I stood up and waved. I really liked Reverend Jackson. He told me that he had American Indian ancestry, but he did not know which tribe. Lydia teased me that when we met there were "minority brown eyes looking deeply into each other."

I still did a lot of hand-shaking on the street, but we also had a number of big events. Ed Garvey, a labor lawyer who represented the National Football League

Ada Deer with Al Gore and Bill Clinton during her congressional campaign, 1992.

Players Association and had run unsuccessfully for the U.S. Senate, emceed a big fund-raiser for me. Gloria Steinem and Wilma Mankiller spoke, and they wowed the attendees. Gloria told Ed that he had done such a good job emceeing that she was making him an honorary woman. I held a fund-raiser at a family planning clinic that also did abortions. Next to my stack of bumper stickers was a basketful of condoms. That attracted publicity! The largest event—one of a different kind—was in October when Bill Clinton and Al Gore came to Madison. Russ Feingold, Democratic candidate for the U.S. Senate, and I were on the capitol steps with them, and there were 30,000 people in the audience. Attorney General Jim Doyle introduced me and said very nice things. There also was a phalanx of media from all across the country.

On election day, polls closed at 8:00 P.M., and we knew that I had lost by about 9:30. I was not really surprised, but I was disappointed. I made a public statement conceding the election and congratulating Scott Klug on his victory. I thanked my supporters and promised to continue the struggle for peace and justice. Overall, it was a good night for Wisconsin Democrats. Feingold won the U.S. Senate seat and Clinton won the presidency. We shared in that victory because my phone-bank callers always said, "I am calling from the Ada Deer campaign. Don't forget to vote. Please vote for Ada as well as Feingold and Clinton." I found their victories very satisfying. Despite my loss, I ended my campaign still determined to make a difference.

Although I never won a state office or a congressional seat, I enjoyed the experience of campaigning. I appreciated the opportunity to promote racial and economic justice. I also met many wonderful people, heard their stories, and thought about what might improve their circumstances. This is a great nation, but it is not a nation without problems. Poverty, racism, sexism, unemployment, large numbers of incarcerated people, underfunded education, unregulated money in politics, foreign intervention—the list goes on. I am convinced, however, that these problems have solutions. Government can be a force for good, but only if we demand it through our participation in the political process.

CHAPTER 8

▪ In the Belly of the Beast ▪

I realize that my optimism about government sounds naïve, but it remained intact. Although I lost the congressional election, Bill Clinton and Al Gore ran a great race and won. Russ Feingold, a Democrat, became Wisconsin's new U.S. senator. After a short break, I huddled with my troops to talk about working in the Clinton-Gore administration. I had worked and lived in Washington before and, although I was not eager to return, I had real hope for change in Indian policy. After twelve years of Republican budget cutting under Presidents Reagan and Bush, I looked forward to greater federal support for education, health care, job creation, and social justice. Furthermore, President Clinton promised that his administration would "look like America," and I wanted to make sure that Indian people were visible and that their ideas were voiced, not just on Indian affairs but on all national issues.

So I embarked on a new campaign, one for an appointment to a policy-level position in Washington. I knew lots of people, of course, from lobbying for Menominee restoration and working for NARF. Lydia Bickford and Jon Holt-shopple, who had run my congressional campaign, began to search *United States Policies and Supporting Positions,* called the "Plum Book" because of its color, for possible positions. I was particularly interested in an appointment as assistant secretary in one of the departments that I thought could benefit from my training and experience as a social worker. In particular, Education, Health, and Human Services; Housing and Urban Development; or Interior seemed good fits. It took a lot of hard work, strategy, and support from my friends. The position I was best suited for in the Department of Education was filled, but I got interviews with

HUD and Interior. Both assistant secretary positions—public and Indian housing at HUD and Indian affairs at Interior—had to do with Indians. I welcomed these opportunities, but I was also a bit irked. If you are an Indian in this society, people tend to put you in a box. Apparently, Indians can only work with Indians, but whites can work with anyone. Nevertheless, I realized that much of my support for an assistant secretary position had come from tribes and Native organizations and that, in either position, I could serve Indian people.

I met with the secretaries of these departments when I was in Washington for the inauguration. The first interview I had was with Secretary Henry Cisneros of HUD. I liked him a lot, and we had a really nice chat. He had already filled the position of assistant secretary for public and Indian housing with a candidate who had extensive experience with urban housing but none, as far as I knew, with Indians. Secretary Cisneros, however, did offer me a job as "special assistant." I replied, "That doesn't sound like 'assistant secretary' to me!" He smiled and asked me why I wanted to be assistant secretary. "Power and money," I replied, and we had a good laugh. But the real reason I wanted such a position was that an assistant secretary can in theory make policy while a special assistant is merely an adjunct to the secretary. As I left, Secretary Cisneros thanked me for the interview, which was very nice. When our paths subsequently crossed, I always enjoyed seeing him.

I next met with Secretary of the Interior Bruce Babbitt about the position of assistant secretary for Indian affairs, the office which heads the BIA. Washington rumors indicated that my chief competition was Peterson Zah, president of the Navajo Nation. An extraordinarily competent leader, Zah reportedly was the choice of Republican Senator John McCain of Arizona. However, the White House, particularly First Lady Hillary Clinton, apparently wanted me in this position, as did Donna Shalala at Health and Human Services. At our meeting, Secretary Babbitt and I exchanged pleasantries and then got down to business. Unlike the position at HUD, this job entailed every aspect of government involvement with Indians—law, politics, culture, economy, education, religion, and so on. Interestingly, we did not talk policy; we only chatted about my experience. I told him that I was an advocate and that, in this position, I would advocate for Native people. He replied, "You can count on leadership from me." He recommended me to President Clinton, who announced my nomination as assistant secretary of the interior for Indian affairs in May 1993.

The next step was Senate confirmation. Several people, including Herman Viola from the Smithsonian; Wyman Babby, who was a BIA area director;

Menominee Michael Chapman; and Faith Roessel, who ran the Navajo Nation's Washington office, helped prepare me for the Senate hearing. They were tough, and they challenged me to think about responses to possible claims that I was not fully prepared, that I saw the BIA as the enemy, and that I "shot from the lips" without thinking. I had individual appointments with some members of the Senate Committee on Indian Affairs, which Senator Daniel Inouye of Hawaii chaired. Senator John McCain of Arizona was one of the members of the committee; he would become chair after the Republicans' 1994 election victories. Colorado Senator Ben Nighthorse Campbell, a Northern Cheyenne and the only Indian in the Senate, was on the committee as well.

In July, I met with the committee as a whole and delivered a speech that my old friend Charles Wilkinson helped me write. I told them about my role in the struggle for Menominee restoration and how that experience led me to a deep appreciation for Indian tribal sovereignty. For the BIA, I envisioned a tribal-federal partnership that rested on recognition of and respect for tribal sovereignty. The days of federal paternalism had ended. I called instead on the federal government to support and help implement tribally inspired solutions to tribally defined problems. I reminded them, however, that tribal sovereignty did not mean one size fits all. Each tribe had its own problems that demanded different solutions. I voiced my support for amendments to the Indian Self-Determination and Education Assistance Act, passed in 1975, in order to give tribes more control over contracting to provide services funded by the federal government. I endorsed working groups to address the Native American Free Exercise of Religion Act. The BIA I envisioned would be a partner with tribes, not a supervisor.

As soon as I completed my remarks, Senator Campbell said, "Let's vote!" Everyone laughed, but the committee did not vote immediately. Instead, they moved on to questions. I found the issues the committee members raised to be very revealing of their attitudes toward Indians and Indian policy. Senator Inouye, for example, asked about impending budget cuts and a recent report on reservation schools that was critical of personnel and school boards. As one of the longest-serving senators, he fully understood the impact of waxing and waning budgets.

Senator McCain was interested in investment tax credits and economic development. He also pointed out that tribal sovereignty and self-government would put the BIA out of business. He was critical of the BIA's budget forecasting, which had led to a significant shortfall in contract support funds, the disarray in the Indian Trust Fund, and the role of the Office of Management and Budget in determining Indian policy. And finally, he brought up the issues of child abuse and alcohol and drug abuse. I appreciated his raising these issues, and I told the committee, "Learning is a two-way process. Sometimes I am the tutor, sometimes I am the tutee." The members laughed again.

Senator Campbell came next. He was concerned about the dramatic cuts that were on the way for the IHS. Indians already were not receiving adequate health care, and in the proposed budget, the IHS was expected to suffer 40 percent of the total cuts to health care. He also raised questions about the federal recognition process. Some tribes had tried to bypass the process, established in 1978, that conferred official status on tribes and made them eligible for BIA services. Instead, these tribes appealed to Congress for legislative recognition. My hope, which I expressed, was to be able to work with the BIA, Congress, and the tribes to reach compromises on these issues.

Senator Mark Hatfield of Oregon cited the termination of Oregon tribes, which happened at the same time as Menominee termination. Restoration for most of these sixty-one tribes, however, came with consolidation into three tribes, without restoration of an adequate land base. He appreciated that I understood their problems firsthand.

Washington Senator Slade Gorton raised the issue of Indian gaming, which was in its infancy, and asked for a timetable for my policy on gaming. I, of course, had no timetable since I did not yet have the job. He pointed out that many non-Indians live on reservations in his state and wanted to know if their views would influence my decisions. I expressed my commitment to hearing all sides and my belief in fairness, but I also pointed out that my primary responsibility was to Indians. I couldn't resist adding that non-Indians on reservations "have you and others to represent them." Senator Gorton was the Washington attorney general who had argued and lost the Boldt Decision that affirmed Native fishing rights. He was not sympathetic to tribal sovereignty; indeed, he was downright hostile.

So was Senator Frank Murkowski of Alaska. He asserted the superiority of the corporate structure imposed on Indigenous Alaskans in which Native villages were grouped into thirteen corporations. Unlike tribes, corporations do not have sovereignty, but Senator Murkowski believed that capitalism was the solution to the "Indian problem" and that this corporate structure was superior to reservations, which made Indians wards of the government. I had been to Alaska several times, and I knew that there were serious problems with these corporations, but I held my tongue.

The hearing finally concluded, and I received a unanimous vote for confirmation as well as a standing ovation. The recommendation to confirm went to the full Senate, where I once again was approved unanimously. I took the oath of office on August 7, my fifty-eighth birthday, at the Menominee powwow, where I received eagle feathers, a symbol of power. I chose the reservation rather than Washington for my public swearing in not only because it was home but also because it represented what Indians could do. Although Congress had dismantled our reservation and revoked our sovereignty, Menominees had worked together to reverse termination and restore our nation. By selecting that location, I intended to send a powerful message about my commitment to tribal sovereignty. Apparently the message got through. A congressional staffer declared, "That lady is a freight train and she's leaving the station!"

Several thousand people attended the public swearing-in ceremony. Among them was my father, who died five months later on January 10, 1994. By then the cabin on the Wolf River had burned, and he lived in a rooming house in Gresham run by a nice woman who took in elderly boarders. Years of alcoholism had taken a toll, and I am not sure he understood what was going on, but I like to believe that he was proud of his eldest daughter.

The challenges were enormous, but the Deer was there to work. The Indian Self-Determination and Education Act of 1975 empowered tribes to exercise their sovereignty and to enter into contracts with the federal government for services. In one sense, Indians now had the authority to shape their own destiny, but the loss of land and resources as well as decades of federal paternalism followed by efforts to terminate tribes had left serious problems in Indian Country. According to the 1990 census, more than 30 percent of American Indians lived below the federal poverty level and one-fourth of working-age adults were unemployed. Indians suffered disproportionately from alcoholism, tuberculosis, diabetes, and other illnesses, as well as from homicide and suicide. I was eager to address these and a host of other problems.

The BIA at that time served approximately one million Native people who belonged to 550 tribes, and it administered more than 42 million acres of tribal land, ten million individually owned acres, and nearly half a million acres of public lands. There were twelve area offices, 83 agency offices, three subagencies, six field stations, and two irrigation projects. The assistant secretary dealt primarily with policy. Administration rested with the deputy commissioner of Indian affairs and the director of the Office of Indian Education Programs. The commissioner supervised directors of economic development, management and administration, tribal services, trust responsibilities, and trust fund management. The director of Indian education programs supervised 26 line officers, 114 day schools, fifty on-reservation and six off-reservation boarding schools, and fourteen dormitories for public-school students. Also under the auspices of the director were the Haskell Indian Nation University, the Southwestern Indian Polytechnic Institute, the Johnson O'Malley program that provided financial support to state-funded schools enrolling Indians, and tribal colleges.

The first thing I needed to do was appoint a staff to fill open positions in the bureau. Michael Chapman had already come onboard as an assistant to manage the transition. Michael was Menominee. His mother had been on the Voting Trust before restoration, and we did not always see eye-to-eye. But Michael was smart and talented, and I have always believed that it is important to bridge gaps between people. During the fight for restoration, Michael edited a newsletter, and he worked on my campaigns. I was comfortable with Michael and trusted him.

Just like the president wanted his administration to "look like America," I wanted the BIA to look like Native America. In some respects it already did. The BIA claimed that 90 percent of employees were Indians but, whatever the proportion of Indians, women were underrepresented, especially in the higher offices. I decided to appoint Indian women to my staff whenever I could. By 1996, I had appointed two women to senior political positions and elevated five career employees of the BIA to the Senior Executive Service. Among these women were Faith Roessel, a Navajo, and Elizabeth Homer, an Osage. Both were lawyers. Faith had been a staff attorney for NARF and director of the Navajo Nation's Washington Office. I appointed her deputy assistant secretary for Indian affairs. Elizabeth moved from the Justice Department to head the Office of American Indian Trust. I also appointed Joann Sebastian Morris, Sault Ste. Marie Chippewa, director of the Office of Indian Education. Nancy Jemison, Seneca, became director of economic development.

I wanted the BIA to reflect Native values of community. For a start, I decided to replace the rectangular conference table in my office. "Do we have any round tables?" I asked the people who handled such things. Back they came with a little round table the size of a postage stamp. I took one look at it and said, "Can you find me the largest round table in the warehouse?" This time they came back with a table that seated twelve. People would come in my office and look around for a place to sit. "Well, sit at the table," I would tell them. "It's a round table. We can work on this together." Almost no one ever got it. They were always wondering who was going to be at the head of the table.

I moved from rearranging the furniture to humanizing the building, which was pretty soulless. One idea came from a meeting that First Lady Hillary Clinton held with women political appointees. She urged us to be sensitive to the special needs of women employees. I thought about that and decided to create a family room where relatives, especially children, could wait and nursing mothers could pump breast milk. I hoped that in this and other ways I could make the BIA less bureaucratic, but I am afraid I was trying to make a silk purse from a sow's ear. Reportedly, when Kevin Gover replaced me, he brought back the long rectangular table. I don't know what happened to the family room. I hope it is still there.

In September 1993, I took a listening tour to New Mexico, South Dakota, Alaska, and Oklahoma. Senator Tom Daschle accompanied me to Pine Ridge, South Dakota. The First Nations Development Institute sponsored a roundtable on economic development, and we listened while tribal leaders described poverty on this reservation, where 63 percent of people lived below the federal poverty line. One of their problems was the fractionalization of land that occurred when people did not write wills and probate courts divided holdings among all heirs. The result was that tracts were too small to support any economic activity. I urged them to take action against this. The big problem, however, was lack of funding, which was going to be difficult to solve, given the funding situation in Washington. I did learn about local initiatives including a micro-banking project that gave small business loans. When I left, Chairman Duane Big Eagle of the Crow Creek Sioux told me, "We pray that your heart will always remain Native American, and that you don't get lost in the bureaucratic system somewhere." I hoped so too.

When I arrived in Alaska, Willie Hensley, an Iñupiaq who was first elected to the Alaska House of Representatives in 1966, introduced me: "We used to have a Great White Father, but now we have a Big Brown Mama!" I did not need an introduction since I had been to Alaska many times, and I was well acquainted with Alaska Natives' situation. But I really appreciated that introduction.

When the United States purchased Alaska in 1867, officials discovered that the Russians had not made treaties with Native peoples, so there was no legal recognition of tribal sovereignty or Native land. Although the Alaska Statehood Act pledged to recognize Native land claims, the federal government began to transfer title of 104.5 million acres to the state without paying much attention to Native claims. The Alaska Native Claims Settlement Act of 1971 tried to resolve the problem by creating twelve regional corporations. (Congress added a thirteenth in 1975.) Each Alaska Native received one hundred shares in a corporation, and the corporations received a total of 44 million acres and nearly one billion dollars.

Doc Tate Nevaquaya, Comanche artist and musician, and
Ada Deer in a Gourd Dance during her visit to Oklahoma.

What the Alaska people did not retain was their ability to govern themselves as sovereign peoples. They were merely stockholders in corporations. The Alaska Natives' situation reminded me of that of the Menominees during termination. MTE had controlled our forests and mills. We had no political institutions through which we could govern ourselves or manage our property, much less carry on government-to-government relations with the federal government. Essentially, Native Alaskan tribes and villages had been terminated. I was interested in trying to help them gain sovereign status.

Secretary Babbitt accompanied me for part of this trip, but he did not sit in on the meeting with the Alaska Inter-Tribal Council where I pledged my support for tribal—not corporate—rights. When we stopped at Togiak, local Native people confronted us about the plan to remove the reindeer herd from Hagemeister Island and begged us to leave fifty reindeer there for subsistence hunting. The reindeer, which had been introduced a century earlier, were destroying the native lichen. The previous year there had been a controversial slaughter of reindeer that left edible carcasses to rot and left injured reindeer to die on the island. Secretary Babbitt promised to consider their views. We then went to Fairbanks, where we attended the annual meeting of the Alaska Federation of Natives. I addressed the group and made it clear that I supported federal recognition of Alaska Native villages and tribes. Such a move would validate their sovereignty, a status that the Native corporations did not confer. But before we even left Alaska, Secretary Babbitt ordered all reindeer removed from Hagemeister Island.

In Shiprock, New Mexico, I attended a groundbreaking ceremony for a Navajo museum and library. I pledged to heed President Zah's suggestion that I turn the BIA upside down and shake it, but I also made a plea that the tribes stop bickering among themselves and direct their energy toward lobbying for change. All tribes have distinct interests, many of which compete with those of other tribes. For the Navajos, tribal differences included a long-standing land dispute with their Hopi neighbors, which I wanted them to resolve. Despite dispensing advice, which I tend to do freely, I promised to consult with tribes, seek their guidance, and shift Indian policy away from paternalism.

Not long after I got back to Washington I heard a rumor that the White House was going to hold a meeting of Indians. I called a staff person in Interior and said, "I hear that there's going to be some kind of meeting in the White House involving Indians, and I don't know about it. I would like to because I am the assistant secretary for Indian affairs." She told me that yes, indeed, there was to be such a meeting. I told her that if the president was going to hold a meeting in the White House, he had to invite all tribes, not just the "Washington Redskins" and their buddies. (By "Washington Redskins," I meant Indians who lived and worked permanently in the District of Columbia, not the football team with the appallingly racist name.) The White House listened and invited all the tribes.

In April 1994 more than three hundred Indians came to the White House. I don't think that there had ever been that kind of meeting of tribal leaders. They pitched a huge tent on the White House lawn, and put out rows of chairs, including chairs at the front for federal officials. The funny thing is that there was no chair for me. Everyone else was sitting down, and there I was, standing up. Finally, Secretary Cisneros got me a chair from somewhere. We both laughed about it. Nothing could spoil this wonderful meeting.

President Clinton addressed the audience in his usual charming way: "Welcome to the White House. Welcome home.... This great historic meeting today must be the beginning of our new partnership, not the end of it." Gaiashkibos, president of the National Congress of the American Indian and chairman of the Lac Court Oreilles, and Wilma Mankiller, principal chief of the Cherokee Nation of Oklahoma, presided. Leaders from all over the country had an opportunity to raise issues with the president of the United States, who took notes throughout the meeting. Tribal leaders spoke on a variety of subjects including religious freedom, jurisdiction over natural resources, law enforcement, reservation poverty, education, and housing. They also raised funding issues, especially budget cuts. But one issue seemed to undergird the entire discussion. Cheyenne River Sioux Chairman Greg Bourland perhaps said it best: "Sovereignty burns in my heart. I look around me and I see sovereignty." He received a standing ovation. President Clinton signed two executive orders. The first instructed departments to work with tribes to accommodate requests for eagle feathers to use in religious ceremonies. The second mandated agencies to remove barriers to working with tribes and to consult with tribes on any issue that affected trust lands.

Soon after this event, I attended an Interior Department meeting about a water project in the West. I had not received a briefing, which was not unusual. I sat quietly and listened until I just couldn't stand it. "Excuse me," I said. "I would like to ask a question." Everyone stared at me. "Have the tribes been consulted?" There was a long silence, and I thought that no one had heard me. I raised my voice, "Have the tribes been consulted?" No one answered, so I said, "I can conclude from the silence that they haven't. This is the Clinton administration. There is a policy of consultation, and the tribes need to be consulted on this. All these decisions cannot be made in area offices or the central office here. We need to consult the tribes." That was the end of the meeting. I thought to myself, "Well, I didn't make any friends in that room, but at least they heard the message."

The administration followed up on the Washington meeting with a National American Indian Listening Conference in Albuquerque, which drew about six hundred people from 240 tribes. We had developed a list of possible topics for discussion in small groups, and tribal leaders selected those they found most relevant. The first was responsibility for the use and management of tribal land, water, and natural resources with particular focus on water rights; the scope of tribal control over resources; the application of the Endangered Species Act to Indian tribes; and the development of tribal environmental codes for Indian Country. Second was the Native American Free Exercise of Religion Act with questions concerning the use of eagle feathers and the applicability of the act to non-federally recognized tribes and the Bureau of Prisons. Next was the status of tribal governments and courts; in particular, the relationship between tribal, federal, and state courts. The next two were criminal justice and law enforcement and delinquency prevention. Sixth was gaming, including state compacts and organized crime.

Attorney General Janet Reno, Secretary Babbitt, IHS Director Michael Trujillo, and I attended. Tribal Chairman Eddie Tullis, of the Poarch Creeks in Alabama, raised the issue of states like his that refused to enter into gaming compacts with tribes, recalcitrance he attributed to racism. Members of the Jemez Pueblo brought up several issues that included the teaching of tribal history in Pueblo schools, public access to archaeological sites, and increases in fees for grazing livestock on public lands. Hopi Chairman Ferrell Secakuku cited long-standing conflicts with the Navajos; in particular, the lack of drinking water caused by the Peabody Coal Company's diversion of water for coal slurry. The secretary of the interior was aware of many of these issues, but now they were all being thrown at him at the same time. I think the attorney general, whose experience with Indians had been limited largely to the Seminoles, was in shock. I already admired Attorney General Reno, but I gained additional respect for her at that meeting. She listened carefully to the delegates, answered their questions thoughtfully, and interacted with them respectfully. Her presence deeply touched many of the people there. When she returned to Washington, she established the Office of Native American Affairs to assist in intertribal disputes and conflicts with the federal government.

I visited as many Indian tribes as I could. By the end of 1995, I had traveled to eighteen states and held more than 250 meetings with tribes. There is nothing quite like meeting people personally and seeing where they live and work. Looking back, it seems like I was constantly packing and unpacking, but visiting Indian tribes and communities was among the most satisfying parts of my job. I got to hear about the specific problems of tribes and see firsthand the remarkable things they were doing. These visits were also frustrating because they made clear what the BIA should be doing, but between bureaucratic hurdles and budget cuts, not much of it was likely to get done. My experiences further convinced me that tribes needed more control over their own budgets, the right to determine their own priorities, and the ability to contract for the services they decided they needed.

When I was in Washington, I was constantly on the go. For example, one day in the fall of 1993, I began my day at the office, as I usually did, at 8:00 A.M. I met with Wyman Babby, acting deputy commissioner of Indian affairs. At

8:45, I chaired a staff meeting and then attended a conference on the Office of Indian Education Programs budget. By 10:30, I was discussing the Circle of Women film project with the filmmakers. Forty-five minutes later, I met with the regional director for the Eastern Area Region, which included all federally recognized Indian tribes east of Texas, Oklahoma, and Kansas and north to and including Maine. I had only fifteen minutes with the regional director, just enough time to say "Hello, Goodbye," to quote the Beatles. At 11:00 there was a Management Control and Audit follow-up. I often had lunch appointments, but that day I must have eaten at my desk because there is nothing on the calendar until 1:30 P.M. Then I met with the chairwoman of the Ute Mountain Ute Tribal Council, Judy Knight-Frank, who had been elected the previous year in a very contentious election in which her opponents had resorted to personal attacks and complaints to the FBI. A difficult conference with Madeleine Jeffery followed. She was a white woman from North Stonington, Connecticut, who opposed Pequot acquisition of land. I had visited her community earlier in the fall and had little sympathy for her position. I had to leave at 3:45 for the Department of Education for a meeting on Indian education. I did not have a dinner or reception that night, so I was able to go home and collapse. This was just one day pulled from my calendar, but I could not call it typical. There was no such thing as a typical day: the script and the cast of characters constantly changed. What remained the same was how packed full every day was.

Budget issues, however, cropped up most days. Federal funding reached tribes in several ways. Traditionally, the BIA provided services, such as education, directly to tribes by, for example, setting curriculum and hiring teachers. Since passage of the 1975 Self Determination and Education Assistance Act (Public Law 93-638), however, some Indian tribes had begun contracting with the BIA to run their own schools, law-enforcement agencies, housing authorities, resource management, and other programs. BIA provided the funding but tribes administered the programs. As well as expanding the exercise of sovereignty, contracting meant that a higher percentage of funding went to tribes rather than remaining under the auspices of federal agencies. In 1993, nineteen tribes had contracts with the BIA; by 1994 the number had risen to twenty-nine. Contracting, I thought, was central to enhancing tribal sovereignty. At the same time, since it was federal money, the BIA needed to provide some supervision, at least in the short term.

In 1994 Congress amended the 1975 act to enable tribes to enter into self-governing compacts that broadened their discretionary authority and simplified the process by which they provided their own services. Compacts set forth the terms of tribal self-government and the tribe's relationship with federal entities. Compacting, it seemed to me, moved the BIA even further away from the old pattern of paternalism. At first, tribes were inexperienced in managing programs for themselves. Indians were not born capitalists, and many of them grew up in societies that operate on a more cooperative basis. There were some bumps along the road. But ultimately contracting and compacting enabled Indians to exercise their sovereignty more fully. A number of Republicans in Congress, including Arizona Senator John McCain, favored a third scheme—block grants—that essentially would have done away with the BIA.

We managed to stop the block grant proposals. Because tribal circumstances vary so dramatically, no one system is likely to work well for all tribes. The really small tribes usually did not have the human resources or technical expertise to meet the needs of their members, so they required more BIA help, while the larger tribes and those with a cohort of highly educated members needed the BIA less. In Indian Country, one size does not fit all. Nevertheless, my emphasis on sovereignty meant shifting more of the responsibility for designing and implementing programs to tribes.

I had barely warmed the seat of my desk chair when the White House asked every federal agency to make a 10 percent budget cut. Instead, I asked for a one-billion-dollar increase in the BIA budget. I did not get it. This cut marked the beginning of the budget wars. President George H. W. Bush's administration had ended with the economy in recession. President Clinton proposed to counter the economic downturn by cutting the budget so that he could lower taxes, spur private investment, and stimulate the economy. He succeeded (and ended up with three fiscal years of budget surpluses), but the human cost was substantial.

President Clinton took office with a Democratic majority in both houses of Congress. Budget negotiations for fiscal year (FY) 1994 were well underway when I took office, and I was largely excluded from developing the budget for FY 1995. (Federal budget years run October 1 to September 30, and fiscal years bear the date of the concluding year.) Requests came up to the BIA from the tribes, agencies, and area offices. The BIA budget director sent our requests to the Interior Department, which incorporated whatever they saw fit into their request, which went to Congress. Somewhere along the way the Office of Management and Budget came in. This happened annually and took up an enormous amount of employee time. My job was basically defensive—I had to defend the BIA budget before the House Appropriations Committee. Doing so became increasingly difficult.

The real budget crisis came when the Republicans took control of both houses of Congress in January 1995 and, later that year, presented their budget for FY 1996. There had not been such an all-out attack on tribal sovereignty since termination. The proposed budget that Congress presented contained massive cuts, especially to the BIA. These cuts included funding for tribal courts, business development on reservations, drug and alcohol programs, education, housing, welfare, summer youth programs, and job training. More than a third of BIA jobs were threatened. In addition to BIA personnel, many reservation jobs held by Indians were on the chopping block. With reservation unemployment at 46 percent, these cuts promised to be disastrous. It was termination by appropriation. I began preparing to lay off between 2,600 and 4,000 of the BIA's 12,000 employees. I pledged to make cuts that spared teachers, but this threatened the administration of programs guaranteed by treaty.

In September 1995, approximately two hundred tribal leaders arrived in Washington for a weeklong lobbying effort. They held a rally on the steps of the Capitol and pitched a teepee, but this did little to resolve the impasse. I went over there to lend my support, an act that Secretary of the Interior Bruce Babbitt frowned upon. But how could I serve the tribes and not join them? Ultimately, the budget crisis did bring many tribes and the BIA together in the same struggle because most tribes realized that the cuts to the BIA directly affected them.

Anti-Indian prejudice on Capitol Hill was obvious. At one hearing of the Senate Appropriations Committee, Washington Senator Slade Gorton asked me how long these welfare payments to Indians were going to continue. I could not believe it. I was certain he knew better. "Excuse me, Senator," I said. "These are not welfare payments. As you know, this country was built on Indian land with Indian resources, and treaties lay out the nation's obligations to Indians, and treaties are the supreme law of the land. These are permanent obligations and will continue." I could hear the air being sucked out of the room, but I would not cave in to Slade Gorton. I realized that he was expressing the views of many people, that Indians are just welfare dependents who should be grateful for what they got and that government was doing too much for them, but silence on my part might have been interpreted as acceptance. I was *not* having that!

Some people held me responsible for the budget cuts. The chairman of the Cheyenne River Sioux, for example, claimed that I did not advocate for Indians and accused me of being "meek," a word I don't think anyone else has ever used to describe me. But others realized that I was doing all I could. I was in an extraordinarily difficult position. Both the Republican Congress and President Clinton wanted to balance the federal budget and make a significant reduction in the deficit. They disagreed on where cuts should be made and how quickly, but their goal hamstrung those of us who were trying to meet the nation's legal commitments. I found little sympathy in Secretary Bruce Babbitt, who blocked me from going to Capitol Hill to defend the BIA's budget while he permitted other Interior agencies to lobby for theirs. Plans were afoot in Indian Country to press for direct funding so that tribes could then decide whether they wanted to contribute to support of the BIA, and Congress floated the idea of funneling money to tribes through the states, a clear violation of tribal sovereignty and federal treaties.

Budget negotiations for FY 1996 dragged on for seven months and through twelve continuing resolutions. When the president vetoed the spending bill Congress sent him, the government closed twice for a total of twenty-seven days. Finally, in February 1996, I ordered a reduction in force in order to live within the budget finally approved. Nearly 900 BIA employees accepted a buyout, and approximately 1,000 vacant positions remained unfilled. I reassigned, downgraded, or dismissed another 700 people. The final federal budget cut the BIA spending by 15 percent over the FY 1995 budget. This affected a wide range of services for which the BIA was responsible, among them an education system for 51,800 elementary and secondary school students, twenty-four tribally controlled colleges, law enforcement and detention on more than 200 reservations, social service programs, management of more than 56 million acres of trust land, and 25 thousand miles of roads on isolated reservations.

The money problems confronting the BIA extended beyond budget cuts. I inherited an investigation into the mismanagement of Indian trust funds that required an accounting of the funds and the development of a more responsible management plan. The BIA is accountable for more than two thousand trust accounts belonging to two hundred tribes, and 17,000 accounts belonging to 288,000 individual Indians, which had been fractionalized through inheritance. The funds in the accounts came from leases that the government had negotiated for the sale of timber, oil, minerals, and other natural resources on Indian land. Long before I took office, Congress had recommended that the BIA reform its management of these accounts, but apparently no one at BIA took these recommendations seriously. Indians were largely in the dark about what was going on until the mid-1980s when Elouise Cobell, the treasurer of the Blackfeet

Nation, discovered that the money literally did not add up. Tribes demanded a full accounting, which, due to poor record keeping, proved impossible to do.

By the time I took office, a plan to reorganize the trust funds office had been languishing for two years with little effort to implement it. Among the many letters I received concerning individual trust funds was one from a Comanche man in Oklahoma who was one of thirty heirs to his grandfather's allotment. The allotment included a spring, which the BIA held in trust and had leased to a rural water district for forty-five years. He had just discovered that his family received only 13 percent of the fair market value for the water. His situation illustrated two problems that were widespread in Indian Country—the fractionalization of family holdings and the BIA's shortcomings in fulfilling its trust responsibilities. He had written the BIA many times, asking them to correct the problem, but had heard nothing. Unlike this man, many Indians did not even realize how badly managed their trusts were until Elouise Cobell and others began to ask questions. They organized the Intertribal Monitoring Association, and contacted NARF.

In 1994 as a result of the irregularities exposed, Congress enacted the Indian Trust Fund Management Reform Act, introduced by Democratic Representative Mike Synar of Oklahoma. Among other things, the legislation required accounting for and reporting of trust fund balances as well as making payments from the funds. Tribes gained a role in management of their accounts and the right to withdraw funds from them. A grant program enabled tribes to receive training to manage their accounts and invest the proceeds from their trust funds.

The legislation also provided for the appointment of a special trustee to conduct an investigation over the next year. That job fell to Paul Homan, who described record keeping for the Indian trust accounts as "the worst that I have ever seen." Between 1973 and 1992, there was $2.4 billion in tribal trust funds that could not be accounted for. Thousands of individual accounts contained money for which there was no documentation and/or no addresses for the holders. Interior provided little help, and Congress coughed up little money. It was a mess. As a result, in 1996, NARF filed suit against Secretary Babbitt, the secretary of the treasury, and others on behalf of 300,000 individual Indian Money Account holders. Although I was named in the suit, I realized that this was not personal. They were suing the office of the assistant secretary, not Ada Deer individually. My office shared responsibility for the debacle and had to be held accountable. As for NARF, I continued to have a good relationship with them.

The case, *Cobell v. Salazar,* dragged on for years after I left office, and my successors took my place in the suit. Finally, in 2009, President Barack Obama signed a settlement that pledged $1.5 billion to 300,000 account holders. The settlement also provided an additional $1.9 billion to pay Indians who wanted to sell fractionalized land to the federal government to be held in trust for their tribes. This enabled Indians to unload tracts too small to be profitable and tribes to consolidate tracts for economic development projects. In 2012 the federal government resolved the claims of forty-one tribes in a settlement that amounted to $1.023 billion.

Assistant secretary was a hard job. My days and often evenings were packed with appointments and events, and I always seemed to be traveling. Furthermore, the budget cuts were a source of constant anxiety. Every time the budget came up, I felt like I was singing just another depressing verse of the same song. But I also knew I was doing something important by constantly reminding the government that the United States had obligations to the Native people whose land the nation occupied.

I was surprised by the lack of interest in, ignorance of, and even hostility toward Native people at the highest levels of government. When budget cuts came, Indian programs suffered disproportionately under the acquiescence and perhaps direction of the secretary of the interior. When the White House decided to hold a conference on Indians, the planners thought they could choose a handful of participants drawn from local Indians or a few tribes without appreciating that tribes have elected representative and that each tribe has a unique set of concerns. Whenever an opportunity arose, people like Senator Slade Gordon and other like-minded members of Congress tried to impoverish Native people and deny tribal sovereignty.

The BIA was also beset with internal problems. Many wonderful, sincere people worked there, but in an institution that large and complex, friction occurred. Budget cuts exacerbated tensions as offices, programs, and agencies competed for funding and jockeyed for influence. A majority of the personnel at the BIA were Native, and sometimes there was tension between Indians and non-Indians. In one ugly incident, an anonymous flyer circulated demanding that African Americans (but using a pejorative term) leave the bureau. I was appalled. Furthermore, the Indians came from many different tribes, so they did not necessarily share the same views and priorities. Yet the diversity, I thought, was a source of the BIA's strength—it really did look like Native America. And I recognized that Indians, like other people, do not always agree.

CHAPTER 9

▪ Sovereignty ▪

The defense and expansion of tribal sovereignty were the priorities of my administration. Sovereignty is the right of a people to govern themselves, and tribal sovereignty is the cornerstone of Native relations with the United States. The U.S. Constitution implies tribal sovereignty by granting the federal government exclusive power to regulate trade with Indian tribes, just as it does with foreign governments and the states. Treaties negotiated between the United States and the tribes express and validate sovereignty since treaties are made only between sovereign powers. The U.S. Supreme Court, in cases dating from the 1830s, has upheld tribal sovereignty. Because tribes are sovereign, the United States has had to coerce or deceive them into agreeing to removal from ancestral homelands, confinement to reservations, allotment of tribally owned land to individuals, or termination of their sovereign status as Indian tribes. I had seen firsthand what happens when the United States deprives a tribe of its sovereignty, and I was determined not to let that happen to any tribe on my watch. In fact, my administration saw an expansion of tribal sovereignty, often after hard-fought battles.

My most significant accomplishment in this area was the acknowledgment of 226 Alaska Native villages and tribes. Alaska villages and tribes had acted as sovereign entities before the 1971 Native Claims Settlement Act, although they had no treaty relationship with the United States. The U.S. failure to recognize their sovereignty in that act had troubled me during my September 1993 visit to Alaska with Secretary Babbitt. Therefore, when I returned to Washington, I started the wheels moving to make things right. In October, I attended the annual conference of the Alaska Federation of Natives and announced that I had officially acknowledged them as sovereign. Federal recognition of these villages and tribes, however, did not confer on them authority over the corporations that controlled their land, an issue with which they still struggle. I feel some satisfaction in making a degree of progress on this issue, although much still remains to be done in terms of securing Native Alaskans the right to control their resources. The federal government also has a trust responsibility to protect tribes, but tribal sovereignty means that tribes have the right to manage their own affairs and to set citizenship criteria and determine who meets those criteria.

Problems arose, however, when tribes did not seem to be following their own rules and instead admitted people who did qualify for citizenship according to tribal constitutions. Few non–Native Americans wanted to be Indians until the 1990s. The "*Dances with Wolves* syndrome" was perhaps partly responsible for this shift: this 1990 film gave a sympathetic, romanticized version of nineteenth-century Native life. But more compelling was gaming income. The U.S. Supreme Court's decision in *California v. Cabazon Band of Mission Indians* (1987) freed federally recognized tribes from state restrictions on gaming, and a few tribes began raking in big profits from tribal casinos. Almost everyone with a tentative claim to tribal citizenship wanted in. And unscrupulous tribal leaders were not above admitting them in order to secure their own political and economic power.

One of the most contentious cases I had to deal with, but by no means the only one, came from the Shakopee Mdewakanton Dakota Community in Minnesota. The Shakopee people were descendants of the Sioux who had suffered defeat in the 1862 uprising against the United States, which subsequently revoked their treaties. In 1969 the federal government once again recognized them as a tribe, an act that restored their sovereignty. At that time, the Shakopee tribe had thirteen members, but by 1994, the population had risen to 255. A group of tribal members contested the legitimacy of some enrollees and filed suit in federal court against the tribal government, the BIA, and the Interior Department. The suit alleged that these parties had violated the tribal constitution and several federal laws including the Indian Gaming Regulatory Act. The plaintiffs contended that 71 percent of the tribe's population, including many who lacked the required one-fourth blood quantum requirement, had been enrolled illegally while the tribal government, with the knowledge of the BIA, had delayed enrollment of legitimate applicants for citizenship. For new enrollees, a motivating factor almost certainly was the six-figure annual per-capita payment to tribal members from the proceeds of the tribe's Mystic Lake Casino. For tribal officials who were enrolling them, the motivation probably was control of the tribal government. The BIA, plaintiffs contended, had failed to protect tribal sovereignty by permitting unscrupulous elected officials to continue in office. The federal court dismissed the complaint.

The BIA, however, did rescind an ordinance enacted by the Shakopee General Council, which consisted of all tribal members, most of them recent enrollees. The ordinance had turned enrollment over to the representative tribal council and prohibited any appeal to the tribal court. The tribal constitution permitted changes in enrollment requirements by three-fourths majority vote, which the ordinance did not have. The council then presented a new constitution, which passed by a margin of eight votes with twenty-three votes being contested. I asked the Interior Department to appoint an administrative court judge to determine the voters' qualifications based on the current constitution. Then the tribal government sued me and Secretary Babbitt, but the tribe lost. In an unusual twist, AIM backed the BIA, because both AIM and the BIA advocated for tribal sovereignty and did not want to see it perverted by an unscrupulous tribal court. On the other hand, there was a limit to what the BIA could do while still respecting tribal sovereignty. I rejected the next tribal enrollment ordinance for a number of reasons, including a provision that would have submitted an enrollment application to popular vote and prohibited an appeal of disenrollment to the BIA. The whole mess dragged on long after I left office, and deep divisions in the tribe remain.

The Shakopee were by no means the only people to struggle with enrollment issues, and I cite them merely as an example. Most Indian tribes had lots of citizens with mixed ancestry, tribally, racially, and internationally. In my own family, my mother was white, my younger sister and brother married whites, another sister married a Sioux, and my older brother married a Wisconsin Oneida. According to the Menominee constitution, enrolled citizens had to be one-fourth Menominee. Because my paternal grandmother had some French ancestry, my siblings' children are less than one-fourth Menominee and, therefore, not entitled to Menominee citizenship. Ancestry from other tribes does not count. I am sorry that after my generation my family no longer will be Menominee citizens, but I honor the constitution and the tribe's right to determine who belongs.

Like U.S. citizens, not all tribal citizens agree on who is eligible for citizenship. When there is no consensus or clear majority, the BIA has to be the final arbiter, an act that jeopardizes tribal sovereignty. But exceedingly acrimonious disagreements that threaten tribal integrity require involvement by the BIA, which has a responsibility to protect tribes. We could not stand by and let tribal governments admit patently unqualified people to their rolls when doing so harmed legitimate citizens by cutting the per-capita pie, federal services, and other benefits into smaller pieces.

Another issue involving tribal citizenship emerged in 1996, but this one united Indian people of all nations. The House of Representatives considered the Adoption Promotion and Stability Act, which threatened to gut the 1978 ICWA. Congress had enacted the ICWA in 1978 to prevent the separation of Indian children from their families and tribes. In the 1960s and 1970s, effective contraception and changing attitudes about unmarried mothers had led to a decline in the number of infants, especially white infants, available for adoption. Therefore, families that wanted to adopt children sought infants from overseas or from nonwhite parents. Of the choices available to them, many prospective parents preferred American Indian babies, in part because of romantic images of Indians and in part because social workers often viewed Indian families as dysfunctional and sought to remove infants they believed to be in danger.

American Indians were (and are) the most impoverished group of Americans. They suffer disproportionately from unemployment, alcoholism, and other problems. All of this made child welfare officials suspicious of their parenting skills. But Indian children frequently lived with the members of their extended family best able to care for them instead of with their parents, a practice that reflected a broader interpretation of "family" than that to which most non-Indians subscribed. In the decades when termination was at the heart of federal Indian policy, tribes were largely powerless to intervene when authorities removed Indian children from their homes. Courts severed their legal ties to their tribes and gave them to non-Indian couples.

The ICWA put a stop to this practice. This law is based on the principle that the tribe to which an Indian child belongs is in a better position than a state or federal court to make decisions about what is best for that child. Congress intended to defer to Indian tribes on issues of cultural and social values and their role in bringing up a child. Furthermore, the ICWA preserves the integrity of tribes by preventing the loss of tribal members through adoption. If a tribe decides that a child meets its citizenship criteria, the child comes under the jurisdiction of the tribe and the provisions of the ICWA.

In 1996 Representative Susan Molinari, a Republican from New York, introduced the Adoption Promotion and Stability Act, which proposed to make interracial adoptions easier and to provide tax credits for adoptive families. The bill had broad support on both sides of the aisle and from President Clinton. But there also was opposition from both political parties. Representatives Don Young, a Republican from Alaska whose wife was Native (Gwich'n), and George Miller, a Democrat from California, recognized immediately that this one provision would gut the ICWA and resolved to defeat it. The ICWA had given tribes jurisdiction over Indian adoption cases in Indian Country and concurrent jurisdiction with state courts elsewhere. The proposed law also, in some cases, gave state courts the right to determine whether or not a child was a tribal member, a serious violation of sovereignty. In the fifteen years the law had been in effect, less than .1 percent of the adoption cases handled by tribal courts had been contested, largely because these courts understood tribal rules of kinship and the importance of extended families. Ultimately, we succeeded in getting these objectionable provisions stricken from the act, and the ICWA and tribal sovereignty remained intact.

Washington Senator Slade Gorton and his cronies in Congress continued to attack tribal sovereignty. In 1995 Senator Gorton succeeded in getting an amendment attached to the appropriations bill that cut federal funding to any tribe that "takes any unilateral action that adversely impacts the existing rights of non-Indians" who lived on the reservation. The senator was intending to punish the Lummi Nation, whose reservation was on the northwest coast of Washington. Over the years Lummis had sold parcels of land to non-Indians, but the land remained part of the reservation. Construction of a high-end housing development on that land sparked concern over the aquifer from which both the Lummi Nation and the housing development drew water. The tribe feared an increase in salinity in the aquifer and reduced the amount of water homeowners in the development could use. Senator Gorton retaliated with the amendment, which apparently went unnoticed, and President Clinton signed the appropriations act into law. The Lummis lost $5 million for trying to limit water use to preserve the aquifer. The case ultimately ended up in court, and in 2007, long after my time, they reached a settlement that restored Lummi funding. Under the settlement, the Washington State Department of Ecology monitors salinity and sets maximum water usage by non-Lummi residents of the reservation, and Lummis can have what is left. More recent developments have jeopardized that settlement, so the saga continues.

Threats to sovereignty came from many directions, some of them quite surprising. In 1994 the Solicitor's Office of the Interior Department (yes, the same department that houses the BIA) issued an opinion distinguishing between "historic" and "non-historic" tribes. "Historic" tribes lived undivided on land that they had occupied from time immemorial; "non-historic" tribes included those that had divided, that lived under a single government on multi-tribe reservations, that no longer lived on ancestral land, that had "tribe" or "band" in their names, and other ridiculous and pernicious provisions. I immediately announced that I could not support the opinion since it would revoke federal recognition and infringe on tribal sovereignty. The opinion listed twenty-one tribes as examples, including the Mississippi Choctaw who had been separated from the Choctaw Nation by removal, and it threatened more than two hundred tribes. I would not be a party to this disenfranchisement. In response Senator McCain introduced a bill prohibiting new restrictions on federally recognized tribes, and although his bill never got out of committee, it was not needed. The Solicitor's Office let this ludicrous opinion die a quiet death.

One of the problems that had long confronted the BIA was how to regard Indian communities and tribes that did not have treaties with the federal government. These peoples did not have treaties with the United States because they had established relations with the colonizers before the American Revolution, or they had never been at war with the United States, sold land to the United States, or engaged in anything that required a treaty with the United States. These groups tended to be very small, some had intermarried extensively with non-Indians, and some lived in places other than where they appeared in the historical record. Most had few resources and struggled to survive as individuals and as a people. Congress occasionally had extended recognition to one of these groups, but there was no systematic approach to tribal recognition.

In 1978 the BIA set up the Bureau of Acknowledgment and Research (BAR, currently called the Bureau of Federal Acknowledgment) to examine petitions from such peoples for federal recognition and make recommendations to the assistant secretary of the Interior for Indian affairs. Petitioners had to demonstrate that that since 1900 they had existed as a distinct community that dated to "historical times." They had to prove that there was political control over members, that membership criteria existed, that their members descended from a historic tribe, and that members belonged to no other tribe. In 1994, Congress passed an act requiring an annual list of federally recognized tribes. The act also ensured that federal funds earmarked for Indians would go to legitimate tribes. During my tenure, BAR acknowledged four tribes: the Mohegan Tribe in Connecticut, the Jena Band of Choctaws in Louisiana, the Huron Potawatomi, Inc., in Michigan, and the Samish Indian Tribe in Washington.

These tribes clearly deserved recognition. For example, the Jena Choctaws first appeared in the historical record in 1880, living on a Louisiana plantation. The

Dawes Allotment Roll of 1903 lists them along with Choctaws in Indian Territory, which became the state of Oklahoma in 1907, and in Mississippi, where most Choctaws who had not gone west in the 1830s still lived. Twentieth-century federal censuses listed the Jenas as Choctaws. The local storekeeper recorded their debts in his ledger book by their first names and "Indian" as a title (for example, Indian William, Indian John). The community buried their dead in the White Rock Indian Cemetery according to Choctaw traditions as late as the 1930s. Between 1820 and 1950, 85 percent of marriages were with other Jena Choctaws, and until the 1930s, the local headman married couples. These people also spoke Choctaw exclusively. For six years in the 1930s, their children attended a separate Indian school partially funded by the federal government. At the time of their petition for recognition, 72 percent of the members lived within thirty miles of Jena. Until 1968, a traditional chief had governed them, but after his death, they wrote a constitution, established a tribal council, and built a tribal center. In 1974 the tribe incorporated under state law, and Louisiana recognized the Jena Choctaws as an Indian tribe distinct from the federally recognized Mississippi Band of Choctaw Indians and the Choctaw Nation. Like the documentation of the other tribes acknowledged, the evidence for the federal recognition of the Jenas was incontrovertible.

Signing recognition petitions that BAR approved gave me great pleasure. These tribes, such as the Jena Choctaws, had managed to maintain their identities and communities through decades and even centuries without any external recognition or support. They often had continued to act as sovereigns without any formal recognition of sovereignty, a situation that made them vulnerable to unscrupulous people. Unfortunately, recognition sometimes became a divisive issue, not just in Congress but also among tribes. The BIA pie was only so big (and was shrinking), so tribes resented attempts to get a slice by groups whom they did not consider to be tribes. I thought the cases BAR made were so well documented that there could be no doubt that the tribes they approved were entitled to recognition.

Federal courts had expanded the principles of tribal sovereignty and enabled greater self-determination in the 1980s largely through cases involving gaming. In 1979 the Florida Seminoles opened a high-stakes bingo parlor, which the local sheriff promptly closed. Federal courts ruled in favor of the Seminoles in *Seminole Tribe of Florida v. Butterworth* (1981). The issue reached the U.S. Supreme Court in *California v. Cabazon Band of Mission Indians* (1987), which established the right of federally recognized tribes to operate casinos. In 1988, Congress passed the National Indian Gaming Regulatory Act, which established the National Indian Gaming Commission (NIGC) and three classes of gaming. Class I exempted traditional games of chance from state or federal regulation. Class II, bingo and related games, was not subject to state regulation as long as the state permitted similar gaming, such as church bingo, and the tribe enacted a gaming ordinance approved by the NIGC. Class III was casino gaming—slot machines, poker, roulette, and so on. Such games had to be legal in the state in which a tribe was located, and the tribe had to have a gaming ordinance. Furthermore, the tribe and the state had to agree to a compact and secure the approval of the Secretary of the Interior.

The negotiations that led to gaming compacts between tribes and states were often difficult. States frequently came up with last-minute proposals for changes. The National Indian Gaming Association (NIGA), an industry organization of gaming tribes, did its best to sort out compact terms, but states resisted. In 1994 the National Governors Association voted forty-nine to one to oppose Indian gaming. The Indian Gaming Regulatory Act required states to have gaming regulatory systems, but these only existed in New Jersey and Nevada. States in which anti-gaming sentiment was particularly strong forced tribes to pay for these systems. Some states seemed to look for opportunities to infringe on tribal sovereignty, and a general opposition to gaming began to take a decidedly anti-Indian focus.

Non-Indian casino owners protested, even though Indian gaming accounted for less than 3 percent of gaming nationwide. On October 5, 1993, Donald Trump, owner of three casinos in New Jersey, testified before the House Subcommittee on Indian Affairs. He insisted that there was no such thing as tribal sovereignty and that Indians should have to pay the same taxes he did. When tribal leaders who also testified pointed out that income from casinos supported schools, social services, and public works, Trump rolled his eyes. Then he charged that the mafia ran Indian casinos, despite the fact that the FBI had provided evidence that such allegations were false. If anything, Trump's blatant self-interest and ludicrous claims garnered support for Indian gaming. Trump and other prominent figures in the gaming industry, in the words of NIGA chair Rick Hill, "launched a campaign noted for its misinformation against Indian gaming and racism as to Indians generally."

Other threats loomed. The state of South Carolina insisted that the Catawba Nation limit gaming to two bingo halls before the state would agree to settle a land-claim case dating back 150 years. The gaming limitations infringed on tribal sovereignty, but the impoverished tribe, which had ceded its land to the state in an unconstitutional treaty, desperately needed the $50-million settlement. So tribal officials accepted the settlement, which is still in effect.

In 1995 the House Ways and Means Committee proposed taxing tribal—but not state—gaming revenue at a rate of 34 percent. This tax threatened to compound problems created by deep budget cuts. It failed. In 1997, a proposed amendment to an appropriations bill prohibited the Secretary of the Interior from taking tribal land in trust unless the tribes agreed with state and local governments to collect sales and excise taxes from which they were exempt. Even though the legislation failed, I had to be constantly vigilant because I never knew what the anti-Indian forces in Congress and elsewhere would spring next.

At the same time, the number of gaming tribes and the revenue they collected from gaming continued to increase. In 1992 gaming tribes brought in $1.2 billion in gross income; by 1996 this had reached $6 billion. In 1997, 142 tribes in 24 states engaged in gaming. Tribes primarily used that income to offset BIA cuts and to support social services, education, and economic development. Tribes had the right to make per-capita payments to tribal members, but the vast majority did not choose to do so.

Gaming is often a mixed blessing for the non-Indian communities surrounding reservations. Casinos bring jobs, often with wages and benefits better than those offered elsewhere in the area. But casinos often disturb the peace and tranquility in rural areas and increase noise and traffic in urban ones. Furthermore, casinos can be built only on land that the United States has taken into trust, which removes it from the tax base and restricts non-Indian ownership and development. Tribes sometimes own land that is not held in trust, but gaming venues cannot be built on non-trust land. Therefore, for a tribe to construct a casino on one of these tracts, the BIA must agree to accept that land in trust. This sometimes becomes a controversial issue.

Not long after I took office, the Mashantucket Pequots in Connecticut petitioned the BIA for authorization to add 245 acres to their reservation for construction of a resort and golf course that would complement their highly profitable casino. Many of their non-Indian neighbors opposed the expansion of the reservation, and I went to Connecticut to meet with that group. They cited many problems associated with an increase in reservation visitors, including traffic, noise, and litter. But the neighbors clearly had mixed feelings about the Pequots, and most appreciated their economic contribution to the entire region. One woman at the meeting recounted how she had been unemployed for three years before the casino opened. Now she had a good-paying job at the casino with free health insurance and educational benefits. I urged the Pequots and their neighbors to work out a compromise rather than force the BIA to make the decision. Ultimately, Secretary of the Interior Bruce Babbitt accepted most of the Pequot land in trust.

Indian tribes occasionally competed against each other for the right to open casinos. Even before I took office, a controversy was brewing among tribes in my home state. A dog track in Hudson, Wisconsin, was having financial difficulties and entered into an agreement with the St. Croix Chippewa Band for the tribe to purchase the track with a view toward placing the land in trust and opening a casino. Governor Tommy Thompson, a Republican, opposed the plan. Since governors have the final say over Indian casinos, the St. Croix abandoned the plan.

Three years later, the Lac Courte Oreille, Red Cliff, and Mole Lake Chippewa Bands revived the scheme. Other tribes in Wisconsin (including the St. Croix) and in Minnesota joined together in opposition. They charged that the development company which had contracted with the three tribes had mafia connections, and they began to exert political influence. The Clinton administration opposed the casino, perhaps because the seven opposing tribes had contributed $400,000 to the DNC in the 1995–96 election cycle. Secretary Babbitt was implicated in this influence-peddling scheme, but ultimately he and the administration were cleared. Wisconsin Governor Scott McCallum's position was unclear. He insisted that he too opposed the casino, but rumors flew, including one that he, being a Republican, actually favored it since the Clinton administration opposed it. As for me, I recused myself since I was from Wisconsin and was a member of a Wisconsin tribe. In 2001 the BIA reached a settlement with the three tribes and approved the casino, but Governor McCallum vetoed it. What a mess!

Gaming sometimes caused problems within tribes as well. When I took office, a representative from each clan of five Iroquois tribes—Mohawk, Onondaga, Seneca, Cayuga, and Oneida—composed the Grand Council of the Haudenosaunee Confederacy (Tuscaroras belonged to the Confederacy but had no representatives on the Grand Council). The council chiefs of the Oneida Nation, located in New York, included Ray Halbritter, who had spearheaded the construction of a recently opened casino. This was a controversial move since the Confederacy generally opposed gaming. The April before I took office, the Grand Council ousted him.

The Oneidas were divided over the issue, with Halbritter's critics claiming that he did not receive tribal approval before entering into negotiations for the casino. There also were charges of corruption, and prominent members of other Iroquois nations, including Onondaga spiritual leader Oren Lyons, opposed gaming. My predecessors at the BIA backed the Grand Council, which seated Wilbur Homer instead. However, more than four hundred out of six hundred adult Oneidas signed statements of support for Chief Halbritter. The signatures could not be verified, so I stayed the order to unseat him for forty-five days and gave the Oneida Nation 120 days to conduct a referendum on the issue. Halbritter claimed that the referendum was a violation of tribal sovereignty. The controversy raged on throughout my tenure, with the Grand Council refusing to seat Halbritter again. The question was, Did the issue rest with the Oneidas or with the Confederacy, whose authority the Oneidas recognized?

This was not the end of the controversy. The Oneidas located their casino on land they had bought, but in 1985 the Supreme Court ruled that New York had illegally taken the land from them in the aftermath of the American Revolution and granted the tribe permission to sue. The Oneidas interpreted this ruling as confirmation of the tract as "Indian Country," which exempted it from state regulatory laws and taxes. However, the U.S. Supreme Court subsequently ruled that the BIA had to take the land formally into trust for these exemptions to apply. Finally, in 2013, long after my departure from the BIA, the state of New York and the Oneida Nation came to an agreement.

Treaties and Indians' trust relationship with the United States define tribal sovereignty, but the trust relationship involves a federal fiduciary responsibility to tribes. To balance sovereignty with this responsibility, the BIA allows tribes with a good management record to receive funds directly rather than through intermediate agencies. The Cherokee Nation enjoyed this status. In 1995 after a bitter election, the Cherokee Nation elected Joe Byrd principal chief. Animosity and suspicion lingered. In 1996 Cherokee Nation marshals searched Byrd's office looking for evidence of misuse of funds, which given the nation's status with the BIA, would have been easy. It turns out that the chief had paid $65,000 out of the Cherokee treasury to a law firm headed by his brother-in-law. That was a no-no.

The chief fired the marshals and appointed his own marshals. By April 1997, there were three different law-enforcement authorities on the Cherokee Nation— the Cherokee Nation marshals, the Byrd marshals, and the BIA police. The tribal council then impeached the justices of the Cherokee Supreme Court, and in the middle of the night, Chief Byrd's marshals seized the historic Cherokee Courthouse. A group of prominent Cherokees, including lawyer Chad Smith, who succeeded Byrd as chief, then stormed the courthouse and were arrested. Then Cherokee Nation marshals sued the BIA, naming me in the suit. The case was thrown out, and soon thereafter I left office. This was an example of tribal

Assistant Secretary of the Interior for Indian Affairs Ada Deer.

dysfunction so severe that the BIA had to intervene. Fortunately, the Cherokee Nation's long tradition of stable government enabled a rapid recovery, but the episode provided an example of conditions under which the BIA would intervene in tribal affairs. Fortunately such episodes were rare.

The examples of BIA interference I have given are not really typical of Indian Country or of the relationship between the BIA and the tribes. But, of course, nothing is really typical for American Indians because of the vast differences in their cultures and histories. What federally recognized tribes do have in common is tribal sovereignty and the BIA. For all the times that the BIA intervened, there were hundreds, perhaps thousands, of tribal actions that progressed seamlessly without a peep from the BIA. And as irksome as some of the problems were, the tribes and the BIA managed to work them out without compromising the basic principles of tribal sovereignty. I consider that to be success for both the tribes and the BIA.

Although I continued to accomplish a great deal, in the fall of 1994 my situation at the BIA seemed to change for reasons that I never could figure out. A gulf appeared to be opening between the secretary of the interior and me. The first indication was his appointment of Hilda Manuel as deputy commissioner without consulting me. Hilda was a lawyer who had worked at the BIA for about five years. She had served as staff director of the Indian Gaming Management Office, director of the Office of Tribal Government Services, and head of the Branch of Judicial Services. The deputy commissioner worked under the assistant secretary. The assistant secretary's responsibility was developing policy while the commissioner implemented policy. Hilda, in my opinion, tended to overstep her authority and try to subvert mine. Among other things, I think she also drove a wedge between me and Michael Chapman, who had been my first appointee at the BIA.

Then in January 1995 Secretary Babbitt decided to move Faith Roessel, whom I trusted and depended on, out of the BIA. She became "special assistant" to the secretary. He told me that his support of me depended on my acceptance of this transfer. I simply could not bring myself to tell her, so eventually his chief of staff informed her of the transfer. The number of people I trusted was declining. I know this sounds paranoid, but I also discovered that emails that were supposed to be private were getting broader circulation, so I changed my password and sent out instructions that only my assistant was to read them. At times I felt like I had arrows in my back from the Indians and spears in my front from the whites!

In January 1997, after President Clinton's victory in November, Secretary Babbitt asked for my resignation. Then he said the most astonishing thing: "You can fight this if you like." I can't imagine why he thought I would do such a thing. Leading the BIA had become so difficult with his unspoken resistance that there was no way I would continue with his public opposition. I addressed my letter of resignation to President Clinton. It began, "I have been blessed with a full and happy life with good friends, wonderful opportunities, and meaningful work. I am especially happy that I have had the opportunity to serve in your Administration as Assistant Secretary for Indian Affairs. It has been one of the most challenging and rewarding experiences of my life." I meant every word of it.

Then Secretary Babbitt asked me to stay on until a successor was named. I agreed because I could not leave the tribes in the lurch. Next the chairman of the NIGC resigned, and Secretary Babbitt asked me if I would serve as interim chair of the NIGC as well. Once again, I said yes. I split my days between the two

offices. Finally, in October Kevin Gover from the Pawnee Tribe of Oklahoma was named assistant secretary, and Tadd Johnson, Bois Forte Band of the Minnesota Chippewa Band, became head of NIGC. I was free.

When I look back over my career at the BIA, I think about an editorial in a 1995 issue of *Indian Country Today*: "Deer is 'damned if she does and damned if she don't.'" That is how I felt much of the time. I was pleased, however, that this newspaper, which usually criticized the BIA, its policies, and its personnel, appreciated that I had done my very best: "Ada Deer took this job with high hopes. She had always managed to get things done by her quick mind and selfless determination. She didn't reckon on an unstoppable force meeting an immovable object. . . . Ada Deer is a good woman. She has fought the good fight and if there is an American Indian in this nation who could have and should have won the battle, it is Ada Deer." Some battles I did win. During my tenure, the Clinton administration established government-to-government relationships with 226 Alaska Native Villages, expanded self-governance to 180 tribes through annual funding agreements, and approved gaming compacts between 130 tribes and 24 states. Fifty-two percent of Indian schools came under tribal, rather than BIA, management, and I approved the federal recognition of four tribes. My work had been exciting, rewarding, and sometimes frustrating, but I was looking forward to whatever challenges the future might bring.

CHAPTER 10

▪ Still an Activist ▪

I returned to Wisconsin with a sense of accomplishment. It was good to be home among my friends, family, and people. I resumed my position at the University of Wisconsin School of Social Work and the American Indian Studies Program. In 2000 the Dean of Letters and Sciences appointed me director of the American Indian Studies Program. Indian Studies was not a department, and the faculty who taught its courses held appointments in other departments. At the time I became director, there were only three faculty members other than me who offered American Indian studies courses—one in literature, one in history, and one in linguistics. I was appalled. Wisconsin was home to eleven federally recognized Indian tribes as well as a considerable number of urban Indians. I concluded that the program needed to expand. Indians had not been at the top of anyone's hiring priorities in the past, but the university recently had embarked on an effort to diversify the faculty. By the time I retired in 2007, the university had added twelve faculty members who held joint appointments in academic departments and the American Indian Studies Program. Students could take courses in comparative literature and folklore, anthropology, art, law, life sciences, communication, literature, history, and linguistics to earn a certificate in American Indian Studies. I also succeeded in getting Denise Wyaka, a Yankton Sioux lawyer, appointed associate director of the program. Denise taught an undergraduate law course and helped provide leadership for the program. We were there for Indian students, who were a tiny minority at the university, but also for non-Indians who wanted a more diverse perspective on the world. Our doors were always open, and we tried to be available to anyone—students, faculty, staff, and the public—who had a question or needed help.

I also had interests beyond the university, and by 2007, those had begun to take up more and more time. As much as I enjoyed teaching and chairing the program, I retired from the university in 2007. I did not retire, however, from my social justice causes. My commitment to tribal sovereignty and self-determination remained strong. NARF reappointed me to its National Support Committee. I also had a busy speaking schedule at colleges, universities, civic clubs, and other venues. One of the more interesting experiences was at West Virginia University where, in 2016, I served for a week as Elder in Residence. I delivered a public lecture, spoke to classes in Native American studies, English, history, and social work, talked to student groups, and met with faculty members. Such activities kept me involved with national Indian issues, but day-to-day, I focused on issues closer to home. I became immersed in problems confronting American Indians, especially Indian people in Wisconsin. When I retired, I hoped that my schedule would go from frantic to hectic to too busy and ultimately reach busy. That hasn't happened yet.

I had not been retired for long when I discovered that Wisconsin had a prison population twice the size of that in neighboring Minnesota, and that it cost the state $30,000 a year to incarcerate one person. This seemed like a terrible waste of human lives and taxpayers' money. Furthermore, Wisconsin's Indians were overrepresented among prisoners. Although they comprised only 1 percent of the state's population, Indians made up 4 percent of Wisconsin's prison population. This disparity was probably due to a number of factors, including the high rate of alcoholism and poverty in Indian communities, but racism and racial profiling almost certainly played a role. Furthermore, American Indians released from Wisconsin prisons had a higher recidivism rate than any other ethnic/racial group. Difficulty in finding jobs and lack of institutional support contributed to this recidivism, as did alcohol and drug problems. Continually throwing people back into prison and doing little to help them find jobs and overcome substance abuse problems made no sense to me. They needed help to become contributing members of the tribes and the broader society.

I worked with Judicare and the Great Lakes Inter-Tribal Council to address this problem. We contacted the eleven Wisconsin tribes, and obtained resolutions of support from the Oneida Nation of Wisconsin, the Stockbridge-Munsee Community, and Menominees. We had lots of meetings and decided to apply to the state for funding. The legislature awarded us $250,000, but the governor authorized only $50,000. Fortunately, in 2010 we were able to get a Second Chance grant of $287,200 from the Bureau of Justice Assistance.

We hired four people to work with male prisoners who were about to be released and who intended to return to tribal communities. These caseworkers met with inmates before they were released and guided them through the process. Once their clients were released, caseworkers helped them identify possible employment, write résumés, develop interview skills, find housing, manage their money, obtain drug and alcohol counseling, reunite with their families, and become involved in the community. The program got off to a successful start, but unfortunately funding ceased after three years. That was the end of the program.

New causes always seemed to find me, however. Just before I left academic life, the Encampment for Citizenship, the program that had meant so much to me as a young woman, became inactive. This summer program for youths of all races, ethnicities, and religions emphasized critical thinking, leadership, and activism. Young people who have participated in the Encampment include Barney Frank, Eleanor Holmes Norton, Floyd Westerman, Clara Sue Kidwell, and Peter Yarrow, as well as many other notable Americans. Disappointed by the program's apparent demise, Encampment alumni began trying to revive it. Former director Margot Gibney invited me to a reunion of former participants, and I joined the effort. We raised money and recruited personnel, and in 2013, we held a two-week encampment in Richmond, Virginia. Since then, a three-week encampment has taken place every summer in a different locale. I always attend for a few days. If the country ever needed the citizenship skills the encampment teaches, it is now.

In June 2015, an environmental and cultural crisis threatened not just the Menominees, but all the people who live along the Menominee River and Green Bay. A Canadian company, Aquila Resources, Inc., applied for a permit to dig an open pit mine in Michigan within 150 feet of the Menominee River. The pit will be 700 feet deep, 2,000 feet long, and 2,500 feet wide. The Menominee River forms the boundary between Wisconsin and Michigan and empties into Green Bay, twenty-five miles away, and ultimately into Lake Michigan. In recent years, many people have worked very hard to clean up earlier pollution of the river, and native lake sturgeon are making a comeback. Aquila plans to mine gold, zinc, copper, silver, and whatever other minerals are there. One of the dangers is that sulfide deposits are present, and upon exposure to air and water, these deposits will produce acidic mine drainage, which will flow into the river.

Furthermore, cyanide will be used in the mining process, and leeching of this toxin threatens the river. The federal government has been largely powerless since it gave Michigan the right to grant construction permits without approval from the U.S. Environmental Protection Agency (EPA). All the mine needed was four state approvals, which it recently secured.

The mine threatens the mouth of the Menominee River where the Menominees believe we originated as a people. Here Eagle, Bear, Wolf, Moose, and Crane transformed themselves into humans and became the progenitors of our five clans. Although Menominees have not lived there since the seventeenth century, we still regard it as our birthplace. Evidence suggests that our ancestors once lived on both sides of the river and that this is the place where they met with French explorer Jean Nicolet in 1632. An archaeological survey has revealed twenty-two sites, including burial mounds, sacred sites, and ancient raised garden beds.

Local whites on both sides of the river have joined Menominees in protesting the mine. In September 2016, the tribe held a gathering, Remembering Our Ancestors, at the mouth of the Menominee River. The event had elements of a demonstration—signs and T-shirts with anti-mine slogans—but we also gathered to commemorate the origins of the tribe. Many people walked at least part of the way from the mouth of the river to near the site of the mine and offered tobacco to the river. Leaders of the tribe and grassroots organizations spoke, as did archaeologists, environmental scientists, and mining experts. I was one of the speakers. As a child, I had heard about this place, and I was glad to be here. I reminded the audience of past struggles, particularly termination and restoration. "We're now about to engage in another big struggle," I said, "And, based on our history, we will win." It was a memorable day. I was moved just to be there with my people.

Demonstrations continued over the next eighteen months. In January 2018 the tribe sued the EPA and the Army Corps of Engineers, and in March, the EPA suspended Aquila's permits while it investigated. Much to our disappointment, the EPA approved the permits for the mine three months later. I do not know what more can be done, but I think that putting a mine so close to this beautiful river where sturgeon, bass, cranes, and other wildlife thrive is a travesty. It represents one more loss to Indian people, one more thing that threatens to disconnect us from our history and culture. If there is a bright side, it is seeing Indians and non-Indians come together to try to stop this mine.

At the same time, another crisis looms closer to home, one involving the sale of carbon offsets. Since 2011 MTE, the Menominee-owned corporation that manages our forest, has investigated three carbon offset proposals. Under these schemes, the Menominees would sell the rights to use our forest, which consumes carbon dioxide, to offset the carbon dioxide pollution produced by industries. MTE had always declined to use its forest as a cover for polluters. Early in 2018, Finite Carbon approached the tribal legislature about selling carbon offsets to British Petroleum. We had just elected a new legislature, which demonstrated more interest in the scheme than MTE or earlier tribal governments had. Some Menominees saw this opportunity as an economic windfall and proposed that the income from such an arrangement could help fund forest management and tribal services. It turns out, however, that the offer is far more complex than it first appeared. Finite Carbon and British Petroleum want a one-hundred-year contract that will give Finite Carbon partial rights to manage the timber on half of our reservation. This offer also involves surrender of our sovereign immunity, which prevents individuals, corporations, or states from suing the tribe without its consent.

On February 14 the Menominee Tribal Legislature and the MTE board of directors met with representatives from Finite Carbon and the Passamaquoddy Indian Tribe of Maine, which has sold 90,000 acres for carbon offsets. Red flags went up all over the reservation. Larry Waukau, chairman of the MTE board of directors, immediately made his views known. First of all, under our constitution, MTE, not the tribal legislature, manages the forest. And second, MTE had already rejected involvement in carbon offset schemes. Tribal members demanded answers to a list of questions. What would be the effect on tribal sovereignty? Could this agreement weaken tribal control over the forest? How would tribal members benefit? What have been the experiences of other tribes? Are carbon offsets compatible with sustainable-yield forestry? Will MTE still manage the forest?

On April 24, the tribe held an informational session at the College of the Menominee Nation. The assistant administrator of the tribe tried to break the audience up into small discussion groups that would then write down their concerns and submit them to the tribal legislature. No! Absolutely not! Menominees hold open discussions in General Council meetings that welcome all tribal members! And that is what we did. Most attendees came for information, but others, including me, made our opposition known. Chairman Waukau conveyed the position of the MTE board: they will no longer consider any proposals for selling carbon credits to big energy companies. "We are delegated, as you elected us, to protect this forest," he told the audience. "We have a fiduciary responsibility, we took an oath of office to protect this forest, and we unanimously oppose any future efforts with carbon credits." I pointed out the role of outside business interests in termination and the threat not only to the forest but also to tribal sovereignty.

The next day the Menominee Tribal Legislature met to discuss the issue. Legislator Myrna Warrington insisted that tribal members needed more information and introduced a motion to reject the carbon credit proposal. Members voted 3 to 3 (two members were absent), and Menominee Chairman Doug Cox broke the tie in favor of pursuing discussions with Finite Carbon. I was horrified. After winning the struggle for our sovereignty and self-determination in the 1970s, it looked like we were about to surrender these rights to an oil company. Other tribal members were also upset, and we started making phone calls. People gradually became aware of the implications of the vote, and opposition began to build, particularly in the reservation community of South Branch. I joined Menominee County board member and community activist Liz Fernandez-Arnold and MTE board chair Larry Waukau in drafting a petition for an ordinance to put an end to such schemes. The proposed ordinance would prohibit selling carbon offsets or agreeing to any other program that would damage our forest or restrict our control of it. We formed a twenty-five-member Petitioners Committee and began to collect signatures on the petition supporting the ordinance, as provided for in our constitution. By July 2018, 1,331 Menominees had signed the petition, a number that exceeded by more than two hundred the 15 percent of eligible voters required by the constitution for submitting a petition.

On May 23 enrolled tribal members met again. Chairman Cox continued to insist that the legislature was simply investigating the issue, not agreeing to carbon offsets, but most of the people in the audience were not buying his claim. Alex Peters from South Branch was among those who spoke: "This is wrong for the tribe. We don't need to proceed with this any further," he said. "What part of 'no' don't you understand?" Jasmine Neosh, a student at the College of the Menominee Nation, demanded to know how much all this research that the legislature was promoting would cost. After most people had had their say, Audrey O'Kimosh, a tribal elder, moved to ban any further consideration of forest carbon offsets, including the current proposal. The motion passed by a vote of 126 to 0 with three abstentions. Unfortunately, the vote was only advisory. The Menominee Tribal Legislature would have the final word. On June 7, 2018, the legislature voted to end their investigation of carbon offsets, followed by a vote on August 2 banning any carbon-offset or cap-and-trade contracts for tribal lands, including the one with Finite Carbon and British Petroleum that had been under consideration. The people won!

This current crisis, like much of my public life, involves principles that I hold near and dear. American Indian tribes retain sovereignty and have the right to determine their own future. American Indians also have the right to education, health care, housing, and employment. Securing these rights is a constant struggle, but if Indian people and Indian tribes work together, we can protect our common good and confront our common enemies. Whether those enemies are multinational corporations, state and national governments, or unscrupulous individuals, we need to keep the principles of tribal sovereignty and self-determination at the forefront of our struggle and the well-being of all Indian people in our hearts.

As I reflect back over my first eighty-three years, I am appalled that a third of American Indian children still live in poverty. Crime, poverty, and suicide rates on reservations remain disproportionately high, and too many reservation schools are underachieving. Tribal governments should be more responsive to the needs of their people. An adequate BIA budget and more self-governance compacts could help them do that, as could further economic development, gaming initiatives, and litigation of tribal claims and water rights. We as individuals cannot simply take up air and space. We need to work as individuals, communities, and tribes to create a better world. We have resources, and we need to protect them. We have talents, and we need to use them. We have histories, and we need to reflect on them. We have cultures, and we need to embrace them. We are citizens of sovereign tribes, and we need to act like it. Ignorance, racism, and greed continue to threaten Native people, tribes, and resources. We must remain vigilant, prepared to defend our rights and ready to make a difference.

▪ Index ▪

Page numbers in italics refer to illustrations. "AD" refers to Ada Deer.